HISTORY
OF THE AMERICAS

A Syllabus with Maps, by
HERBERT EUGENE BOLTON
Sather Professor of History and Director of the
Bancroft Library, University of California

NEW EDITION

GREENWOOD PRESS, PUBLISHERS
WESTPORT, CONNECTICUT

Library of Congress Cataloging in Publication Data

Bolton, Herbert Eugene, 1870-1953.
   History of the Americas.

   Reprint of the "new edition" published in 1935 by
Ginn, Boston.
   Includes bibliographies.
   1. America--History. I. Title.
E18.B7   1979   970   79-15343
ISBN 0-8371-5273-9

970
B694

This edition published in 1935 by Ginn and Company,
Boston

Reprinted in 1979 by Greenwood Press, Inc.
51 Riverside Avenue, Westport, CT 06880

Printed in the United States of America

10 9 8 7 6 5 4 3 2 1

PREFACE

The time has come for a broader course in American history, to supplement the type of course in national history traditionally given. European history cannot be learned from books dealing alone with England or France or Germany, nor can American history be adequately taught if confined to the United States or Brazil or Canada or Mexico. Most present-day political boundary lines in America are of recent origin; culture and commerce quite generally ignore them. In this country the study of thirteen English colonies and the United States in isolation has obscured many of the larger factors in their development. Similar distortion has resulted from the teaching of national history alone in other American countries. The day of isolation is past. The increasing importance of inter-American relations makes imperative a better understanding by each of the history and culture of all. This is so patent that it needs no demonstration, and for the future I foresee two types of college courses in American history: an introductory, synthetic course, embracing the entire Western Hemisphere, analogous to courses in general European history; and courses on the traditional lines, dealing with the history of the United States or of any other individual American nation.

One shortcoming of the usual first-year college course in United States history given in this country is that it covers essentially the same ground as the courses taught in the grammar grades and again in the high school. It lacks freshness. This element of freshness is admirably provided by a synthetic course in the history of the Western Hemisphere in which the United States is put in a new setting.

Entertaining these views, in 1918 I launched at the University of California a course in the history of the Americas for freshmen and sophomores. For the course I prepared a Syllabus, first in mimeographed form and later printed (not published) by the University press, for the use of my own students. The course succeeded far beyond my expectations and has rapidly spread to other institutions. Originally I had no thought of publishing the Syllabus, but the demand for it has become so widespread that I have now consented to do so.

This Syllabus presents a general survey of the history of the Western Hemisphere from the discovery to the present time. Emphasis is placed in the first semester on the European inheritance and the planting of colonial societies in the New World, the influence of native civilizations and of geographical environments, colonial policies, commerce, industry, and culture, colonial expansion and international rivalry; and in the second semester, on the wars of independence in English America and in Hispanic America, the development of the independent American nations, their relations with one another and with the rest of the world.

The Syllabus, like the course for which it was prepared, is a pioneer, and pioneer trails generally are neither smooth nor straight, but those who come after me will remedy these defects. The Syllabus makes no pretence of finality. It merely presents a survey of Western Hemisphere history in the form of sixty lectures. The introductory paragraphs at the beginning of each topic indicate the main ideas to be presented in each lecture; the outlines which follow, being much more detailed, serve as a guide to the students for further study. Presumably no lecture and no recitation will cover all the points in any single outline. Users of the Syllabus will doubtless vary the emphasis of the course at many points. One of the great library problems connected with the teaching of history is that of providing an adequate supply of atlases. They are expensive and they are soon mutilated or destroyed. Moreover, students need maps conveniently at hand for every lecture, recitation, or study exercise. To meet this need in part, the Syllabus has been liberally supplied with maps, many of which are original and not to be found elsewhere. For the drafting of most of the maps, under my direction, I am greatly indebted to Mr. W. H. Edie.

Certain apparent inconsistencies in the spelling of proper names that may be noticed in the Syllabus are intentional and follow the historical changes which occurred as different nations came into control.

The course as given at the University of California consists of two lectures and one discussion hour each week. The students meet all together for the lectures, and in sections of twenty or twenty-five for discussion. Each student provides himself with a Syllabus. The lectures aim to present general ideas, to stimulate, and to interpret. The discussions are designed to guide the work of individual students and to afford them an opportunity for self-expression. In other institutions a different procedure may be found desirable.

In this new edition of the Syllabus the reading lists have been revised to include new books and new editions of some of the older books. In the textbook assignments, references to both new and old editions make it possible to use either. Special effort has been made to improve the list of monthly Topical Readings, with a view to substituting books of greater human interest and better literary style for some which by experience have proved to be unsuitable for the main purpose, which is to encourage students to read historical books for pleasure. A List of Atlases has been added. In revising the Syllabus I have been greatly aided by Mr. Charles L. Stewart, who for three years assisted me in giving the course on the History of the Americas at the University of California.

CONTENTS

LIST OF LECTURES

PART ONE. COLONIAL AMERICA

INTRODUCTORY

The Scope and Significance of American History.
The Discovery of America.

THE SPANISH AND PORTUGUESE COLONIES

The Beginnings of the Spanish Colonial Empire.
The Occupation of Central America.
Cortés and the Conquest of Mexico.
The Mines and the Northern Borderlands.
Pizarro and the Conquest of Peru.
Venezuela and New Granada.
Valdivia and the Founding of Chile.
The La Plata Colonies.
The Founding of Brazil.
The Enemies of Philip II and Defensive Spanish Expansion.
Spanish Colonial Administration.
Commerce and Industry in the Spanish Colonies.
Social, Intellectual, and Religious Life in the Spanish Colonies.

THE FRENCH, DUTCH, SWEDISH, AND DANISH COLONIES

The Founding of New France.
The Old Régime in Canada.
The French in the Heart of the Continent (1670–1763).
The Dutch, Swedish, and Danish Colonies.

THE ENGLISH COLONIES

The Beginnings of English Expansion.
The Swarming of the English.
The English Colonies in the Caribbean.

ix

LIST OF MAPS

THE DISCOVERY OF AMERICA

THE SPANISH AND PORTUGUESE COLONIES

THE FRENCH, DUTCH, SWEDISH, AND DANISH COLONIES

THE ENGLISH COLONIES

EXPANSION AND INTERNATIONAL RIVALRY

THE FOUNDING OF THE UNITED STATES

LIST OF MAPS

READING PLAN

Provision is made for three types of reading. (1) For each lecture brief textbook assignments are made — the briefer the better. (2) For topical reading one interesting small book (or an equivalent portion of a larger book) is assigned as a minimum to each student each month. For convenience of administration, if classes are large, the library should provide enough copies of a few selected titles so that the same book may be assigned to all students of one section at the same time. With small classes this is not necessary; but experience shows that duplicate copies of a few select titles are preferable to single copies of a wider range of less readable and less useful books. (3) Lists of books are provided in the Syllabus to guide students in more extended reading. With few exceptions, only books in English are listed.

Teachers may wish to substitute other books for those assigned. For Hispanic America the list of good textbooks is limited. For the United States and Canada there are many good texts. For the topical reading two excellent series of little books are available — The Chronicles of Canada and The Chronicles of America. For South America good books in English for young students are not so plentiful. There are numerous good syllabuses for the history of the United States. R. G. Trotter has published an admirable one for Canadian history. For Hispanic America and international relations the syllabuses prepared by Hoskins, Mecham, Pierson, Priestley, and Wilgus will prove useful.

REQUIRED TOPICAL READINGS

FIRST SEMESTER

First Month. (One of the following assigned to each student)

BENSON, E. F. *Ferdinand Magellan.*
BISHOP, M. *The Odyssey of Cabeza de Vaca.*
DARK, RICHARD. *The Quest of the Indies.*
GRAHAM, R. B. C. *The Conquest of New Granada* (Quesada).
GRAHAM, R. B. C. *The Conquest of the River Plate.*
GRAHAM, R. B. C. *Pedro de Valdivia, Conqueror of Chile.*
HELPS, ARTHUR. *The Life of Hernando Cortés.*
HELPS, ARTHUR. *The Life of Pizarro.*
LUMMIS, C. F. *The Spanish Pioneers.*
MACNUTT, F. A. *Fernando Cortés and the Conquest of Mexico.*
MAY, S. B. *The Conqueror's Lady.* (A novel.)
NILES, BLAIR. *Maria Peluna.* (A novel.)
OBER, F. A. *Pizarro and the Conquest of Peru.*
RICHMAN, I. B. *The Spanish Conquerors.*
SEDGWICK, H. D. *Cortés the Conqueror.*
STEPHENS, KATE. *The Mastering of Mexico.*
THOMPSON, J. E. *Mexico before Cortés.*
WALLACE, LEW. *The Fair God.* (A novel.)
WILLARD, T. A. *The Lost Empire of the Itzaes and Mayas.*

Second Month. (One of the following assigned to each student)

BENSON, E. F. *Sir Francis Drake.*
BOURNE, E. G. *Spain in America,* 202–319.
DAWSON, T. C. *The South American Republics* (200 selected pages).
GOSSE, PHILIP. *Sir John Hawkins.*
GRAHAM, R. B. C. *A Vanished Arcadia* (the Jesuits in Paraguay).
HELPS, ARTHUR. *The Life of Las Casas, the Apostle of the Indies.*
MACNUTT, F. A. *Bartholomew de las Casas.*
VAN LOON, H. W. *The Golden Book of the Dutch Navigators.*
VERRILL, A. H. *The Real Story of the Pirate.*
WOOD, WILLIAM. *The Elizabethan Sea-Dogs.*

Third Month. (One of the following assigned to each student)

BURPEE, L. J. *Pathfinders of the Great Plains.*
CATHER, WILLA. *Shadows on the Rock.* (A novel.)
CHAPAIS, THOMAS. *The Great Intendant.*
COLBY, C. W. *The Fighting Governor.*
COLBY, C. W. *The Founder of New France.*
JACKS, L. V. *La Salle.*
KIRBY, WILLIAM. *The Golden Dog.* (A novel.)
LEACOCK, STEPHEN. *The Mariner of St. Malo.*
MARQUIS, T. G. *The Jesuit Missions.*
MUNRO, W. B. *Crusaders of New France.*
MUNRO, W. B. *The Seigneurs of Old Canada.*
PARISH, J. C. *The Man with the Iron Hand.*
PARKMAN, FRANCIS. *La Salle and the Discovery of the Great West.*
REPPLIER, AGNES. *Father Marquette.*
WOOD, L. A. *The War Chief of the Six Nations.*

Fourth Month. (One of the following assigned to each student)

ANDREWS, C. M. *Colonial Folkways.*
ANDREWS, C. M. *The Colonial Period.*
ANDREWS, C. M. *The Fathers of New England.*
BOAS, R. P. and L. S. *Cotton Mather.*
BOLTON, H. E. *Outpost of Empire.*
BOLTON, H. E. *The Padre on Horseback.*
BOLTON, H. E. *The Spanish Borderlands.*
CATHER, WILLA. *Death Comes for the Archbishop.* (A novel.)
CHATTERTON, E. K. *Captain John Smith.*
DOBIE, J. F. *Coronado's Children.*
DOUGHTY, A. G. *The Acadian Exiles.*
FIERRO BLANCO, ANTONIO DE. *The Journey of the Flame.* (A novel.)
FISHER, S. G. *The Quaker Colonies.*
GOODWIN, M. W. *Dutch and English on the Hudson.*
HART, F. R. *Admirals of the Caribbean.*
JOHNSTON, MARY. *Pioneers of the Old South.*
LAUT, A. C. *Adventurers of England on Hudson Bay.*
MARQUIS, T. G. *The War Chief of the Ottawas.*
MORROW, H. W. *Beyond the Blue Sierra.* (A novel based on Bolton's *Outpost of Empire.*)
PARKMAN, FRANCIS. *A Half-Century of Conflict.*
POWYS, LLEWELYN. *Henry Hudson.*
REPPLIER, AGNES. *Junipero Serra.*
WOOD, WILLIAM. *The Great Fortress.*

Wood, William. *The Passing of New France.*
Wood, William. *The Winning of Canada.*
Wrong, G. M. *The Conquest of New France.*

SECOND SEMESTER

Fifth Month. (One of the following assigned to each student)

Becker, C. L. *The Eve of the Revolution.*
Bodley, Temple. *George Rogers Clark.*
Churchill, Winston. *The Crossing.* (A novel.)
Corwin, E. S. *John Marshall and the Constitution.*
Farrand, Max. *The Fathers of the Constitution.*
Fiske, John. *The Critical Period of American History, 1783–1789.*
Gibbs, G. F. *The Shores of Romance* (Lafitte, New Orleans, in 1812). (A novel.)
Henderson, Archibald. *The Conquest of the Old Southwest.*
Johnson, Allen. *Jefferson and his Colleagues.*
Ogg, F. A. *The Old Northwest.*
Paine, R. D. *The Fight for a Free Sea.*
Skinner, C. L. *Pioneers of the Old Southwest.*
Thwaites, R. G. *Daniel Boone.*
Wrong, G. M. *Washington and his Comrades in Arms.*

Sixth Month. (One of the following assigned to each student)

Bradley, A. G. *Canada.*
Decelles, A. D. *The Patriotes of '37.*
Grant, W. L. *The Tribune of Nova Scotia.*
Laut, A. C. *Pioneers of the Pacific Coast.*
Laut, A. C. *Vikings of the Pacific.*
MacMechan, Archibald. *The Winning of Popular Government.*
Raymond, E. T. *Tecumseh.*
Skinner, C. L. *Adventurers of Oregon.*
Skinner, C. L. *Beaver, Kings, and Cabins.*
Wallace, W. S. *The Family Compact.*
Wallace, W. S. *The United Empire Loyalists.*
Wood, L. A. *The Red River Colony.*
Wood, William. *The Father of British Canada*
Wood, William. *The War with the United States.*

Seventh Month. (One of the following assigned to each student)

Caesar, Count Corti Egon. *Maximilian and Charlotte of Mexico.*
Dawson, T. C. *The South American Republics* (the portions dealing with the movement for independence).

FRANCK, H. A. *Tramping through Mexico.*
FRANCK, H. A. *Vagabonding down the Andes.*
FRANCK, H. A. *Working North from Patagonia.*
GARCÍA CALDERÓN, FRANCISCO. *Latin America.*
GRAHAM, R. B. C. *A Brazilian Mystic: the Life and Miracles of Antonio Conselheiro* (nineteenth century).
HUDSON, W. H. *The Purple Land.*
LATANÉ, J. H. *From Isolation to Leadership.*
LATANÉ, J. H. *The United States and Latin America.*
MITRE, BARTOLOMÉ. *The Emancipation of South America.*
MITRE, BARTOLOMÉ, and PETRE, F. L. *Simón Bolívar.*
NOLL, A. H., and McMAHON, A. P. *Life and Times of Miguel Hidalgo y Costilla.*
OLIVEIRA LIMA, MANOEL DE. *The Evolution of Brazil compared with that of Spanish and Anglo-Saxon America.*
PAXSON, F. L. *The Independence of the South American Republics.*
ROBERTSON, W. S. *Rise of the Spanish-American Republics,* chaps. 1, 3, 4, 6, 7.
SHEPHERD, W. R. *The Hispanic Nations of the New World.*
SHERWELL, G. A. *Simón Bolívar.*
VANDERCOOK, J. W. *Black Majesty: the Life of Christophe, King of Haiti.*
VAUCAIRE, M. *Bolívar the Liberator.*
WHITE, E. L. *El Supremo* (Dr. Francia of Paraguay). (A novel.)
YBARRA, T. R. *Bolívar, the Passionate Warrior.*

Eighth Month. (One of the following assigned to each student)

BURNS, W. N. *The Saga of Billy the Kid.*
BURNS, W. N. *Tombstone: an Iliad of the Southwest.*
COLQUHOUN, A. H. U. *The Fathers of Confederation.*
DODD, W. E. *The Cotton Kingdom.*
DUNN, H. H. *The Crimson Jester.*
FISH, C. R. *The Path of Empire.*
FLEMING, W. L. *The Sequel of Appomattox.*
HENDRICK, B. J. *The Age of Big Business.*
HOUGH, EMERSON. *The Passing of the Frontier.*
JAMES, MARQUIS. *The Raven, a Biography of Sam Houston.*
LAUT, A. C. *The Cariboo Trail.*
MOODY, JOHN. *The Railroad Builders.*
NEIHARDT, J. G. *The Splendid Wayfaring.*
OGG, F. A. *The Reign of Andrew Jackson.*
PAXSON, F. L. *The Last American Frontier.*
PINCHON, E. *Viva Villa.*
SEYMOUR, CHARLES. *Woodrow Wilson and the World War.*
SKELTON, O. D. *The Canadian Dominion.*

SKELTON, O. D. *The Day of Sir Wilfrid Laurier.*
SKELTON, O. D. *The Railway Builders.*
STEPHENSON, N. W. *The Day of the Confederacy.*
STEPHENSON, N. W. *Texas and the Mexican War.*
THOMPSON, HOLLAND. *The New South.*
VESTAL, STANLEY. *Kit Carson: the Happy Warrior of the Old West.*
WERNER, M. R. *Brigham Young.*
WHITE, S. E. *Folded Hills.* (A novel.)
WHITE, S. E. *The Forty-niners.*
WHITE, S. E. *Long Rifle.* (A novel.)
WHITE, S. E. *Ranchero.* (A novel.)

ATLASES

General

BARTHOLOMEW, J. G. *The Citizen's Atlas of the World.* Edinburgh, 1924.
CRAM, C. S., and Co. *Cram's Modern Reference Atlas of the World.* Chicago and New York, 1922.
GOODE, J. P. *Goode's School Atlas, Physical, Political, and Economic.* Chicago and New York, 1923.
GOODE, J. P. *Rand McNally World Atlas.* Chicago and New York, 1932.
HAMMOND, C. S., and Co. *World Atlas.*
JOHNSTON, G. H. *The Handy Royal Atlas of Modern Geography.* Edinburgh and London, 1921.
MUIR, RAMSAY. *Putnam's Historical Atlas.* New York, 1927.
SHEPHERD, W. R. *Historical Atlas.* New York, 1929.
STIELER, ADOLF. *Stieler's Hand-Atlas.* Gotha, 1925–1926.
London Times. *The Times Survey Atlas of the World.* London, 1922.
Rand McNally Commercial Atlas (64th ed.), New York, 1933.

Canada

BURPEE, L. J. *An Historical Atlas of Canada.* Toronto, 1927.
CHALIFOUR, J. E. (Editor). *Atlas of Canada.* Department of the Interior, Ottawa, 1915.

Hispanic America

BIEDMA, J. J., and BEYER, C. *Atlas Histórico de la República Argentina.* Buenos Aires, 1909.
GENERAL DRAFTING COMPANY. *Atlas América Latina.* New York, 1919.
SÁNCHEZ, P. C. *Atlas Geográfico de la República Mexicana.* Mexico, 1929–1930.

United States

Fox, D. R. *Harper's Atlas of American History.* New York, 1920.

PAULLIN, O., and WRIGHT, J. K. *Atlas of the Historical Geography of the United States.* Washington and New York, 1932.

SLOANE, C. S. (Editor). *Statistical Atlas of the United States.* Washington, 1925.

HISTORY OF THE AMERICAS

PART ONE. COLONIAL AMERICA

LEGEND

1. Arctic or Eskimo
2. Northwest or North Pacific Coast
3. California-Great Basin
4. Plateau
5. Mackenzie-Yukon
6. Plains
7. Northeast or Northern Woodland
8. Southeast or Southern Woodland
9. Southwest
10. Mexico
11. Colombia or Chibcha
12. Andean or Peruvian
13. Patagonia
14. Tropical Forest
15. Antillean

Based on map in A. L. Kroeber's *Anthropology*

THE PRINCIPAL CULTURE AREAS OF PRIMITIVE AMERICA

INTRODUCTORY

Lecture I. The Scope and Significance of American History

Introductory. The discovery of America was the most important event of modern times. It made possible the Euro-American civilization of today and shifted the leadership of the world. America has served as a frontier of Europe, providing a new outlet for energy and commercial enterprise, an expanded food supply and a new home for increasing population, and a laboratory for social, political, and economic experimentation. Settlers have transplanted European cultures to America, but these have become greatly modified by American environment and by contact with native peoples.

For some three hundred years the Western Hemisphere was in a colonial status. European nations occupied the country and devised systems for exploiting natives and natural resources. Rival nations competed for profit and possession. Some of the contestants were eliminated, leaving Spain, Portugal, and England as the chief colonial powers at the end of the eighteenth century.

European colonies in America grew up and asserted their majority. In the half-century between 1776 and 1826 practically all of South America and two thirds of North America became politically independent of Europe, and a score of American nations, republican in form, came into being. Now, with minor exceptions, the entire Western Hemisphere has achieved independent nationality. Since separation these nations have been struggling for national solidarity, stability, and economic strength, and for an adjustment of relations with each other and with the rest of the world. The key note of the nineteenth century was nationalism. In the twentieth century a broader outlook is being manifested.

1. Colonial America. Preliminaries to colonization: native cultures; the discovery; exploration. The transplanting of European cultures: the process, colonial systems; colonial society (Spanish, Portuguese, French, English, Dutch, Swedish, Danish, Russian) as modified by new environments. Colonial expansion and international rivalry: in the Caribbean; in South America; in eastern North America; in western North America; elimination of some nations; three great survivors (Spain, England, Portugal). Colonial America on the eve of independence.

2. Independent America. The separation of America from Europe: the wars of independence; English colonies, Spanish, Portuguese; causes; events; significance. The founding of the American nations: the United States; Canada; the Spanish American republics; Brazil. A century of development in North, South, and Central America: the struggle for stability, unity, democracy; economic and territorial expansion; culture; national ambition. International relations: the relations of the American nations with one another (neutrality, recognition, the Monroe Doctrine, territorial aggression, and boundary disputes); the control of the Caribbean; peaceful intercourse; Pan-Americanism; Pan-Hispanism. The Western Hemisphere today: America and Europe; America and Asia: the United States as a world power.

REFERENCES

Bolton, H. E. "The Epic of Greater America," in *American Historical Review*, Vol. XXXVIII, No. 3, April, 1933, pp. 448–474.

Chapman, C. E. *Colonial Hispanic America*, "Foreword."

Priestley, H. I. *The Coming of the White Man*, "Foreword."

Turner, F. J. *The Frontier in American History*, chap. 1.

Lecture II. The Discovery of America

Introductory. Columbus was not the first visitor from the Old World to the New. The American Indians doubtless migrated from Asia in prehistoric times. There are faint traces of early Chinese visits to American shores; Norse journeys from Europe in the ninth century are better attested; and there are indications of voyages by Europeans in the years just before the discovery by Columbus. But these visits had no important results. It was Columbus who made America known to Europe.

Columbus's voyage was not a sudden event. On the contrary, it was the result of a long process of growth in nautical skill, geographical knowledge, and commercial enterprise. It was especially an incident in the effort of Europeans to promote trade with the Orient. Interest in the East, never lacking since ancient times, was greatly stimulated by the Crusades. Commerce increased, but routes and profits were dominated by Italian cities. Western Europe therefore looked in other directions. Portugal turned south and developed trade with Africa. Columbus, sailing west in the service of Spain, stumbled upon America, and gave Europe a thrill such as Lindbergh four centuries later gave the whole world.

The voyage of Columbus set in motion a race for the Orient. Portuguese adventurers sailed round Africa, reached India, and set up a colonial empire there. Spain, finding the American continent in the way, sought a route through or around the obstacle. As a result the coast line was rapidly explored, but it took over two centuries to show that America was not a part of Asia.

6

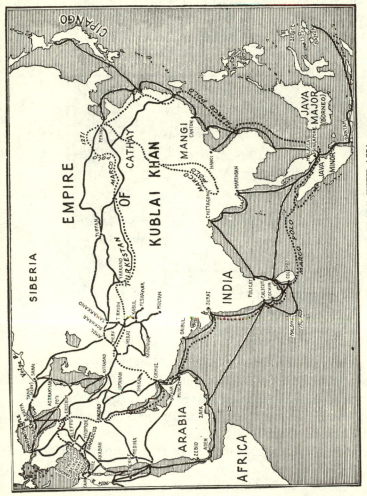

ROUTES OF EUROPEAN TRADE WITH ASIA

1. Pre-Columbian discovery of America. Prehistoric contact:
   the Indians, the Chinese, the Northmen.
2. The Columbian discovery. The result of a long process
   of growth in nautical skill (the compass, the astrolabe),
   in geographical knowledge, and in commercial enterprise.

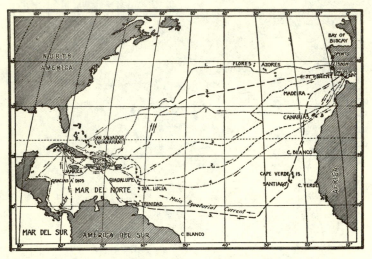

THE FOUR VOYAGES OF COLUMBUS

3. Medieval trade and travel in the East. Effect of the Crusades; travelers (Carpini, Rubruquis, the Polos); trade
   of Italian cities; routes to the East not cut off by Turks;
   Eastern routes monopolized by Italian cities; Portugal
   and Spain turn elsewhere.
4. Portuguese expansion. Lisbon and Oporto; capture of
   Ceuta (1415); Prince Henry the Navigator; trading
   voyages on the African coast; trading posts; voyages
   after the death of Henry (Díaz, 1486; Vasco da Gama,
   1497); colonies in the East (Goa).

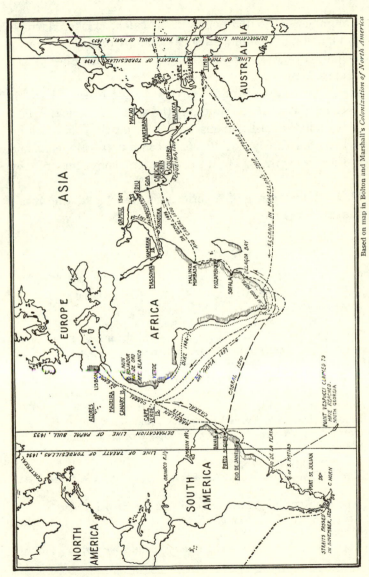

PORTUGUESE EXPANSION AND MAGELLAN'S VOYAGE

Based on map in Bolton and Marshall's *Colonization of North America*

5. Columbus. Disputed points in his career (Fiske, Harrisse, Vignaud); Columbus's ideas and preparation; aim of first voyage; what he thought of it; the Line of Demarcation.
6. New coasts and a strait. Portuguese successes: Vasco da Gama; Cabral; Vespuccius, the name "America"; Portugal in the East. Spanish voyages: pearls, gold; Columbus's fourth voyage; Pinzón (1509, 1515); Magellan and Elcano (1519–1522). Entire eastern coast line run by 1525.
7. Slow understanding of American geography; Bering Strait explored (1728).

REQUIRED READING

One of the following:

BOLTON, H. E., and MARSHALL, T. M. *The Colonization of North America*, chap. 1.
BOURNE, E. G. *Spain in America*, 3–32.
CHAPMAN, C. E. *Colonial Hispanic America*, chap. 1.
FISKE, JOHN. *The Discovery of America*, I, chap. 3, 4, or 5.
LUMMIS, C. F. *The Spanish Pioneers*, 25–42.
MARTIN, A. E. *History of the United States*, I, Enlarged Edition, 1–23.
PRIESTLEY, H. I. *The Coming of the White Man*, 1–16.
RICHMAN, I. B. *The Spanish Conquerors*, chaps. 1–2.
RIPPY, J. F. *Historical Evolution of Hispanic America*, chap. 2.
ROBERTSON, W. S. *History of the Latin-American Nations*, 1922 ed., 60–70; 1932 ed., 64–74.
SWEET, W. W. *History of Latin America*, 1919 ed., 32–42; 1929 ed., 42–55.
WEBSTER, HUTTON. *History of Latin America*, 52–64.
WILGUS, A. C. *A History of Hispanic America*, chaps. 3, 4 (selections).
WILLIAMS, M. W. *People and Politics of Latin America*, 102–110.

REFERENCES

Growth of Geographical Knowledge

Beazley, C. R. *The Dawn of Modern Geography.*

Fischer, Joseph. *The Discoveries of the Norsemen in America.*

Fiske, John. *The Discovery of America,* I, 151–256, 363–381.

Gillespie, J. E. *A History of Geographical Discovery, 1400–1800.*

Gray, E. F. *Leif Eriksson, Discoverer of America,* A.D. 1003.

Hovgaard, William. *The Voyages of the Norsemen to America,* 221–255.

Kendrick, T. D. *A History of the Vikings.*

Lawrence, A. W., and Young, Jean. *Narratives of the Discovery of America.*

Merriman, R. B. *Rise of the Spanish Empire,* II, chaps. 16–18; III, chap. 27.

Newton, A. P. (Editor). *The Great Age of Discovery.*

Polo, Marco. *The Book of Ser Marco Polo, the Venetian* (Yule Edition).

Richman, I. B. *The Spanish Conquerors,* chap. 1.

Thordarson, Matthias. *The Vinland Voyages.*

Vahl, M., and others. *Greenland.* Vol. III. (The colonization of Greenland and its history until 1929.)

Winsor, Justin. *Narrative and Critical History of America,* I, 1–58.

Asiatic Contact with America

Vining, E. P. *An Inglorious Columbus; or Evidence that Hwui Shan discovered America in the Fifth Century.*

Portuguese Discoveries

Beazley, C. R. *Prince Henry the Navigator,* 125–307.

Benson, E. F. *Ferdinand Magellan.*

Bourne, E. G. "Prince Henry the Navigator," *Essays in Historical Criticism,* 173–189.

Cheyney, E. P. *European Background of American History,* 60–70.

Cleven, N. A. N. *Readings in Hispanic American History,* 71–78, 111–126.

Helps, Arthur. *The Spanish Conquest in America,* I, 1–54.

Jayne, K. G. *Vasco da Gama and his Successors,* 7–240.

Lybyer, A. H. "The Ottoman Turks and the Routes of Oriental Trade," *English Historical Review*, XXX, 577–588.

Major, R. H. *The Discoveries of Prince Henry the Navigator.*

Martins, J. P. O. *The Golden Age of Prince Henry the Navigator*, 66–84, 205–231.

Prestage, Edgar. *The Portuguese Pioneers.*

Stephens, H. M. *Portugal*, 115–240.

Columbus

Biggar, H. P. "The New Columbus," Annual Report of the American Historical Association (1912), 97–104.

Bourne, E. G. *Spain in America*, 8–32.

Channing, Edward. *History of the United States*, I, 14–25.

Cleven, N. A. N. *Readings in Hispanic American History*, 62–70.

Hart, A. B. *American History told by Contemporaries*, I, 28–41.

Helps, Arthur. *The Spanish Conquest in America*, I, 55–68.

Jane, Cecil (Editor). *Select Documents Illustrating the Four Voyages of Columbus.*

Jane, Cecil (Editor). *The Voyages of Christopher Columbus.* Being the journals of his first and third, and the letters concerning his first and last voyages, to which is added the account of his second voyage written by Andrés Bernáldez.

Major, R. H. *Select Letters of Columbus.*

Markham, Clements. *Life of Columbus.*

Merriman, R. B. *Rise of the Spanish Empire*, II, chap. 17.

Nunn, G. E. *The Columbus and Magellan Concepts of South American Geography.*

Olson, J. E., and Bourne, E. G. (Editors). *The Northmen, Columbus, and Cabot* (Original Narratives), 89–585.

Peter Martyr. *De Orbe Novo.* (F. A. MacNutt, translator.)

Richman, I. B. *The Spanish Conquerors*, chap. 2.

Thacher, J. B. *Columbus.*

Ulloa, Luis. *Christophe Colomb, Catalán.*

Vignaud, Henry. *Toscanelli and Columbus.*

Winsor, Justin. *Columbus.*

Christopher Columbus: Documents and Proofs of his Genoese Origin (English-German edition, authorized by the city of Genoa).

THE SPANISH AND PORTUGUESE COLONIES

LECTURE III. THE BEGINNINGS OF THE SPANISH COLONIAL EMPIRE

The West Indies

Introductory. America, at first an obstacle in the way to the Orient, soon proved to be of interest itself, and the discovery was quickly followed by colonization. European efforts turned first to trade with the natives, the exploitation of their labor, the raising of tropical crops, and the opening of mines. In the exploration and colonization of the Western Hemisphere Spain and Portugal led the way. They not only explored and exploited but colonized extensively, and their experience was utilized by the later comers. Their colonizing results were permanent, and two thirds of the Western Hemisphere today is dominantly Hispanic.

Spain was prepared for leadership by a vigorous process of unification and a brilliant position in Europe, and by experience in the Canary Islands. Her first American center of colonization was in the West Indies. Here she first set up agencies for the governing of Spaniards in the New World. Here she first encountered and attempted to solve the problem of dealing with the natives. The West Indies constituted a commercial center for trade, a base for expansion to the mainland, and a strategic outpost for the protection of Spanish commerce and possessions from European rivals. Spain's West Indian colonies were tropical plantations.

1. Spain the pioneer colonizer in America; did not merely
   explore, but planted colonies and transplanted Spanish
   civilization; Spain's experience utilized by other nations.
2. Spain's preparation for her task. The unification of Spain
   by Ferdinand and Isabella. Territorial: marriage of
   Ferdinand and Isabella; conquest of Granada. Administrative (displacement of feudal by royal agencies):
   royal treasury (taxation, Grand Masterships of the
   military orders); royal army and police (the Santa
   Hermandad); royal justice; royal supervisors of local
   government (corregidores, visitadores); royal councils
   of state, justice, finance, the Inquisition. Religious: the
   Inquisition; expulsion of the Moors and Jews. The
   prestige of Charles V.
3. The importance of the Caribbean area in American history;
   Española (Haiti) the "Mother of America"; the seventeenth-century struggle in the Caribbean; the present-
   day problem.
4. The rule of Columbus in Española. Columbus first ruler in
   America; his explorations; colonies planted (Navidad,
   Isabela, Santo Domingo). His successors (Ovando,
   Diego Columbus).
5. Expansion to other islands. Porto Rico (Ponce de León);
   Jamaica (Esquivel); Cuba (Velásquez).
6. Beginnings of colonial institutions and policy. Towns
   (Santo Domingo, San Juan, Havana); industries (native,
   European); commerce (the treasure fleets); Indian
   policy (encomiendas, negro slavery); administration
   (Fonseca, Casa de Contratación, Council of the Indies,
   governor and captain general, the Audiencia of Santo
   Domingo); the Church; social institutions; the first
   tropical colonies in America.

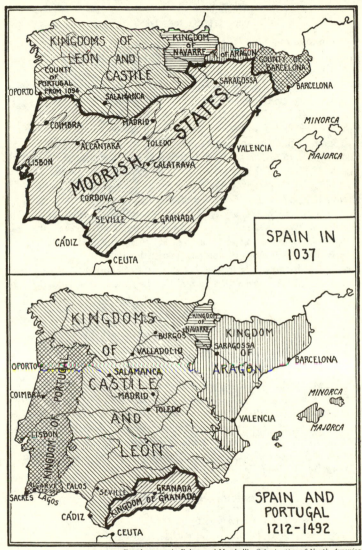

KINGDOMS OF LEÓN AND CASTILE

KINGDOM OF NAVARRE

K. OF ARAGON

COUNTY OF BARCELONA

COUNTY OF PORTUGAL FROM 1094

OPORTO

BARCELONA

SARAGOSSA

SALAMANCA

MINORCA

COIMBRA

MADRID

MAJORCA

ALCÁNTARA

TOLEDO

VALENCIA

LISBON

MOORISH STATES

CALATRAVA

CORDOVA

SEVILLE

GRANADA

CÁDIZ

CEUTA

SPAIN IN 1037

KINGDOMS OF CASTILE AND LEÓN

KINGDOM OF NAVARRE

KINGDOM OF ARAGON

BURGOS

VALLADOLID

SARAGOSSA

OPORTO

BARCELONA

KINGDOM OF PORTUGAL

SALAMANCA

COIMBRA

MADRID

MINORCA

TOLEDO

MAJORCA

LISBON

VALENCIA

ALGARVE 1253-1263

PALOS

SACRES

LAGOS

SEVILLE

GRANADA

KINGDOM OF GRANADA

CÁDIZ

CEUTA

SPAIN AND PORTUGAL 1212-1492

Based on map in Bolton and Marshall's *Colonization of North America*

THE RECONQUEST AND UNIFICATION OF SPAIN AND PORTUGAL

REQUIRED READING

One of the following:

BOLTON, H. E., and MARSHALL, T. M. *The Colonization of North America*, 13–23.

BOURNE, E. G. *Spain in America*, 33–35 (Spain in the West Indies), 202–219 (beginnings of colonial institutions).

CHAPMAN, C. E. *Colonial Hispanic America*, chap. 2.

CHEYNEY, E. P. *European Background of American History*, 79–103 (Spain during the conquest).

FISKE, JOHN. *The Discovery of America*, I, 460–516 (the West Indies).

JAMES, H. G., and MARTIN, P. A. *The Republics of Latin America*, 1–17 (Spain's preparation).

RIPPY, J. F. *Historical Evolution of Hispanic America*, chap. 3.

ROBERTSON, W. S. *History of the Latin-American Nations*, chap. 3.

SWEET, W. W. *History of Latin America*, 1919 ed., 7–20; 1929 ed., 56–60 (Spain during the conquest); 1919 ed., 94–100; 1929 ed., 105–112 (beginnings of colonial institutions).

WEBSTER, HUTTON. *History of Latin America*, chap. 2.

WILLIAMS, M. W. *People and Politics of Latin America*, chap. 3.

REFERENCES

SPAIN DURING THE CONQUEST

CHAPMAN, C. E. *A History of Spain*, 202–233.

HALE, E. E., and SUSAN. *Spain*, 298–320.

HUME, M. H. S. *Spain, 1479–1788*, 1–30.

LOWERY, WOODBURY. *The Spanish Settlements, 1515–1561*, 79–101.

MERRIMAN, R. B. *Rise of the Spanish Empire*, II, 5–166.

PRESCOTT, W. H. *Ferdinand and Isabella*.

ROBERTSON, W. S. *History of Latin-American Nations*, chap. 2.

STONE, J. S. *The Cult of Santiago: Traditions, Myths, and Pilgrimages*.

WALSH, W. T. *Isabella of Spain, the Last Crusader*.

BEGINNINGS IN THE WEST INDIES

FISKE, A. K. *The West Indies*, 1–65.

FISKE, JOHN. *The Discovery of America*, I, 460–516.

HELPS, ARTHUR. *The Spanish Conquest in America*, I, 127–200.

NEWTON, A. P. *The European Nations in the West Indies*, chaps. 1–3.

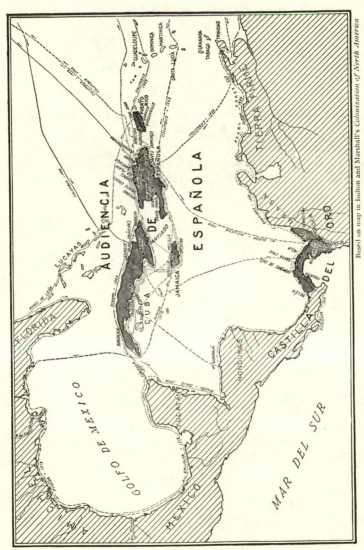

THE OCCUPATION OF THE WEST INDIES (1492–1519)

Based on map in Bolton and Marshall's *Colonization of North America*

Sweet, W. W. *History of Latin America*, 1919 ed., 46–54; 1929 ed., 56–60.

Van Deusen, R. J. and E. K. *Porto Rico, a Caribbean Isle.*

Wright, I. A. *The Early History of Cuba.*

Wright, I. A. *Historia Documentada de San Cristóbal de la Habana en el Siglo XVI.* 2 vols.

Beginnings of Spanish Colonial Institutions

Bancroft, H. H. *History of Central America*, I, 247–268.

Keller, A. G. *Colonization*, 168–313.

Priestley, H. I. *The Coming of the White Man*, chaps. 4, 5.

Simpson, L. B. *The Encomienda in New Spain.*

LECTURE IV. THE OCCUPATION OF CENTRAL AMERICA

The Maya Country

Introductory. While exploring the coasts of the Gulf of Mexico the Spaniards found natives in different stages of development. The advanced peoples were the most worth exploiting, and among them the Spaniards first settled on the mainland. It happened too that the areas of advanced cultures in America were the areas containing the great mineral deposits. To the Isthmus the Spaniards were led by rumors of wealth and a South Sea. To the more northern portions of Central America they were attracted by the remarkable Maya culture, already decadent when they arrived. Panama became a base for a rapid advance south to Peru, and northwest into the Maya country. The north-moving column, directed by Pedrarias, soon met a south-moving column from Mexico. By the middle of the sixteenth century Central America was largely under Spanish control, and permanent centers of Spanish civilization had been established — the beginnings of the five Central American republics of today.

1. The Mayas. Culture centers (Chichén Itzá, Uxmal, Palenque, etc.); the Quichés of Guatemala (Utatlán); Maya culture; Maya history (the "golden age," A.D. 472–620; the "renaissance," A.D. 1000–1200; decline).
2. Expansion from the West Indies to the Isthmus. Gold, pearls, and the Strait; the Ojeda and Nicuesa grants (Urabá, Darién, Castilla del Oro), 1507; Darién, 1509: Nombre de Dios.

Based on map in Bolton and Marshall's *Colonization of North America*

THE COLONIZATION OF CENTRAL AMERICA (1509–1526)

3. The discovery of the South Sea, and the founding of
   Panamá. Balboa in a barrel; becomes the "strong man"
   at Darién; Enciso and Nicuesa banished; marriage with
   chief's daughter; expedition to the South Sea (1513);
   plans for exploration; Pedrarias at Darién; Balboa
   executed (1519); capital moved to Panamá (1519); new
   rush, north and south.

4. The northward advance into Central America. Exploration
   of the west coast: Espinosa (1519); Niño and González
   (1522–1523). Beginnings of Costa Rica and Nicaragua:
   Córdova sent by Pedrarias (León, Granada, and Bruselas
   founded); Córdova beheaded; Pedrarias governor;
   San Juan River explored. González in Honduras.

5. The contest with Cortés's men. In Honduras: struggle of
   González with Olid and Casas; Cortés in Honduras.

Alvarado in Guatemala and San Salvador; Father Las Casas in Chiapas (the "Land of War" becomes the "Land of True Peace").

REQUIRED READING

One of the following:

BOLTON, H. E., and MARSHALL, T. M. *The Colonization of North America*, 26–32.
CHAPMAN, C. E. *Colonial Hispanic America*, chap. 3 (selections).
FISKE, JOHN. *The Discovery of America*, I, 131–139, or II, 454–482.
JAMES, H. G., and MARTIN, P. A. *The Republics of Latin America*, 24–28.
RICHMAN, I. B. *The Spanish Conquerors*, chaps. 3, 5.
RIPPY, J. F. *Historical Evolution of Hispanic America*, 48–54.
ROBERTSON, W. S. *History of Latin-American Nations*, 1922 ed., 26–29, 72–73; 1932 ed., 28–31, 77–78.
SWEET, W. W. *History of Latin America*, 1919 ed., 50–54; 1929 ed., 60–64.
WEBSTER, HUTTON. *History of Latin America*, 17–27.
WILGUS, A. C. *A History of Hispanic America*, chap. 2 (selections).
WILLIAMS, M. W. *People and Politics of Latin America*, 21–47, 111–114.

REFERENCES

ANDERSON, C. B. G. *Old Panama and Castilla del Oro*, 1–28.
BANCROFT, H. H. *History of Central America*, I, 182–202, 202–247, 358–412, 478–511, 522–643.
BRIGHAM, W. T. *Guatemala, the Land of the Quetzal.*
FERNÁNDEZ GUARDIA, RICARDO. *History of the Discovery and Conquest of Costa Rica.*
FORTIER, ALCÉE, and FICKLEN, J. R. *Central America and Mexico*, 1–102.
GANN, THOMAS. *Maya Cities, a Record of Exploration and Adventure in Middle America.*
HELPS, ARTHUR. *Las Casas.*
HELPS, ARTHUR. *The Spanish Conquest in America*, III, 23–48, 48–57, 164–289.

KELLY, J. E. *Pedro de Alvarado, Conquistador.*

KOEBEL, W. H. *Central America,* 56–82.

KROEBER, A. L. *Anthropology.*

MACNUTT, F. A. *Las Casas.*

MERRIMAN, R. B. *Rise of the Spanish Empire,* III, 467–473, 519–522.

NILES, BLAIR. *Maria Peluna.* (A novel.)

RADIN, PAUL. *The Story of the American Indian.*

SPINDEN, H. J. *Ancient Civilization of Mexico and Central America.*

STRAWN, ARTHUR. *Sails and Swords.* Being the golden adventures of
Balboa and his intrepid company, freebooters all, discoverers of the
Pacific.

VERRILL, A. H. *Great Conquerors of South and Central America.*

WINSOR, JUSTIN. *Narrative and Critical History of America,* II,
187–201.

LECTURE V. CORTÉS AND THE CONQUEST OF MEXICO

The Nahua Country

Introductory. The conquest of Mexico by Hernán Cortés and his little band of followers was one of the boldest exploits in all history. The Valley of Mexico at that time was the center of the most powerful Indian state in North America, but Cortés arrived at an opportune moment for success. The peoples subject to the Aztecs were restless, and Montezuma II was not a strong ruler. Cortés turned this unrest to his account, and led against the Aztec capital a large native army, without whose help he could not have succeeded. The fall of Mexico City (Tenochtitlán), in 1521, was only the beginning of the conquest, and it took twenty years for Cortés and his associates to bring the Nahua peoples under control. From Mexico Cortés and his lieutenants turned south, conquered Guatemala, and in Honduras met and disputed the way with the lieutenants of Pedrarias coming from the Isthmus. The conquest was not wholly a work of destruction, but was one of construction as well. Wherever they went the Spaniards founded cities, built churches, developed industries, and set up Spanish political institutions. The Indians were exploited, but the missionaries worked nobly to Christianize and educate them. Nahua culture was badly shattered but not wholly destroyed, and many of its finest features are preserved today in the mixed race which has resulted from the conquest. Mexico City became the capital of the viceroyalty of New Spain, embracing most of Spanish North America. Over the viceroyalty Antonio

Based on map in Bolton and Marshall's *Colonization of North America*

CORTÉS AND HIS COMPANIONS IN MEXICO

de Mendoza, one of Spain's ablest men, was sent to rule. Cortés was supplanted by Mendoza in the first place, but he was made Marquis of the Valley and granted vast estates.

1. The mapping of the Gulf Coast. Two movements: north-westward (León); westward (Córdova, 1517; Grijalva, 1518; Pineda, 1519; Cortés, 1519).
2. Mexico on the eve of the conquest. The Nahua migration; Nahua culture; the city of Mexico; struggle of the valley tribes; the triple alliance (Mexico, Texcoco, Tlacopán); the Aztec conquests; tribute and human sacrifice; resistance by Tarascans and Tlascalans; unrest; Montezuma II a fatalist; belief in the "Fair God"; arrival of Spaniards opportune.
3. The fall of Mexico City. Hernán Cortés; the expedition; Aguilar and Doña Marina; alliance with the Totonacs;

Vera Cruz; presents for the Emperor; iconoclasm; the march over the mountains; Tlascala; Cholula; Montezuma in custody; Narváez; Noche Triste; the valley subdued; the fleet on the lake; siege and fall of the capital (August, 1521).

4. The spread of the conquest. Reasons for rapidity: unrest; fear of horses; firearms; genius of Cortés; his companions; aid of allies. General features: destruction of life and monuments; encomiendas; constructive work (cities, churches, monasteries, industries, audiencias); the viceroyalty of New Spain; the New Laws. Steps in the spread of the conquest (1521-1543): the companions of Cortés; Sandoval in southern Vera Cruz (1521); Orozco in Oaxaca (1521); Olid in Michoacán and Colima (Tzintzuntzán, Zacatula, Amazon Island, Queen of Jalisco), 1522-1524; Cortés and Garay in Pánuco (1522-1524); Alvarado in Tehuantepec, Guatemala, and San Salvador (1522-1524); Olid and Las Casas in Honduras (1524); the march of Cortés to Honduras (1524-1525); the burning of Cuauhtémoc; Montejo in Yucatán (first conquest, revolt, Campeche, Mérida, Valladolid), 1527-1545; Guzmán in Sinaloa (Culiacán), 1529-1531; Cortés in California (1533-1535).

REQUIRED READING

One of the following:

BOLTON, H. E., and MARSHALL, T. M. *The Colonization of North America*, 27-28, 32-40.

BOURNE, E. G. *Spain in America*, 149-158.

CHAPMAN, C. E. *Colonial Hispanic America*, 34-41.

FISKE, JOHN. *The Discovery of America*, I, 94-131 (ancient Mexico), or II, chap. 8 (the conquest of Mexico).

MERRIMAN, R. B. *Rise of the Spanish Empire*, III, 459-512.

PRIESTLEY, H. I. *The Mexican Nation*, chap. 2 or 3.

RICHMAN, I. B. *The Spanish Conquerors*, chap. 4.
ROBERTSON, W. S. *History of Latin-American Nations*, 1922 ed., 30–35, 70–90; 1932 ed., 32–38, 74–95.
SWEET, W. W. *History of Latin America*, 1919 ed., 55–65; 1929 ed., 65–75.
WEBSTER, HUTTON. *History of Latin America*, 64–73.
WILGUS, A. C. *A History of Hispanic America*, chaps. 2, 5 (selections).
WILLIAMS, M. W. *People and Politics of Latin America*, 114–119.

REFERENCES

THE AZTECS AND THE CONQUEST OF MEXICO

ABBOTT, J. S. C. *Hernando Cortez.*
AITON, ARTHUR. *Antonio de Mendoza, First Viceroy of New Spain.*
BANCROFT, H. H. *History of Mexico*, I and II, 1–515.
BANCROFT, H. H. *Popular History of Mexico*, 152–208.
BIART, LUCIAN. *The Aztecs; their History, Manners, and Customs.*
BRADEN, C. S. *Religious Aspects of the Conquest of Mexico.*
BRITTAIN, ALFRED. *Discovery and Exploration*, I, 315–384.
CAVO, ANDRÉS. *Los Tres Siglos de México.*
CLEVEN, N. A. N. *Readings in Hispanic American History*, 43–62, 126–138.
DÍAZ DEL CASTILLO, BERNAL. *True History of the Conquest of New Spain.*
FISKE, JOHN. *The Discovery of America*, II, 212–295; also III, 1–92.
HALE, SUSAN. *The Story of Mexico*, 135–202.
HELPS, ARTHUR. *Life of Cortés.*
HELPS, ARTHUR. *Life of Las Casas.*
HELPS, ARTHUR. *Spanish Conquest in America*, II, 160–365; III, 1–164.
HONEYMAN, A. V. *The Aztecs.*
JOHNSON, W. H. *Pioneer Spaniards in America*, 126–192.
JOYCE, T. A. *Mexican Archaeology.*
KEATINGE, MAURICE (Editor). *The True History of the Conquest of Mexico*, by Captain Bernal Díaz del Castillo. 2 vols.
LEÓN, NICOLÁS. *Historia General de México.*
MACNUTT, F. A. *Cortés and the Conquest of Mexico.*
MACNUTT, F. A. *The Letters of Cortés to Charles V*, I–II.
MAYER, BRANTZ. *Mexico*, I, 14–147.

NOLL, A. H. *Short History of Mexico*, 47–101.
PRESCOTT, W. H. *The Conquest of Mexico.*
PRIESTLEY, H. I. *The Mexican Nation*, chaps. 1–7.
RIPPY, J. F. *Historical Evolution of Hispanic America*, chap. 2.
ROBINSON, H. M. *Stout Cortez.* A Biography of the Spanish Conquest.
SPENCE, LEWIS. *The Civilization of Ancient Mexico.*
SPINDEN, H. J. *Ancient Civilizations of Mexico and Central America.*
STEPHENS, KATE. *The Mastering of Mexico.* (An abridged translation
of Bernal Díaz's *True History of the Conquest.*)
WINSOR, JUSTIN. *Narrative and Critical History of America*, II, 249–306.
ZAMACOIS, NICETO DE. *Historia de Méjico.*

LECTURE VI. THE MINES AND THE NORTHERN BORDERLANDS

Introductory. While the men of Pedrarias were pioneering Central America, and Cortés was establishing Spanish rule in southern Mexico, exploring expeditions scoured the northern interior, following up tales of gold and great cities. They hoped, with reason, to find in the north "another Mexico." Armored men on armored horses, like crusading knights they moved from village to village, abandoning one will-o'-the-wisp to follow another. Few in number, they secured safety through spreading terror, seizing chieftains as they went, and holding them as hostages. There was little hard fighting, but the adventurers showed endurance beyond belief. Like apparitions, Narváez and De Soto flitted through the vast region called La Florida, only to find watery graves. Coronado sought wealth and fame in Gran Quivira, and returned to Mexico discredited. Cabrillo, trusting his fate to the South Sea waves, was lured to his death by the California Lorelei. These bold adventurers gained little wealth, but their heroic marches were by no means wild-goose chases. They quieted for a time the extravagant tales of great cities in the north and taught Europe an important lesson in American geography.

Next the Spanish pioneers advanced into the mining area north of the Aztec country, a region which proved to be one of America's richest treasure chests. Great captains — men of means — directed the forward movement. Guzmán, Ibarra, and Carbajal were conquistadores of only lesser fame than Cortés. Agents of the king, they were made feudal rulers of vast frontier provinces, unlimited on the north. Patriotic to their home lands, they recorded this affection by naming their jurisdictions New Galicia, New Vizcaya, and New León. In this north country there were "strikes," "rushes," and "boom towns," the prototypes of later ones all the way from Mexico to Alaska. Zacatecas, Durango, Guanajuato, and Monterrey became flourishing towns. The society established there was permanent, and sixteenth-century mining camps have become capitals of thriving states today. The wealth of these mines, and of those opened simultaneously in Peru, gave Spain a brilliant position and stimulated all Europe.

From southern Chihuahua the frontier of permanent settlement leaped across the wide desert to the Pueblo region of the upper Rio Grande. Here lived sedentary Indians like the Aztecs, and the province was therefore called New Mexico. Thither Oñate led a colony with paternal care. Franciscan friars built missions, soldiers warded off the attacks of Apaches, and civilians founded a semipastoral society. Meanwhile Menéndez occupied Florida to restrain the French, and Legazpi founded Manila as a base for Oriental commerce and an outpost of Mexico. Of the Indies Florida was the right wing and the Philippines the left.

1. The Northern Mystery (1513–1543). Influence of fabulous tales on northern exploration : Fountain of Youth ; Strait of Anian ; Amazon Island ; Seven Cities ; Quivira ; "Otro México" and "Otro Perú." Exploration of the northern interior : by way of Florida (Ponce de León, Ayllón, Narváez, Vaca, De Soto, Moscoso) ; by way of the Pacific slope (Cortés, discovery of California, his colony, the name "California," Coronado expedition (Friar Marcos), Cíbola, Grand Cañon, Tiguex, Quivira). Up west coast

and across the Pacific: Alvarado; Cabrillo in California;
Saavedra; Villalobos; the Philippines. Not wild-goose
chases (fabulous tales exploded, geographical knowledge).
2. The mines of north Mexico. Characteristics of later
sixteenth-century expansion: mines; stock-raising;
missions; defense; the adelantados, or great captains

THE MINES AND THE NORTHERN MYSTERY

(Ibarra, Carbajal, Urdiñola, Oñate). New Galicia (1540-
1560): Mixton War; the mines of Zacatecas and Guanajuato. New Vizcaya (1563-1590): Ibarra (Durango,
Santa Bárbara); expedition up coast (1567); Urdiñola
(Mazapil, Saltillo, Tlascaltecan colonies). New León
(1579-1590): Carbajal (Monterrey, the Inquisition).
3. New Mexico (1580-1609). The Pueblo Indians; renewed
expeditions (Rodríguez, 1581; Espejo, 1582; Sosa, 1590;
Humaña in Kansas, 1593); Oñate and the founding
of the colony (his contract, his expedition, revolt at

Ácoma, Villagrá's history, Oñate's explorations); Santa
Fé founded (1609).
4. Florida, California, and the Philippines. Increasing importance of defense: presidios and missions. The colonization of Florida: early attempts (Coosa, Santa Elena,
Cancer, De Luna, Villafañe), 1549-1561; French intrusion (Ribaut and Laudonnière); Menéndez de Avilés
(French expelled; settlements up Florida, Georgia, and
Carolina coasts; St. Augustine); Jesuit and Franciscan
missions; interior explorations. The Philippines and
California: Legazpi and the conquest of the Philippines;
the Manila galleon; foreign intrusion (Drake, Cavendish); California (Cermeño, 1595; Vizcaíno, 1602-
1603; plans to occupy Monterey Bay).

NOTE. Some of this ground is covered from a world point of view in
Lecture XII.

REQUIRED READING

One of the following:

BOLTON, H. E. *Outpost of Empire*, chaps. 1 and 2.
BOLTON, H. E. *The Spanish Borderlands*, chap. 1, 2, 3, 4, or 5.
BOLTON, H. E., and MARSHALL, T. M. *The Colonization of North Amer-
ica*, 40-47, 54-61, 61-71, 72-75.
BOURNE, E. G. *Spain in America*, 133-148, 158-189.
LUMMIS, C. F. *The Spanish Pioneers*, 125-148.
MECHAM, J. L. *Francisco de Ibarra* (selections).
PRIESTLEY, H. I. *The Coming of the White Man*, 51-84.
WEBSTER, HUTTON. *History of Latin America*, 78-85.
WILGUS, A. C. *A History of Hispanic America*, chaps. 5, 7 (selections).
WILLIAMS, M. W. *People and Politics of Latin America*, 119-129.

REFERENCES

THE NORTHERN MYSTERY

BANCROFT, H. H. *Discovery of the Northwest Coast*, I, chaps. 2-4.
BANDELIER, FANNY R. *The Journey of Álvar Núñez Cabeza de Vaca*.
(Original narrative in translation.)

BISHOP, MORRIS. *The Odyssey of Cabeza de Vaca.*
BOLTON, H. E. *Spanish Exploration in the Southwest,* 1–39.
CLEVEN, N. A. N. *Readings in Hispanic American History,* 194–206.
DELLENBAUGH, F. S. *Breaking the Wilderness,* 103–238.
DELLENBAUGH, F. S. *The Romance of the Colorado,* 1–35.
FISKE, JOHN. *The Discovery of America,* III, 312–342.
HODGE, F. W., and LEWIS, T. H. *Spanish Explorers in the Southern United States.*
JOHNSON, W. H. *Pioneer Spaniards in North America,* 77–126, 195–299.
KING, GRACE. *De Soto and his Men in the Land of Florida.*
LOWERY, WOODBURY. *Spanish Settlements in the United States, 1513–1561,* 123–283.
MAYNARD, THEODORE. *De Soto and the Conquistadores.*
NUNN, G. E. *Origin of the Strait of Anian Concept.*
PUTNAM, RUTH. *California, the Name.*
ROBERTSON, J. A. (Editor). *True Relation of the Hardships Suffered by Governor Fernando de Soto and Certain Portuguese Gentlemen during the Discovery of the Province of Florida, now newly set forth by a Gentleman of Elvas.*
SAUER, C. O. *The Road to Cibola.*
SCHAFER, JOSEPH. *The Pacific Slope and Alaska,* 3–24.
SEDGWICK, MRS. W. T. *Acoma, the Sky City.*
WAGNER, H. R. *Spanish Voyages to the Northwest Coast of America in the Sixteenth Century.*
WINSHIP, G. P. *The Coronado Expedition.*

FLORIDA

BAIRD, C. W. *Huguenot Emigration to America,* I, 60–77.
BOLTON, H. E. *Spain's Title to Georgia.*
BOLTON, H. E. *The Spanish Borderlands,* 120–164.
BOLTON, H. E., and MARSHALL, T. M. *The Colonization of North America,* 61–67.
BOLTON, H. E., and ROSS, MARY. *The Debatable Land,* 1–68.
BOURNE, E. G. *Spain in America,* 175–189.
CHAPIN, G. M. *Florida,* I, 16–34.
CONNOR, J. T. *Colonial Records of Spanish Florida.*
HAMILTON, P. J. *Colonization of the South,* 3–41.

JOHNSON, J. G. "The Spanish Period of Georgia and South Carolina History, 1566–1702," *University of Georgia Bulletin*, May, 1923.
JOHNSON, J. G. "The Yamassee Revolt of 1597, and the Destruction of the Georgia Missions," *Georgia Historical Quarterly*, March, 1923.
KENNY, MICHAEL, S.J. *The Romance of the Floridas.*
LOWERY, WOODBURY. *Spanish Settlements, 1513–1561*, 351–377 (De Luna, Villafañe).
LOWERY, WOODBURY. *Spanish Settlements. Florida, 1562–1574* (Menéndez).
PARKMAN, FRANCIS. *Pioneers of France in the New World*, 16–162. (Revised Edition, 20–181.)
PRIESTLEY, H. I. *The Luna Papers.*
ROSS, MARY. "French Intrusions in Georgia and South Carolina, 1577–1580," *Georgia Historical Quarterly*, September, 1923.
ROSS, MARY. "The French on the Savannah, 1605," *Georgia Historical Quarterly*, September, 1924.
WINSOR, JUSTIN. *Narrative and Critical History of America*, II, 254–283.

PHILIPPINES AND CALIFORNIA

ALESSIO ROBLES, VITO. *Acapulco en la Historia y en la Leyenda.*
BANCROFT, H. H. *History of California*, I, 81–94 (Drake), 94–105 (Gali, Cermeño, Vizcaíno).
BARROWS, D. P. *History of the Philippines*, 74–84 (Magellan), 114–119 (Loaisa, Villalobos), 125–140 (Legazpi).
BLAIR, E. H., and ROBERTSON, J. A. *Philippine Islands*, II, 23–330 (Loaisa, Saavedra, Villalobos, Legazpi).
BOLTON, H. E. *The Spanish Borderlands*, 105–119.
BOLTON, H. E. *Spanish Exploration in the Southwest*, 41–134.
BURNEY, JAMES. *Chronological History of Discoveries in the South Sea.*
CLEVEN, N. A. N. *Readings in Hispanic American History*, 207–218 (Drake).
CORBETT, J. S. *Sir Francis Drake.*
FISKE, JOHN. *The Discovery of America*, II, 184–211 (Magellan). (Three-volume edition, II, 419–450.)
GUILLEMAND, F. H. H. *Ferdinand Magellan.*
MOSK, S. A. "The Cardona Company and the Pearl Fisheries of Lower California," in *Pacific Historical Review*, III (1934), 50–61.

RICHMAN, I. B. *California under Spain and Mexico*, 12–30.

ROBERTSON, J. A. "Legazpi and Philippine Island Colonization," Report of the American Historical Association (1907), I, 145–155.

WAGNER, H. R. *Sir Francis Drake's Voyage around the World.*

THE NORTH–MEXICAN FRONTIER IN THE SIXTEENTH CENTURY

ALESSIO ROBLES, VITO. *Francisco de Urdiñola.*

ALESSIO ROBLES, VITO. *Saltillo en la Historia y en la Leyenda.*

BANCROFT, H. H. *Arizona and New Mexico*, 74–146.

BANCROFT, H. H. *History of Mexico*, II, chaps. 22, 24, 34.

BANCROFT, H. H. *North Mexican States and Texas*, I, chap. 5.

BLACKMAR, F. W. *Spanish Institutions of the Southwest*, chap. 10.

BOLTON, H. E. *Spanish Exploration in the Southwest*, 137–280 (especially 137–141, 163–167, 199–206).

BOLTON, H. E., and MARSHALL, T. M. *The Colonization of North America*, 52–61.

CAMPBELL, T. J. *The Jesuits, 1534–1921.*

CAUGHEY, J. W. *A History of the Pacific Coast.*

HACKETT, C. W. (Editor). *Historical Documents relating to New Mexico, Nueva Vizcaya, and Approaches Thereto, to 1773.*

HAMMOND, G. P. *Don Juan de Oñate and the Founding of New Mexico.*

HAMMOND, G. P., and REY, AGAPITO (Editors). *Obregón's History of Sixteenth Century Explorations in Western America.*

MECHAM, J. L. *Francisco de Ibarra.*

SAUER, C. O. *The Distribution of Aboriginal Tribes and Languages in Northwestern Mexico.*

SHIELS, W. E. *Gonzalo de Tapia, 1561–1594.*

TWITCHELL, R. E. *Leading Facts of New Mexican History*, 234–273.

LECTURE VII. PIZARRO AND THE CONQUEST OF PERU

Land of the Incas

Introductory. The Spanish conquest spread simultaneously into South America and North America. Rumors of Peru reached the Isthmus before Balboa crossed the mountains. His discovery of the South Sea started a rush south as well as north. Panama was the base for both. The conquest of Peru presented numerous analogies and notable contrasts with that of Mexico. In each case a culture was weakened or destroyed that was well worth preserving. With fewer men Pizarro performed a feat of boldness equal to that of Cortés. The "empire" of the Incas was far greater in extent and in some respects more advanced than that of the Montezumas. Both Cortés and Pizarro were aided by firearms, horses, native superstitions, and native disunion. The capture of Cuzco ended only the first stage in the conquest of Peru, and several decades were required to bring the whole Inca realm into subjection. The conquest was bloodier and more turbulent in Peru than in Mexico. But here as well as there destruction was accompanied by constructive work. Gradually the royal agents obtained control; conquerors were followed by colonists, and Spanish institutions were established on a stable basis. In spite of the harshness of the conquest, most of the natives were preserved, and their descendants form a prominent element in Peruvian society today.

1. The discovery of Peru by the men of Pedrarias. Rumors of the Incas; Andagoya in Birú (1522); Pizarro, Almagro

35

and Luque; personalities; expedition to San Juan River
(1524); the contract; expedition across the equator
(1525); Pizarro on Gallo Island; a skein of cotton; the
rescue ships; "Peru and riches, or Panama and poverty";
the expedition to Túmbez (1527); llamas, gold, and vi-
cuña shawls.

2. Peru on the eve of the conquest. Rise of Inca rule: Lake
Titicaca, the "Tibet of the New World"; monuments
of prehistoric civilization (monoliths of Tiahuanaco);
consolidation of the four tribes in the thirteenth century
(Incas, Quechuas, Canas, Cauchis); Cuzco built as the
capital. Spread of the Inca conquests (fourteenth and
fifteenth centuries) from Popayán to Río Maule: Quito
a second capital; nature of the Inca rule (military occupation, roads, couriers, assimilation, language, religion,
the temple of Pachacamac); meanings of "Inca"
(the tribe, the caste, the God-King "Viracocha").
Civil war: Huascar becomes Inca (1525); rebellion
of Atahualpa; Huascar captured, and Atahualpa
enthroned.

3. Pizarro in Spain (1528–1529). His patent; titles; two
hundred leagues from Santiago River; his brothers; five
vessels equipped; Almagro's jealousy of Fernando Pizarro.

4. The overthrow of Atahualpa. The expedition of 1531; two
hundred men and fifty horses; followed by Benalcázar and
De Soto; the march to Túmbez; San Miguel founded;
the march to Caxamarca (1532); "Sons of Viracocha";
Atahualpa captured; Valverde's sermon; the ransom;
Huascar murdered at Atahualpa's order; trial and death
of Atahualpa; on to Cuzco (1530); Manco becomes
Inca; Benalcázar and Alvarado in Quito; Lima founded;
other cities, colonies; Pizarro's constructive work.

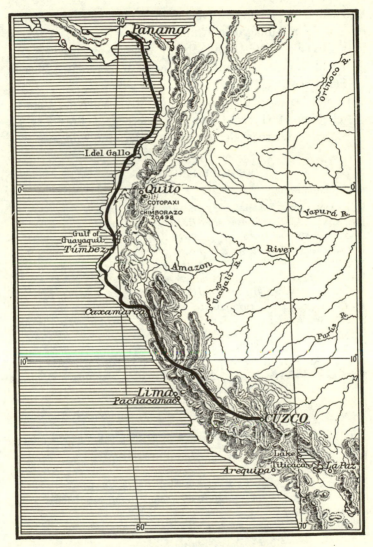

THE PIZARRO EXPEDITION TO PERU

5. Rebellion and civil war. New grants (New Castile and New Toledo); Almagro in Chile; Manco's revolt; Almagro seizes Cuzco; Battle of Salinas; Almagro executed (1538); Fernando Pizarro imprisoned in Spain; Francisco Pizarro murdered (1541).

6. The new laws, audiencia, and viceroy. Vaca de Castro; rebellion of Gonzalo Pizarro; victory of President La Gasca; Mendoza viceroy; law, order, and progress.

REQUIRED READING

One of the following:

CHAPMAN, C. E. *Colonial Hispanic America*, 45–53.
DAWSON, T. C. *South American Republics*, II, 20–57.
FISKE, JOHN. *The Discovery of America*, II, chap. 10.
LUMMIS, C. F. *The Spanish Pioneers*, 238–264.
MERRIMAN, R. B. *Rise of the Spanish Empire*, III, 541–576.
RICHMAN, I. B. *The Spanish Conquerors*, chap. 6.
ROBERTSON, W. S. *History of the Latin-American Nations*, 1922 ed., 18–24, 35, 72–77; 1932 ed., 19–25, 78–81.
SWEET, W. W. *History of Latin America*, 1919 ed., 65–74; 1929 ed., 75–83.
WEBSTER, HUTTON. *History of Latin America*, 27–32, 73–76.
WILGUS, A. C. *A History of Hispanic America*, chaps. 6, 8 (selections).
WILLIAMS, M. W. *People and Politics of Latin America*, 49–64, 131–137.

REFERENCES

PIZARRO AND THE CONQUEST OF PERU

BANCROFT, H. H. *History of Central America*, II, 1–43, 122–132, 246–273.
BINGHAM, HIRAM. *Machu Picchu, a Citadel of the Incas.*
CLEVEN, N. A. N. *Readings in Hispanic American History*, 1–43, 153–174.
DAWSON, T. C. *South American Republics*, II, 20–57.
ENOCK, C. R. *Peru*, 31–57.
HELMHOLT, H. F. *History of the World*, I, 373–380.

HELPS, ARTHUR. *Life of Pizarro.*

HELPS, ARTHUR. *The Spanish Conquest in America*, Books XVI–XIX.

HERNÁNDEZ ALFONSO, LUÍS. *El Virreinato del Perú.*

MARKHAM, CLEMENTS. *History of Peru*, 65–135.

MEANS, P. A. *Ancient Civilizations of the Andes.*

MEANS, P. A. *The Fall of the Inca Empire.*

MOSES, BERNARD. *Spanish Dependencies in South America*, I, 93–120, 204–229.

OBER, F. A. *Pizarro and the Conquest of Peru.*

PRESCOTT, W. H. *Conquest of Peru*, Books II–IV.

SINCLAIR, J. H. (Editor). *The Conquest of Peru as Recorded by a Member of the Pizarro Expedition.*

Lecture VIII. Venezuela and New Granada

The Search for Meta, El Dorado, and Omagua

Introductory. Like a fan the Spanish conquest opened out in all directions, until a half-circle was described around the West Indies. Southward from Española the frontier of settlement advanced to Tierra Firme, the northern mainland of South America. At first all this area was subject to the Audiencia of Santo Domingo. Then for a time the Venezuela district was in the control of the German business house of Welsers, who held the area as a fief from Charles V. The emperor needed money; the bankers furnished it and took land in return.

Pearl-fishing, gold-hunting, trade, and slave-catching raids made the vast stretch of shore line known. Settlements on the coast became bases for forays into the interior. There, as in North America, belief in fabulous tales hastened exploration. Cortés had found a great city and Pizarro had captured a ruler who paid for his ransom a room full of gold. So while some adventurers sought in the north "another Mexico," others hoped to find in the south "another Peru." In search of these fabled lands heroic expeditions were made by seekers of treasure. In the Orinoco valley some sought Meta. "I do not think that any of those who took part in the enterprise would have taken so much trouble to get into Paradise," says Oviedo. Over the sky-touching Andes others pursued the gilded chieftain, El Dorado, to the plains of Bogotá. He was no longer there; so eastward they turned and looked for Omagua in the valley of the Amazon. In these adventures the

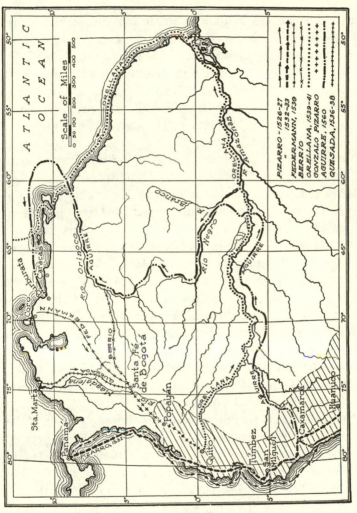

THE SEARCH FOR META, EL DORADO, AND OMAGUA

Germans of Venezuela took a prominent and reckless part. Like those in North America, these great marches served a useful purpose. They made known the geography of the northern half of South America and resulted in the permanent colonization of Venezuela and New Granada. Later a similar belief in extravagant tales led English explorers into Guiana to seek the fabled city of Manoa.

1. New centers of expansion; extension from Peru, south, east, and north; meeting of the different movements.
2. Early settlements on Tierra Firme. The region under the Audiencia of Santo Domingo; pearl fisheries and slave-catching raids (Margarita, Trinidad, Cubagua, and the Paria coast); beginnings of New Granada; Santa Marta district; Ojeda's colony, Santa Marta (1525), Cartagena (1533); beginnings of Venezuela; "Little Venice"; Las Casas' attempt (1521); Coro founded (1527); German rule in Venezuela (the Welsers, Alfinger, Speyer, Federmann; harsh rule; Tocuyo founded; grant rescinded, 1545).
3. Belief in the fabulous as a cause of rapid exploration. North America (Amazon Island, the Seven Cities, Quivira, Copper-Crowned King); South America (Meta, Omagua, El Dorado, White King).
4. The search for Meta and Omagua and the exploration of the Orinoco. From the Paria district (Ordaz (1531–1535) up the Orinoco, Herrera (1534) up the Orinoco, Ortal (1535) overland to the Orinoco); from Coro (Federmann (1530) to Apure River, Speyer (1535–1538) across Caqueta River); the search for Meta fuses with the quest of El Dorado.
5. The search for the Gilded Man and the founding of New Granada. Legends of El Dorado (basis of the legend, Cundinamarca, Lake Guatavitá); Alfinger's attempt

from Coro (1529–1530); Quesada's expedition from Santa Marta (Santa Fé de Bogotá founded), 1536–1538; Benalcázar's expedition from Quito (Popayán and Antioquía); Federmann's expedition from Coro; the agreement; New Granada; attempts to drain Lake Guatavitá.

6. The eastward quest. Von Hutton, from Coro, seeking Meta reaches Caqueta River, and turns east to Guaviare River (1541); Gonzalo Pizarro; the "Land of Cinnamon"; Orellana deserts; Orellana's expedition down the Amazon (1539–1541); Ursua and Aguirre (1560); later expeditions (Raleigh, 1595; Manoa).

REQUIRED READING

One of the following:

CHAPMAN, C. E. *Colonial Hispanic America*, 54–59.

LUMMIS, C. F. *The Spanish Pioneers*, 181–199.

MERRIMAN, R. B. *Rise of the Spanish Empire*, III, 531–537, 576–588.

ROBERTSON, W. S. *History of the Latin-American Nations* (selections).

SWEET, W. W. *History of Latin America*, 1919 ed., 75–79; 1929 ed., 86–89.

WILLIAMS, M. W. *People and Politics of Latin America*, 47 49, 129 131, 137–138.

ZAHM, J. A. *The Quest of El Dorado*, chaps. 2, 4.

REFERENCES

BANDELIER, A. F. *The Gilded Man*, 1–110.

BORDA, J. J. *Historia de la Compañia de Jesús en Nueva Granada.*

CASTELLANOS, JUAN DE. *Elegías de Ilustres Varones de las Indias.*

DAWSON, T. C. *South American Republics*, II, 297–301, 347–350, 403–416.

GROOT, J. M. *Historia Eclesiástica y Civil de Nueva Granada.*

MARKHAM, CLEMENTS. *Conquest of New Granada*, 80–170.

MOSES, BERNARD. *Spanish Dependencies in South America*, I, 29–79, 121–156, 276–288.

SIMÓN, PEDRO. *Expedition of Pedro de Ursua and Lope de Aguirre.*

Lecture IX. Valdivia and the Founding of Chile

Land of the Araucanians

Introductory. Peru became a base for expansion south as well as north, and Chile was soon brought within the range of Spanish influence. Inca civilization extended to Río Maule; southern Chile was the home of the sturdy and warlike Araucanians. The way to Chile was led by Almagro, Pizarro's rival in Peru. In an epic march, with incredible hardship he led a little army over the snows of the Andes, leaving behind him a trail that was marked by the line of condors which flocked to feed on the bodies of his Indian carriers who fell by the way.

Almagro had spied out the land. Pedro de Valdivia led the colony that permanently occupied the country. Valdivia was a man of restless enterprise, courage, and loyalty, and a veteran of the conquests of Venezuela and Peru. In the face of untold obstacles he founded his colony, of which Santiago became the capital and the center of Spanish culture. Beyond the Bío Bío Valdivia met the determined resistance of the Araucanians. They had maintained their freedom against the Incas, and they now offered a resistance to the Spaniards that was not completely broken till the end of the nineteenth century. Their great chieftains, Lautaro and Caupolicán, became national heroes whose statues now dot the country. The long struggle produced *La Araucana*, an epic poem that ranks with the great epics of literature. In Chile the Spaniards and Indians never fused so completely as in Mexico and Peru, and the modern Chilean race is dominantly Spanish.

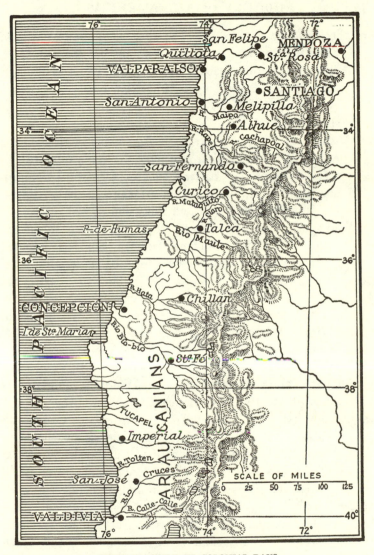

CENTRAL CHILE IN COLONIAL DAYS

1. The land and the people. The Inca conquest of northern Chile to Río Maule; the Araucanians (or Mapuches).

2. Failure of the Alcazaba expedition (1534-1535). Grants of New Castile, New Toledo, and New León; Alcazaba's expedition to Patagonia (mutiny, counter-revolution, shipwreck, failure).

3. Almagro in Chile (1535-1537). Agreement with Pizarro; Almagro's forces; his route over the mountains to Coquimbo; exploring parties sent to Río Maule; disappointment; return by way of Atacama Desert; contest with the Pizarros; trial and execution of Almagro.

4. Valdivia and the founding of Chile (1540-1550). The expedition by way of Atacama Desert; Santiago founded (1541); Valdivia independent (elected governor by cabildo); ship-building and mining; Santiago destroyed; Monroy's mission (the golden stirrup); arrival of aid (Pastene and Monroy); La Serena (Coquimbo) founded, (1543); exploration to 41 degrees south (Pastene); Valdivia in Peru (1547); his return; conquest extended to the Araucanian border (Concepción founded, 1550).

5. The Araucanian War (1550-1557). Valdivia founds posts south of the Bío Bío (Imperial, Valdivia, Angol, Villarica, 1550-1552); Araucanian resistance; Caupolicán and Lautaro; Lautaro's strategy; defeat of Spaniards at Tucapel; torture and death of Valdivia; Angol and Villarica abandoned; defeat at Marigueñu; Concepción abandoned; rivalry of Villagrán and Aguirre.

6. Lost ground temporarily regained. The tide turned by the death of Lautaro (1557); García Hurtado de Mendoza governor; Villagrán and Aguirre expelled ("one bench large enough for both "); new campaign against the Araucanians: the Bío Bío recrossed; Concepción and Villa

Rica reoccupied; advance to Chiloé; Osorno founded; torture and death of Caupolicán (1558); Ercilla y Zúñiga's epic poem, *La Araucana*.

7. Continuation of the Araucanian war; few settlements retained south of the Bío Bío River after 1598; final submission, 1882.

8. Expansion east of the mountains. City of Mendoza founded; Cuyo province.

9. Character of Chilean colonial society: agriculture, immigration, a military frontier.

REQUIRED READING

One of the following:

CHAPMAN, C. E. *Colonial Hispanic America*, 59–63.
DAWSON, T. C. *South American Republics*, II, 135–147.
MERRIMAN, R. B. *Rise of the Spanish Empire*, III (selections).
ROBERTSON, W. S. *History of the Latin-American Nations* (selections).
SWEET, W. W. *History of Latin America*, 1919 ed., 73–74; 1929 ed., 83–84.
WILGUS, A. C. *A History of Hispanic America*, chaps. 6, 8 (selections).
WILLIAMS, M. W. *People and Politics of Latin America* (selections).

REFERENCES

BARROS ARANA, DIEGO. *Historia Jeneral de Chile*, I, 147–443; II, 5–294.
CLEVEN, N. A. N. *Readings in Hispanic American History*, 174–187.
DAWSON, T. C. *South American Republics*, II, 135–147.
ELLIOT, G. F. S. *Chile*, 14–63.
GALDAMES, LUÍS. *Estudio de la Historia de Chile*, 40–47, 56–95.
GRAHAM, R. B. C. *Pedro de Valdivia*.
HANNOCK, A. U. *History of Chile*, 21–72.
MAITLAND, F. J. G. *Chile*, 17–25.
MILLS, G. J. *Chile*, 19–27.
MOLINA, J. I. *History of Chile*, II, 1–174 (especially 1–47, 114–174).
MOSES, BERNARD. *Spanish Dependencies in South America*, II.

Lecture X. The La Plata Colonies

The Beginnings of Paraguay, Argentina, and Uruguay

Introductory. The La Plata valley was a meeting place for different lines of colonial expansion. There Spaniards from the east met Spaniards from the west; there Spaniards contested the ground with Portuguese. True to tradition, Argentina and Uruguay are cosmopolitan today. The La Plata valley at first lay in the path of Spaniards on the way to the Orient and to Peru. Early attempts to occupy the mouth of the great river were defeated by the stronger attractions of Peru, the opportunity to Christianize and exploit the gentle, sedentary Guaraní Indians of the Paraguay country, and the hostility of the wilder tribes of the lower La Plata River. One project after another for settlement down the river was defeated by the stronger pull of Peru and Paraguay. As a consequence Asunción became the first permanent center of occupation on the La Plata, and Paraguay became a well-developed colony before Spanish settlements farther down the stream got a start. Eventually, however, a ranching society pushed down the valley, and Buenos Aires took new root. Irala is remembered as the colonizer of Paraguay, and Garay as the founder of a permanent settlement at Buenos Aires. The Banda Oriental, now Uruguay, was long a no man's land, and then it became a bone of contention between Spain and Portugal. The Jesuit missions were characteristic features of Paraguay, and Argentina was marked by Gaucho society and the vast herds of stock which the Gauchos tended.

48

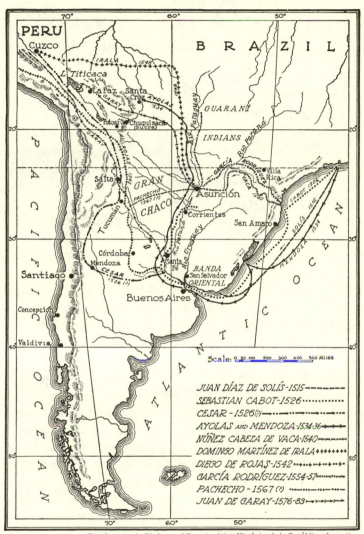

Based on map in Biedma and Beyer's *Atlas Histórico de la República Argentina*

THE OPENING OF THE LA PLATA BASIN

1. The La Plata region the meeting place of different lines of
   colonial expansion. Movements from the Atlantic and the
   Pacific; the Spaniards and the Portuguese; cosmopolitan population today.

2. The land and the people. The La Plata, Uruguay, Paraná,
   Paraguay, and Pilcomayo rivers; the pampas; Gran
   Chaco; the Andean piedmont; the Guaraní Indians.

3. The La Plata region in the path of the voyagers to the
   Spice Islands and of the seekers for the White King
   Solís's voyage (1516); his death. Expedition of Alejo
   García in search of the White King (1516–1524). Se-
   bastian Cabot: pilot major for Spain; expedition to
   Cathay (1526); decides to explore the La Plata (1527);
   post at Sancti Spiritus; explorations above the forks of
   the Paraná.

4. Temporary beginnings at Buenos Aires. Diego de García:
   concession (1526); agreement with Cabot on the Paraná;
   up the Pilcomayo; Sancti Spiritus destroyed; return of
   Cabot and García to Spain. Pedro de Mendoza, adelantado of the La Plata (1534–1537): expedition with eleven
   vessels; Buenos Aires founded (1536); Indian attacks;
   settlers move to Corpus Christi.

5. Efforts to communicate with Peru and the founding of Asunción. "The pull of Peru": Ayolas and Irala sent by
   Mendoza to reach Peru; expedition and death of Ayolas
   (1537); Asunción founded in his absence (Salazar and
   Irala); the Guaraní Indians a factor in Spanish settlement; Corpus Christi colony moved to Asunción.
   Cabeza de Vaca in Paraguay: experiences in North
   America; adelantado of the La Plata; his journey overland (1541); attempt to reach Peru (1543–1544): deposed. Irala in charge in Paraguay: elected by his men;

expedition to Peru; ordered back by La Gasca; his successful rule; Indian policy; efforts to secure the frontiers; Ontiveras founded to hold back the Portuguese; Santa Cruz, on the Peru border; Santa Cruz independent. San Francisco Solano in the Gran Chaco.

6. Expansion down the Paraná and the refounding of Buenos Aires. Zárate adelantado; Santa Fé founded by Garay as a port for Paraguay (1573); Creoles; Zárate founds San Salvador on the Uruguay; Garay refounds Buenos Aires (1580); Creoles; Garay slain; cattle; the Gauchos.

7. The western border (the trans-Andean settlements of Peru and Chile); Charcas and Tucumán; mines; rivalries; cities founded; communication with the La Plata.

8. Paraguay and La Plata separated (1617); the Jesuits in Paraguay.

REQUIRED READING

One of the following:

CHAPMAN, C. E. *Colonial Hispanic America*, 63–69.
DAWSON, T. C. *South American Republics*, I, 19–46.
MERRIMAN, R. B. *Rise of the Spanish Empire*, III, 606–611.
ROBERTSON, W. S. *History of the Latin-American Nations*, 1922 ed., 14–16, 80–81, 107–108; 1932 ed., 16, 85–86, 114–115.
SWEET, W. W. *History of Latin America*, 1919 ed., 79–83; 1929 ed., 89–93.
WILGUS, A. C. *A History of Hispanic America*, chaps. 6, 8 (selections).
WILLIAMS, M. W. *People and Politics of Latin America*, 140–143.

REFERENCES

THE LA PLATA COLONIES

ARCOS, SANTIAGO. *La Plata*, 63–120.
BOURNE, E. G. *Spain in America*, 112–113, 192.
CLEVEN, N. A. N. *Readings in Hispanic American History*, 187–191 (Cabeza de Vaca); 218–221 (English pirates); 238–242 (the Jesuits in Paraguay).

DAWSON, T. C. *South American Republics*, I, 19–46.

DOMÍNGUEZ, L. L., SCHMIDT, ULRICH, and CABEZA DE VACA, ÁLVAR NÚÑEZ. *The Conquest of the River Plate (1535–1555)*. (Hakluyt Society publications.)

ENOCK, C. R. *Republics of Central and South America*.

KIRKPATRICK, F. A. *A History of the Argentine Republic*.

LEVENE, RICARDO. *Investigaciones acerca de la Historia Económica del Virreinato del Plata*. 2 vols.

O'NEILL, GEORGE, S.J. *Golden Years on the Paraguay*.

SCHMIEDER, OSCAR. *Historic Geography of Tucumán*.

SCHMIEDER, OSCAR. *Situation of the Argentine Pampa in the Colonial Period*.

Lecture XI. The Founding of Brazil

Portuguese America

Introductory. Brazil is a monument to little Portugal. By the Line of Demarcation the eastern coast of South America was awarded to her. To this basis of ownership Portugal added important explorations. For a time she was more interested in her colonies in the Orient, but foreign danger soon forced her to protect and colonize Brazil. The vast country was divided into separate grants called capitanias. Each grant had an ocean frontage, and the grantees were endowed with extensive feudal prerogatives and powers of government. Some of the grants were never occupied. The needs of administration and of defense soon resulted in placing them all under a single governor-general, and Souza was sent to rule with powers resembling those of a viceroy.

The colony now took on new life. Sugar-raising flourished on great fazendas, or plantations, worked by Indian and Negro slaves. Commerce was conducted with the home country, and enterprising Portuguese smuggled goods across vast spaces to the Spanish settlements. Jesuit missionaries labored to convert the natives and protect them against aggressive slave-catchers, who pursued their prey far into the interior. São Paulo, Rio de Janeiro, Bahia, and Pernambuco became the principal centers of colonization and culture. French and Dutch intruders settled in Brazil, threatening Portugal's empire, but were expelled by the hardy Brazilians after vigorous contests. For sixty years (1580–1640) Brazil, like Portugal,

was under the Spanish crown,— the "Babylonian captivity,"
the period was called,— but this connection did not greatly
change the current of life in the colony, and Brazil remains
Portuguese in character.

1. Brazil a monument to sixteenth-century Portugal. Portuguese language, institutions, traditions; economic importance of Brazil (area, population, rivers, minerals,
   forests, coffee, rubber, etc.); political stability; foundations laid in the colonial period.
2. The discovery and early neglect. The Line of Demarcation;
   Portuguese interests in the East; voyages of Cabral
   (1500) and Vespucius (1501); the name "America";
   twenty-five years of neglect (Brazil wood, French voyages, castaways and deserters, "Caramurú" at Bahia and
   Ramalho at São Paulo).
3. Affonso de Souza and the beginnings of São Paulo. Foreign
   danger (the French and Cabot); Affonso de Souza
   (1530–1532); São Vicente founded; the Paulistas the
   frontiersmen of Brazil.
4. The capitanias. A feudal arrangement; twelve fiefs created
   (1534); Affonso de Souza at São Paulo; Duarte Coelho
   at Pernambuco; other capitanias not prosperous; São
   Paulo and Pernambuco principal centers till 1549; the
   royal capitania (need of centralization, Thome de Souza
   governor-general; Bahia made the capital), beginnings
   of prosperity; sugar; Indian and Negro slavery.
5. The Jesuits in Brazil. Harsh Indian policy of the Portuguese; arrival of the Jesuits; Fathers Nobrega and
   Anchieta; missions at São Paulo; Jesuits favor Negro
   slavery to protect Indians; the Mamelukes (Paulistas);
   slave-hunting raids; attacks on Jesuits.

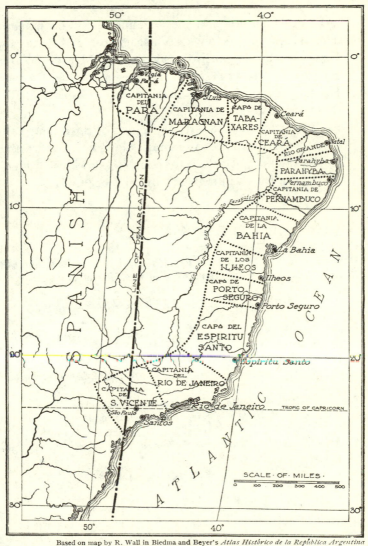

Based on map by R. Wall in Biedma and Beyer's *Atlas Histórico de la República Argentina*

THE CAPITANIAS IN BRAZIL (SIXTEENTH CENTURY)

6. The French intrusion and the founding of Rio de Janeiro. The Huguenot colony; Villegagnon in "Antarctic France" (Rio de Janeiro); victories of Men de Sá and Estacio de Sá (1558–1567); expulsion of the French; Rio de Janeiro founded; Brazil divided (Bahia and Rio de Janeiro capitals, 1572).

7. Brazil under Spain (1580–1640). Union of Spain and Portugal (1580); expansion of Brazil along north coast and in the interior; English freebooters (Hawkins, Cavendish); the Dutch in northern Brazil (1624–1661).

REQUIRED READING

One of the following:

CHAPMAN, C. E. *Colonial Hispanic America*, chap. 5.

DAWSON, T. C. *South American Republics*, I, chaps. 2–7 (one chapter).

JAMES, H. G., and MARTIN, P. A. *The Republics of Latin America*, 18–21, 64–77.

RIPPY, J. F. *Historical Evolution of Hispanic America*, 45–46, 72–76, 116–120.

ROBERTSON, W. S. *History of the Latin-American Nations*, 1922 ed., 61, 82–84, 108–111, 139–148; 1932 ed., 87–89, 115–143.

SCHMIEDER, O. *The Brazilian Culture Hearth*, 159–185.

SWEET, W. W. *History of Latin America*, 1919 ed., 84–93; 1929 ed., 94–103.

WEBSTER, HUTTON. *History of Latin America*, 111–115.

WILGUS, A. C. *A History of Hispanic America*, chaps. 6, 8, 11, 14, 15 (selections).

WILLIAMS, M. W. *People and Politics of Latin America*, 143–148, 245–275.

REFERENCES

THE FOUNDING OF BRAZIL

AKERS, C. E. *A History of South America.*

BULEY, E. C. *North Brazil*, 30–36.

BULEY, E. C. *South Brazil*, 24–29.

DAWSON, T. C. *South American Republics*, I, 287–370.

ELLIOTT, L. E. *Brazil*, 10–25.
ESCRAGNOLLE TAUNAY, AFFONSO DE (Editor). *Historia Geral das Bandeiras Paulistas*. 6 vols.
FLETCHER, D. P., and KIDDER, J. C. *Brazil and the Brazilians*, 46–60.
GARCÍA CALDERÓN, FRANCISCO. *Latin America; its Rise and Progress*.
GRANT, ANDREW. *History of Brazil*, 1–90.
KOEBEL, W. H. *South America*, 35–46.
LUCIO DE AZEVEDO, J. *Os Jesuítas no Grão-Pará: Suas Missões e a Colonização*.
PANDÍA CALOGERAS, JOÃO. *Formação Historica do Brasil*.
PRESTAGE, EDGAR. *The Portuguese Pioneers*.
REPARAZ, GONZALO DE. *La Época de los Grandes Descubrimientos Españoles y Portugueses*.
SOUTHEY, ROBERT. *History of Brazil*, I, 1–58, 221–343, 369–470; II, 1–250.
WATSON, R. G. *Spanish and Portuguese South America*, I, 155–168.
Cambridge Modern History, III, chap. 7.

Lecture XII. The Enemies of Philip II and Defensive Spanish Expansion

Introductory. Spain's exalted position in the New World at the end of the sixteenth century is reflected by the enemies who rose up against her. In Europe Philip II devoted himself to stamping out the Reformation in the Netherlands, France, and England. The English retaliated by attacks on Spanish commerce, which culminated in the destruction of the Spanish Armada. In America, the English, French, and Dutch resisted Spain's monopoly. Freebooters plundered vessels, sacked towns, and destroyed missions. In defense Spain adopted a fleet system, formed a West Indian armada, and walled her towns on the Caribbean coasts. The French intruded into South Carolina, Florida, and Brazil, but were effectively expelled from all three. The English under Raleigh attempted to found colonies in Carolina and at the mouth of the Orinoco but without success. Drake and Cavendish boldly invaded the Pacific Ocean and attacked Spain's commerce there. In the Orient Portugal contested Spain's position. With the opening of the seventeenth century Spain sustained a struggle there with the British East India Company and the Dutch East India Company. These dangers forced Spain to expand her frontiers of occupation for defensive as well as for direct economic purposes, and to give increased attention to defense on the sea.

1. Philip and the religious wars. The European conflict; increased importance of defense of the colonies; attack on commerce; the flota system.

2. The French intrusion and the founding of Florida. Early efforts to colonize Florida (Coosa, Santa Elena, Cancer, De Luna, Villafañe); the French intrusion (Ribaut, Laudonnière); Menéndez de Avilés (French expelled, De Gourgues's revenge); settlements on the coast of Florida, Georgia, and Carolina; St. Augustine; Jesuit and Franciscan missions; interior explorations; the seventeenth-century struggle with the English in Carolina and Georgia.

3. The English sea-dogs. Hawkins (the slave trade); attacks on Spanish commerce; Drake's attacks; voyage around the world; New Albion; Cavendish; other sea-rovers.

4. The defeat of the Spanish Armada. The Armada; the battle off Gravelines; reprisals for the Armada; a blow at Spanish sea power; inroads into Spanish monopoly.

5. Defensive Spanish expansion. New efforts in Florida. California: new explorations (Cermeño, 1595; Vizcaíno, 1602–1603); plans to occupy Monterey Bay.

6. The Anglo-Dutch invasion of the East. Rise of the Netherlands; attacks on Spain; English in the East; English East India Company; Dutch in the East; Dutch East India Company.

NOTE. Some of this ground is covered from a more local point of view in Lecture VI.

REFERENCES

ABBOTT, W. C. *The Expansion of Europe*, I, chaps. 13, 14, 15.

BENSON, E. F. *Sir Francis Drake.*

BESSON, MAURICE. *The Scourge of the Indies: Buccaneers, Corsairs, and Filibusters.*

BOLTON, H. E. *The Spanish Borderlands*, 112–119, or chap. 6.

BOLTON, H. E., and MARSHALL, T. M. *The Colonization of North America*, 61–71, 107–108.

BOLTON, H. E., and ROSS, MARY. *The Debatable Land*, 1–68.

CONWAY, G. R. G. *An Englishman and the Mexican Inquisition, 1556–1560.*

GOSSE, PHILIP. *Hawkins, Scourge of Spain.*

KENNY, MICHAEL, S.J. *The Romance of the Floridas.*

WILLIAMSON, J. A. *Sir John Hawkins.*

WOOD, WILLIAM. *The Elizabethan Sea-Dogs*, chaps. 5, 6, 7, 8, 9.

WRIGHT, I. A. (Editor). *Documents concerning English Voyages to the Spanish Main, 1569–1580.*

For additional references see Lecture VI.

Lecture XIII. Spanish Colonial Administration

Introductory. To manage her vast American empire Spain developed a colonial system. At home, the king, the Council of the Indies, and the Casa de Contratación were the chief agencies of colonial administration. America was erected into the viceroyalties of New Spain and Peru, to which two more were subsequently added. The viceroys were personal representatives of the king. The audiencias were administrative courts, which assisted in government and acted as checks on the viceroys. A corps of oficiales reales looked after the royal revenue. The audiencias were divided into provinces under governors with a variety of titles. Municipalities had elective cabildos, or councils. The cabildo abierto, or open cabildo, was a bulwark of local self-government that never completely lost its force. At the end of the eighteenth century Charles III made many reforms in colonial government, but most of them came too late to achieve their aims.

1. Spanish and Portuguese achievement : extent of exploration, geographical knowledge, settlement (200 Spanish towns and 160,000 Spaniards by 1574); transmission of culture; comparison with English, French, Dutch; efforts to civilize natives.
2. Home agencies of government. The king: the colonies a personal possession of the crown of Castile. Council of the Indies : supreme governing body for the Indies; the Recopilación de Leyes; decline of authority in eighteenth century. The House of Trade (Casa de Contra-

tación): controlled trade monopoly; warehouse at Seville; moved to Cádiz; decline in later eighteenth century; abolished (1790).

3. The viceroys. Personal representatives of the king; functions; kept detached from colonies (three-year term, forbidden to bring family, marry, or hold property there) ; the residencia. The viceroyalties: New Spain (Mexico), 1535; Peru (Lima), 1542; New Granada (Bogotá), 1718; Rio de la Plata (Buenos Aires), 1776. Certain districts (captaincies general) became practically independent of viceroyalties: Guatemala, Venezuela (1773), Provincias Internas (1776), Chile (1798).

4. The audiencias. Functions (administrative courts, check on viceroys) ; functions become limited. Audiencia districts in New Spain: Santo Domingo (1526), Mexico (1527), Guatemala (1543), Guadalajara (1548), Manila (1583). In Peru: Panama (1536), Lima (1542), Bogotá (1549), Los Charcos (1559), Quito (1563), Santiago de Chile (1609), Buenos Aires (1661), Caracas (1786), Cuzco (1787). Others in nineteenth century.

5. The fiscal officials (real hacienda). Importance of American gold and silver; the revenue-gatherers; the royal revenues (tribute, fifths, or quinto, half-annates, taxes on sales, imports, etc.; the royal monopolies of quicksilver, playing cards, tobacco, bullfighting, stamped paper, salt, etc.).

6. The provinces. Ruled by governors of various classes (adelantados, governors, corregidores, alcaldes mayores).

7. The towns. Independent spirit at first ; crushed by Charles V and Philip II ; the town councils (cabildos or ayuntamientos), elective in theory but elections interfered with by higher officials ; offices bought and sold ; open cabildos (cabildos abiertos) a bulwark of popular liberty.

Based on map in Biedma and Beyer's *Atlas Histórico de la República Argentina*

POLITICAL DIVISIONS OF SOUTH AMERICA IN THE
SEVENTEENTH CENTURY

8. Administrative corruption. Graft; nepotism; corruption of justice.

9. Reforms of Charles III. Inspectors (Gálvez); fiscal and commercial reforms; Intendancies.

REQUIRED READING

One of the following:

AITON, A. S. *Antonio de Mendoza* (selections).

BOLTON, H. E., and MARSHALL, T. M. *The Colonization of North America*, 19–20, 34, 47–50, 54–55, 75–76.

BOURNE, E. G. *Spain in America*, 220–242.

CHAPMAN, C. E. *Colonial Hispanic America*, chap. 8.

JAMES, H. G., and MARTIN, P. A. *The Republics of Latin America*, 33–41.

MERRIMAN, R. B. *Rise of the Spanish Empire*, III, 618–625, 638–653.

ROBERTSON, W. S. *History of the Latin-American Nations*, 1922 ed., 87–104; 1932 ed., 92–110, 144–159.

SWEET, W. W. *History of Latin America*, 1919 ed., 94–101; 1929 ed., chap. 8.

WEBSTER, HUTTON. *History of Latin America*, 95–99.

WILGUS, A. C. *A History of Hispanic America*, chaps. 9, 12 (selections).

WILLIAMS, M. W. *People and Politics of Latin America*, 149–163.

REFERENCES

SPANISH COLONIAL INSTITUTIONS

AITON, A. S. *Antonio de Mendoza.*

BOURNE, E. G. *Spain in America*, 190–312.

CASTAÑEDA, C. E. "The Corregidor in Spanish Colonial Administration," in *Hispanic American Historical Review*, IX (1929), 446–470.

CLEVEN, N. A. N. *Readings in Hispanic American History*, 331–372.

COLMEIRO, MANUEL. *Historia de la Economía Política en España.*

CUNNINGHAM, C. H. *The Audiencia in the Spanish Colonies.*

DESDEVISES DU DEZERT, G. H. *L'Espagne de l'ancien régime.*

FISHER, L. E. *The Intendant System in Spanish America.*

FISHER, L. E. *Viceregal Administration in the Spanish-American Colonies.*

HAEBLER, KONRAD. "The Colonial Kingdom of Spain," in H. F. Helmholt's *History of the World*, I.

HILL, R. R. "The Office of Adelantado," in *Political Science Quarterly*, XXVIII (1913), 646–668.

KELLAR, A. G. *Colonization*, 207–316.

MOSES, BERNARD. *The Establishment of Spanish Rule in America*, 17–312.

PIERSON, W. W. "Some Reflections on the Cabildo as an Institution," in *Hispanic American Historical Review*, V (1922), 573–596.

PRIESTLEY, H. I. *The Coming of the White Man*.

PRIESTLEY, H. I. *José de Gálvez, Visitor-General of New Spain, 1765–1771*.

PRIESTLEY, H. I. *The Mexican Nation*, chaps. 4, 6, 7, 9.

RIPPY, J. F. *Historical Evolution of Hispanic America*, chap. 6.

ROBERTSON, WILLIAM. *The History of America*, II, 345–434.

ROBERTSON, W. S. *Rise of the Spanish-American Republics*, 10–25.

RÖSCHER, W. G. F. *The Spanish Colonial System*. (Translated by E. G. Bourne.)

SHEPHERD, W. R. *Latin America*, 19–69.

SIMPSON, L. B. *The Encomienda in New Spain*.

SMITH, D. E. *The Viceroy of New Spain*.

SWEET, W. W. *History of Latin America*, 84–118.

ZIMMERMANN, ALFRED. *Die Kolonialpolitik Portugals und Spaniens*.

Lecture XIV. Commerce and Industry in the Spanish Colonies

Introductory. Spain, like other nations, held mercantilist views of commerce. Colonies were founded for the benefit of the mother country. Colonial trade was restricted to prescribed ports in Spain and America. To protect commerce and facilitate its supervision, a fleet system was established. Land trade in America was conducted largely by pack trains and river boats. Wholesale and retail trade was carried on in fairs and markets. With all her efforts Spain was unable to maintain her trade monopoly. Dutch, English, and French freebooters freely smuggled goods into Spanish ports. Foreign merchants in Spain furnished wares for the colonial markets. Asientos, or contracts, granted trading rights to foreign companies. By one of these asientos, in 1713, English merchants obtained exceptionally important concessions.

The greater part of the labor supply in Spanish America was furnished by natives. The Indian was controlled by the encomienda system, which aimed to convert, civilize, protect, and exploit him. The dominant occupations in Spanish America always were agriculture and stock-raising, but mines attracted more attention and furnished the crown the most revenue. The vast supply of silver and gold from Mexico and Peru had an important influence on the economic life of all Europe. Manufactures were permitted so long as they did not compete with home industries, and in several lines the colonies had considerable industrial enterprises. Mexico City was famous for its fine carriages and coaches.

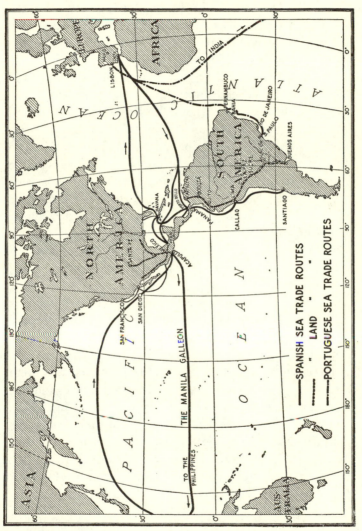

SPANISH AND PORTUGUESE TRADE ROUTES

1. Commerce. The mercantile theory: trade restricted in the interest of the crown to Spanish subjects and to special ports (Seville, Vera Cruz, Porto Bello, Acapulco, etc.); commerce hampered by heavy taxes; intercolonial trade restricted. The fleet system: pirates; the flota and the Tierra Firme galleons; the Peruvian armada; the Manila galleons; the Armada de Barlovento. Overland routes: Indian carriers and mule trains (recuas); Porto Bello to Panama (plans for a canal); Buenos Aires to Lima and Santiago; Quito to Cartagena; Nicaragua to Porto Bello by way of the San Juan River; Acapulco to Vera Cruz; New Mexico and Texas to Vera Cruz. Fairs (ferias): Porto Bello; Jalapa; Mexico (Acapulco, Lima, Santa Fé, Saltillo, etc.) The consulados: Mexico (1604); Lima (1627); control of trade; abuses. Breakdown of the monopolistic system: foreign merchants in Spain; the asientos; the South Sea Company; buccaneers; smuggling; the fleet system abolished (1748); reforms of Charles III (changes in the direction of greater freedom of trade; designed to stimulate commerce and increase revenue).

2. The labor supply. Indian labor: the encomienda system designed to convert, civilize, and exploit the Indian; attention given to exploitation; opposition by Las Casas and others; the New Laws (1542); encomiendas gradually abolished; the mita; enslavement of rebels and cannibals; peonage. Negro slaves: a substitute for Indians; slave-trade asientos; illegal slave trade (John Hawkins); the South Sea Company in the slave trade; Negroes most numerous in Caribbean area and Brazil; numbers; abolitionists (Las Casas; San Pedro Claver, "Apostle of the Negroes"); cimarrones.

3. Agriculture and stock-raising. Encouraged by sovereigns; plants, animals, and laborers sent over; native agriculture continued as main support (maize, potatoes, vanilla, cacao, bananas, maguey, cotton); European crops; sugar-raising in West Indies and Brazil; stock-raising; large ranches (cattle, sheep, goats); the mesta; hide and tallow trade; the vaqueros and gauchos; the long drives; influence on our ranch life; the cayuse, the long-horn, and the razorback.

4. Mining. Temple-robbing and grave-robbing; the great mines (Potosí, Zacatecas, Guanajuato, etc.); value of products; methods; mining rushes; mining law; the Minería of Mexico.

5. Manufacturing. Must not compete with Spanish manufactures; considerable development, largely in native hands; textile arts (Mexico, Peru, Chile); metal work (Peru and Mexico, plateros, the bells of Arequipa, cannon); furniture; carriages; shipbuilding (Guayaquil, Havana, San Blas).

REQUIRED READING

One of the following:

BOURNE, E. G. *Spain in America*, chap. 19.

HARING, C. H. *Trade and Navigation between Spain and the Indies*, 21–45, 123–154, 201–230.

JAMES, II. G., and MARTIN, P. A. *The Republics of Latin America*, 49–57.

MERRIMAN, R. B. *Rise of the Spanish Empire*, III, 626–637.

PRIESTLEY, H. I. *The Coming of the White Man*, 85–103.

ROBERTSON, W. S. *History of the Latin-American Nations*, 1922 ed., chaps. 4–5; 1932 ed., chap. 8.

SWEET, W. W. *History of Latin America*, chap. 9.

WEBSTER, HUTTON. *History of Latin America*, 99–107.

WILGUS, A. C. *A History of Hispanic America*, chaps. 10, 13 (selections).

WILLIAMS, M. W. *People and Politics of Latin America*, 164–178, 193–208.

REFERENCES

ALESSIO ROBLES, VITO. *Acapulco en la Historia y en la Leyenda.*
BANCROFT, H. H. *History of Mexico,* III.
BARRIO LORENZOT, J. F. DEL. *El Trabajo en México durante la Época Colonial. Ordenanzas de Gremios de la Nueva España.*
HARING, C. H. *Buccaneers in the West Indies in the Seventeenth Century.*
LEVENE, RICARDO. *Investigaciones acerca de la Historia Económica del Virreinato del Plata.*
LOOSLEY, A. C. "The Puerto Bello Fairs," in *Hispanic American Historical Review,* XIII (1933), 314–335.
RIPPY, J. F. *Historical Evolution of Hispanic America,* chaps. 4–6.
SIMPSON, L. B. *The Encomienda in New Spain.*
SIMPSON, L. B. *Studies of the Administration of the Indians in New Spain.*

Lecture XV. Social, Intellectual, and Religious Life in the Spanish Colonies

Introductory. In America Spanish civilization was imposed on native culture and based on a caste system. Most of the social and official privileges were reserved to Peninsulars. Creoles, less favored than the Spanish-born, were far more fortunate than mestizos, Indians, and intermediate castes. Colonial Spanish America was by no means devoid of culture. In Mexico and Lima high society was modeled on court life in Madrid. Till near the end of the eighteenth century Mexico was the leading city in the Western Hemisphere. The universities of Mexico, Lima, and Córdova were recognized by contemporary European universities. Not a few men, especially among the clergy, were devotees of learning. Important books were written on historical, ethnological, linguistic, and other subjects. Architecture, especially in church-building and monastery-building, was far ahead of that in other parts of America. Like economic and political life, education was on a caste basis. Instruction was controlled by the Church, and universities and colleges were designed to train men for the priesthood and the professions. The regular orders established monastery schools where mestizos had some chance for learning. On the frontier, where the encomienda was unprofitable, the natives fell largely to the care of the missions, which were designed to Christianize and civilize the Indians and help to hold the frontier against outside invaders. In the interest of their charges Jesuits, Dominicans, Franciscans, and other orders rendered unselfish service.

1. Social classes. The Peninsulars: theory of colonization;
   deterioration of Spaniards in America mentally and politically; hence control must remain in hands of Spanish-born; their privileges. Creoles (criollos): defined;
   their limitations; their opportunities; their general
   characteristics; influence in history. Mestizos: defined;
   their relations with other groups; their employments;
   use in the army and in menial occupations; effect of
   the eighteenth-century system of colonial defense. Mu-
   lattoes: compared with mestizos; Negro status in the
   Spanish colonies; manumissions; the pardos; gente de
   razón. The Indians: conquest of wild and sedentary
   tribes contrasted; admixture of lower castes; the léperos;
   modern pelados, lobos, coyotes, chinos, sambos. Disap-
   pearance of Spaniards at Independence; Creoles and
   mestizos absorb developing citizenry; development of
   Hispanic civilization superimposed upon tribes of
   mixed race.
2. Intellectual life. Society on a caste system; education on a
   class basis; early school ideas of the Church; its industrial education; the maestre; the craft guilds; education
   in holy orders; development of universities in America;
   Universities of Mexico and Lima, influence of Mendoza;
   University of Santiago, planned in 1600, instruction begun
   in 1756; ceremony of inauguration; government of the
   university; privileges of the students and faculty; famous
   students (Marcos Solís y Haro, Pedro de Paz Vasconcelos,
   Antonio Calderón); ceremonials at graduation; ideal of
   the colonial university; its influence.
3. Influence of the Church. Character of the conquest (tem-
   poral and spiritual at expense of Indians); the tithes;
   conflict between the regular and secular clergy over

possession of territory, and the struggles over the tithes; the notable regular orders (Franciscans, Dominicans, Augustinians, Mercedarians, Jesuits); the early monasteries and convents supplemented by the missions; the mission theory; mission contrasted with encomienda; the mission as a frontier institution; its religious inspiration and its political significance; the entradas of the Fathers as service rendered to the crown; the missions as frontier defenses; missions as educational institutions (religious, industrial, and civic education); secularization; estimates of the efficiency of the mission system; contrast with the ideal contemplated; with the systems of other colonial powers.

REQUIRED READING

One of the following:

BOLTON, H. E. "The Mission as a Frontier Institution in the Spanish-American Colonies," *American Historical Review*, October, 1917.

BOURNE, E. G. *Spain in America*, chap. 16, 17, 18, or 20.

CHAPMAN, C. E. *Colonial Hispanic America*, chap. 7.

JAMES, H. G., and MARTIN, P. A. *The Republics of Latin America*, 41–48, 57–64.

LEONARD, I. A. *Don Carlos de Sigüenza y Góngora: a Mexican Savant of the Seventeenth Century* (selections).

MERRIMAN, R. B. *Rise of the Spanish Empire*, III, 654–663.

PRIESTLEY, H. I. *The Coming of the White Man*, 139–172.

RIPPY, J. F. *Historical Evolution of Hispanic America*, 106–115.

ROBERTSON, W. S. *History of the Latin-American Nations*, 1922 ed., chaps. 4–5 (appropriate paragraphs); 1932 ed., chap. 9.

SHEPHERD, W. R. *Latin America*, chap. 3, 5, or 6.

SWEET, W. W. *History of Latin America*, chap. 10.

WEBSTER, HUTTON. *History of Latin America*, 86–95, 107–111.

WILGUS, A. C. *A History of Hispanic America*, chaps. 10, 13 (selections).

WILLIAMS, M. W. *People and Politics of Latin America*, 209–226.

74 HISTORY OF THE AMERICAS

REFERENCES

BANCROFT, H. H. *History of Mexico*, Vol. III.
CAMPBELL, T. J. *The Jesuits, 1534–1921.*
GRAHAM, R. B. C. *A Vanished Arcadia.*
LEONARD, I. A. *Don Carlos de Sigüenza y Góngora: a Mexican Savant of the Seventeenth Century.*
LEONARD, I. A. *Romances of Chivalry in the Spanish Indies.*
MARKHAM, CLEMENTS. *History of Peru.*
MOSES, BERNARD. *South America on the Eve of Emancipation.*
MOSES, BERNARD. *Spain's Declining Power in South America.*
NAVARRO Y LAMARCA, CARLOS. *Historia General de la América.*
OLIVEIRA LIMA, MANOEL DE. *The Evolution of Brazil.*
O'NEILL, GEORGE, S.J. *Golden Years on the Paraguay.*
SHIELS, W. E. *Gonzalo de Tapia, 1561–1594.*

THE FRENCH, DUTCH, SWEDISH, AND DANISH COLONIES

LECTURE XVI. THE FOUNDING OF NEW FRANCE

Brazil, Guiana, the Caribbean, Acadia, St. Lawrence Valley

Introductory. France, England, and the Netherlands established no permanent colonies in the sixteenth century; but all were interested in expansion in similar ways, all desired a share in the trade of America and the Far East, all wished to break Spain's trade monopoly and made intrusions into the Caribbean and the South American mainland. Simultaneously in the seventeenth century all three began to make permanent settlements in North America and the Caribbean. Being late comers they established themselves in left-over areas, for Spain and Portugal had occupied two thirds of the hemisphere.

During the sixteenth century France was absorbed in Italian and domestic wars, and her colonizing efforts failed. Her early seventeenth-century efforts succeeded, but not till the middle of the century did she have a vigorous colonial policy. French success on the mainland was based on the fur trade. Acadia, the first permanent French colony, was a buffer against New England. Quebec, a monument to Samuel de Champlain, became the center of the early fur business of the St. Lawrence valley. By 1670 fur-traders and missionaries had reached the Upper Lakes and prepared the way for entering the vast Mississippi Valley. South of the Great Lakes French expansion was checked by Iroquois hostility and Dutch and English influence. In Guiana and the Lesser Antilles France established tropical plantations, trading stations, and buccaneering bases.

1. France during the colonial period. The consolidation of France; France in the sixteenth century (the Italian wars, the religious wars); reorganization in the seventeenth century (the great ministers, Sully, Richelieu, Mazarin, Colbert); Louis XIV; lack of a colonial policy before Colbert's day.

2. Sixteenth-century attempts at colonization. Attacks on Spanish commerce; the fisheries of Newfoundland; attempts at settlement (Cartier and Roberval on the St. Lawrence, 1534–1543; the Huguenots in Brazil, 1555–1657; the Huguenots in South Carolina and Florida, 1562–1568; later French intrusions).

3. Acadia and the St. Lawrence valley. The fur-trade monopoly (De Monts). Acadia: settlements round the Bay of Fundy (Port Royal, St. Jean, Grand Pré); missions; border rivalry with the English (Acadia captured, 1628–1632, 1654–1667, 1710; ceded, 1713); the land of Evangeline. The St. Lawrence valley: Champlain; the founding of Quebec (1608); alliance with the Algonquins (battle of Lake Champlain, 1609). Westward exploration: Ottawa River, Lake Huron, Lake Ontario (1614–1615); Nicolet in Wisconsin (1634); Radisson and Grosseilliers (1654–1660); Joliet on Lake Superior (1669); Dollier and Galinée up Lake Erie (1670); St. Lusson at Sault Ste. Marie (1670).

4. Guiana and the Caribbean area. Various attempts in East Guiana (Cayenne), 1613–1663; Caribbean Islands settlements (St. Christopher, Antigua, Montserrat, Santo Domingo, Guadeloupe, St. Martin, St. Bartholomew,

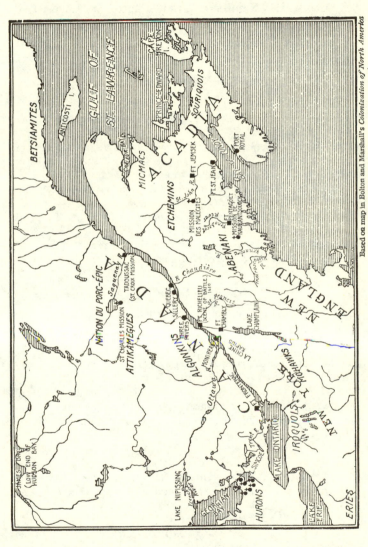

THE FRENCH IN ACADIA AND THE ST. LAWRENCE VALLEY (SEVENTEENTH CENTURY)

Based on map in Bolton and Marshall's *Colonization of North America*

St. Croix, Les Saintes, Marie-Galante, St. Lucia, Grenada); tobacco, sugar, buccaneering; population; the West India Company (embracing all French America), 1664.

REQUIRED READING

One of the following:

BOLTON, H. E., and MARSHALL, T. M. *The Colonization of North America*, 78–96.

BURPEE, L. J. *Historical Atlas of Canada*, maps 12, 17 and accompanying notes.

COLBY, C. W. *The Founder of New France.*

GREENE, E. B. *Foundations of American Nationality*, chap. 10.

MARQUIS, T. G. *The Jesuit Missions* (selections).

MUNRO, W. B. *The Crusaders of New France*, chaps. 1–3.

MUNRO, W. B. *The Seigneurs of Old Canada.*

SCHMIEDER, O. *The Brazilian Culture Hearth*, 169–171.

THWAITES, R. G. *France in America*, chaps. 1–3, 8.

REFERENCES

THE FOUNDING OF NEW FRANCE

BIGGAR, H. P. *A Collection of Documents Relating to Jacques Cartier and the Sieur de Roberval.*

BRITTAIN, ALFRED. *Discovery and Exploration*, chap. 13.

CHAMPLAIN, SAMUEL DE. *Works.* 5 vols.

COLBY, C. W. *Canadian Types of the Old Régime*, chap. 1 (historical background of New France), chap. 2 (the explorer — Champlain), chap. 3 (the missionary — Brébeuf), chap. 4 (the colonist — Hébert).

FISKE, A. K. *The West Indies.*

GRANT, W. L. *History of Canada.*

HANOTAUX, GABRIEL, and MARTINEAU, ALFRED (Editors). *Histoire des Colonies Françaises et de l'Expansion de la France dans le Monde.* Tome I.

HOLMES, H. E. *The Makers of Maine.*

HUGUET, ADRIEN. *Jean de Poutrincourt, Fondateur de Port Royal en Acadie, Vice-roi du Canada, 1557–1615.*

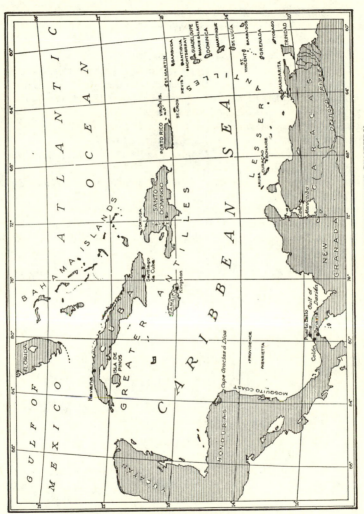

THE CARIBBEAN AREA IN THE SEVENTEENTH CENTURY

KELLOGG, L. P. *The French Régime in Wisconsin and the Northwest,* 1-43.

KINGSFORD, WILLIAM. *History of Canada,* I, 1-295.

MIMS, S. L. *Colbert's West Indian Policy.*

MUNRO, W. B. *The Crusaders of New France.*

PARKMAN, FRANCIS. *The Jesuits in North America.*

PARKMAN, FRANCIS. *The Old Régime in Canada.* (Read especially the third section. Chapter 18 of this section is on Canadian feudalism.)

PARKMAN, FRANCIS. *Pioneers of France in the New World,* 189-456.

PROWSE, D. W. *A History of Newfoundland.*

ROBINSON, P. J. *Toronto during the French Régime.*

RODWAY, JAMES. *Guiana: British, Dutch, and French.*

RONCIÈRE, CHARLES DE LA. *Jacques Cartier et la Découverte de la Nouvelle-France.*

SAINTOYANT, J. *La Colonisation Française sous l'Ancien Régime (du XVe siècle a 1789).* 2 vols.

SHORTT, ADAM, and DOUGHTY, A. G. *Canada and its Provinces,* I.

TROTTER, R. G. *Canadian History: a Syllabus and Guide to Reading.*

WRONG, G. M. *The Rise and Fall of New France.*

LECTURE XVII. THE OLD RÉGIME IN CANADA

Introductory. Acadia and the St. Lawrence valley under France presented a mixture of medieval Europe and an American frontier. It was a land of explorers, missionaries, fur-traders, peasant farmers, feudal lords, and royal officials. Jesuit missionaries worked among the Indians, and the *Jesuit Relations* are a noble monument to their labors. The most successful missions were among the Hurons, but even these were short-lived, for they were destroyed by the Iroquois. When the Hurons fled west the Jesuits followed them and established more slender missions on the shores of the Upper Lakes. Efforts among the Iroquois were rewarded with little success. As elsewhere in America, the Jesuits and other orders established schools, colleges, and hospitals. The heroic work of the Jesuits in Canada has been acknowledged by the Church in the recent canonization of eight of their martyrs.

Feudalism, dead in France, was revived in Canada through the need of settlers and military protection. Great seigneuries, cut up into strips each with a river frontage, were tilled by peasant farmers, or habitants. Many of the seigneuries were granted to soldiers. In spite of the feudal grants, French population grew slowly. For half a century the French colonies were like stepchildren, being controlled largely by trading companies; but in 1663 New France became a royal province and was given increased military protection.

1. The Jesuit missions. Recollect fathers came first (Father le Caron); the Jesuits in America (South America,

81

Mexico, New France); the *Jesuit Relations*; the Huron missions (location, Fathers Brébeuf and Lallemand, headquarters at Ste. Marie), 1625–1629; Iroquois hostility (the destruction of the Huron missions, 1649; the martyrdom of Brébeuf and Lallemand; flight of the Hurons; Black Robes canonized); the Iroquois missions

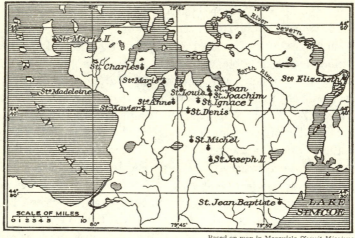

Based on map in Marquis's *Jesuit Missions*

THE HURON MISSIONS

(Iroquois hostility toward the French, Dutch and English control, Father Jogues's efforts and martrydom); later French attempts among Iroquois (the Iroquois punished; De Tracy, Frontenac; a French colony and a new mission attempted in New York; failure); the Upper Lakes missions (the Jesuits follow the Hurons; Allouez, Marquette); missions on the Upper Lakes (Michilli-mackinac, Ste. Marie, Green Bay, La Pointe, St. Joseph, etc.); cultural work of the missionaries (schools, colleges, hospitals; the Sulpician Seminary, the Ursuline Con-

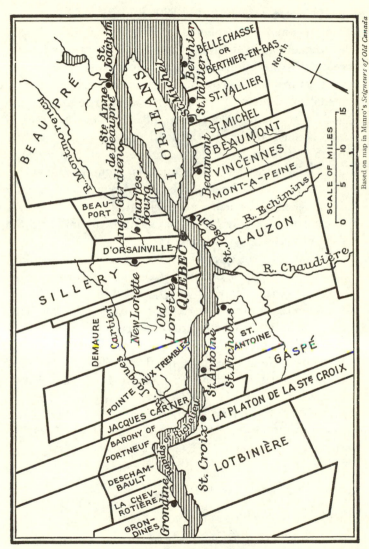

SEIGNEURIAL GRANTS IN THE VICINITY OF QUEBEC

Based on map in Munro's *Seigneurs of Old Canada*

BEAUPRÉ

R. Montmorency

Ste Anne de Beaupré

St. Joachim

I. ORLÉANS

St. Michel

Berthier

St Vallier

BELLECHASSE
OR
BERTHIER-EN-BAS

ST. VALLIER

North

SCALE OF MILES

0   5   10   15

Ange-Gardien

Charles-bourg

Beaumont

ST. MICHEL

BEAUMONT

BEAU-PORT

VINCENNES

D'ORSAINVILLE

MONT-A-PEINE

R. Echimins

R. du Sud

St. Joseph

LAUZON

SILLERY

New Lorette

Old Lorette

QUEBEC

R. Chaudière

DEMAURE

Cartier

Pointe

Jacques

I. aux Tremble

St. Antoine

St. Nicholas

ST. ANTOINE

GASPÉ

JACQUES CARTIER

BARONY OF PORTNEUF

Rapids of Richelieu

Grondine

St. Croix

LA PLATON DE LA STE CROIX

DESCHAM-BAULT

LA CHEV-ROTIÈRE

LOTBINIÈRE

GRON-DINES

vent, Notre Dame, Laval University); the Jesuits as explorers and geographers.

2. The seigneurial system in Canada. Feudal vestiges in colonial America (capitanias, encomiendas, patroons, proprietary English colonies, seigneuries in New France); feudalism dead in France (personal and military bond gone); revived in Canada (need of settlers and protection against Indians); the land system (feudal grants, narrow strips with frontage on the rivers); three hundred seigneuries (grants to officials, Church seigneuries, the Carignan regiment, the Le Moynes, the barony of Longueil); seigneur and habitant (burdens on habitant not heavy; a few cash payments; the mill and the fish pole; the Maypole party).

3. Population small in spite of feudal grants (3000 by 1665; 12,000 by 1700; 60,000 by 1763); settlers mainly Normans; women shipped over (La Hontan's description).

4. Government. Control by private companies till 1663 (the fur companies, the Hundred Associates); Louis XIV and Colbert take hold; De Tracy sent to conquer the Iroquois; New France a royal province, 1663; the Council (governor, intendant, bishop; Frontenac, Talon, Laval).

REQUIRED READING
One of the following:

MARQUIS, T. G. *The Jesuit Missions* (selections).
MUNRO, W. B. *Crusaders of New France*, chap. 4 or chap. 5.
PRIESTLEY, H. I. *The Coming of the White Man*, 210–235.
THWAITES, R. G. *France in America*, 124–142.

REFERENCES

BRYCE, GEORGE. *Short History of the Canadian People*, 171–180.
CAHALL, RAYMOND. *The Sovereign Council of New France.*

CAMPBELL, T. J. *Isaac Jogues.*

CAMPBELL, T. J. *The Jesuits, 1534–1921.*

CAMPBELL, T. J. *Pioneer Priests of North America, 1642–1710.*

COLBY, C. W. *Canadian Types of the Old Régime.*

DELALANDE, J. *Le Conseil Souverain de la Nouvelle-France.*

DOLLIER DE CASSON, FRANÇOIS. *A History of Montreal, 1640–1672.* Edited and translated by Ralph Flenley.

DOUGHTY, A. G. *Quebec of Yester-year.*

FORAN, J. R. *Jeanne Mance, or "The Angel of the Colony."*

GREENOUGH, W. P. *Canadian Folk Life and Folk Lore.*

HENEKER, D. A. *The Seigniorial Régime in Canada.*

JAMET, D. A. (Editor). *Marie de l'Incarnation: Écrits Spirituels et Historiques.* 2 vols.

LANCTOT, GUSTAVE. *L'Administration de la Nouvelle-France.*

MARQUIS, T. G. *The Jesuit Missions.*

MUNRO, W. B. *The Seigneurs of Old Canada.*

MUNRO, W. B. *The Seigniorial System in Canada.*

PARKMAN, FRANCIS. *The Jesuits in North America.*

PARKMAN, FRANCIS. *The Old Régime in Canada.*

PRIESTLEY, H. I. *The Coming of the White Man.*

REPPLIER, AGNES. *Mère Marie of the Ursulines: a Study in Adventure.*

ROBINSON, P. J. *Toronto during the French Régime, 1615–1793.*

ROY, PIERRE-GEORGES. *La Ville de Québec sous le Régime Français.* 2 vols.

VATTIER, GEORGES. *Esquisse Historique de la Colonisation de la Province de Québec, 1608–1925.*

WRONG, G. M. *The Rise and Fall of New France.*

Lecture XVIII. The French in the Heart of the Continent (1670–1763)

The Alabama, Mississippi, and Saskatchewan Basins

Introductory. From two bases, Canada and the Caribbean, the French now entered the Mississippi Valley. Many motives led them, but the two most potent were interest in the fur trade and international rivalry. On the fur trade of the West the prosperity of Canada depended. The home government opposed westward extension, but was forced to yield to actualities and to American opinion. The fur trade was granted to companies, but their control was weakened by the aggressive coureurs de bois. The highways of the fur men were the lakes, rivers, and portages. The trade transformed Indian society and determined the sites of cities. The way to the West was led by explorers, and bands of fur men followed under leaders with business ability. For the fur trade of the Upper Lakes country, Detroit became the principal base. Thence water routes spread out like a fan reaching from Lake Winnipeg to the mouth of the Ohio. Missionaries pushed into the same areas and labored heroically among the tribes.

Rivalry with Spain and England drove France into the Gulf region. La Salle's project of a Gulf colony was carried out by Iberville and Bienville. Louisiana, with Mobile as its capital, soon was extended west to Red River and north to include the Illinois country. Stimulated by John Law's financial schemes, French population increased. Trading posts in the Alabama basin became a bulwark against the Spaniards of Florida and

Based on map in Bolton and Marshall's *Colonization of North America*

THE FRENCH IN THE UPPER LAKES REGION (1670–1727)

the English of South Carolina and Georgia. The Illinois settlements restrained the English traders from the more northern colonies. Louisiana was controlled by trading companies till 1731, when it became, like Canada, a royal province. French traders and explorers did not stop at the Mississippi. West of that stream posts were established all the way from the Gulf to the Kansas River. Explorers and traders went still beyond, reaching the Rocky Mountains and Santa Fé. In the Northwest, under La Vérendrye, trade was extended from Lake Superior into the Canadian prairies and up the Saskatchewan River to the Rockies, thus cutting into the profits of the Hudson's Bay Company.

1. Motives to westward expansion. Search for a passage to Asia; interest in Spanish mines; the fur trade; international rivalry. The fur trade: importance (principal interest of the West for 150 years, stimulated exploration, transformed Indian society, opened highways of communication, fixed sites of cities); the fur-trade monopoly; coureurs de bois; the waterways, the portages, posts, annual journeys.

2. The opening of the Mississippi Valley. Policy divided; Talon, the " Great.Intendant "; Frontenac, the "Fighting Governor"; the advance guard; Joliet and Marquette, 1673 (the "Sea of California"); La Salle in the Illinois country (1679); Accau and Hennepin on the Upper Mississippi (1680); La Salle's colony on the Gulf. The fur trade organized: the Upper Mississippi; Duluth (posts on Nipigon and Pigeon rivers, the St. Croix-Brulé route), 1680–1686; Le Sueur (at St. Anthony's Falls, 1683; posts at La Pointe and St. Croix, 1693–1694; "fool's gold" at Mankato), 1683–1700. Perrot (1686): fur trade and

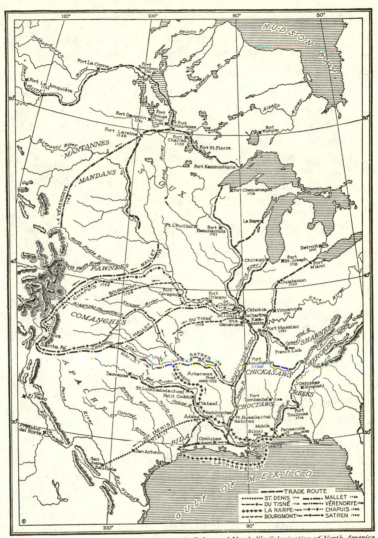

Based on map in Bolton and Marshall's *Colonization of North America*

THE FRENCH IN THE INTERIOR OF NORTH AMERICA (1700–1763)

lead mines (posts at Trempealeau, Lake Pepin, Prairie du Chien, Galena). The Fox wars; posts abandoned. The Illinois country: Tonty; Fort St. Louis; Cahokia and Kaskaskia. English rivalry: Detroit (1701).

3. The founding of Louisiana and the development of the Illinois country. La Salle's project revived (1698); Iberville and Bienville (Biloxi, 1699; Mobile; Spanish rivalry); the trading monopolies (Crozat, the Company of the West); occupation of the Alabama basin; Natchez, Natchitoches, New Orleans (1718); the "Mississippi Bubble"; the Illinois country attached to Louisiana; new posts (Fort de Chartres, Ste. Geneviève, St. Charles); the "Garden of New France"; English rivalry (Vincennes, Ouiatanon).

4. The trans-Mississippi west. Motives (Indian trade, horse trade, Spanish mines); the Texas border (the coast tribes, Opelouzas, Attakapa); the Red River valley (Natchitoches, Cadodacho, Taovayas); St. Denis; the Arkansas valley (La Harpe, the Arkansas post); the Missouri valley (Du Tisné, Bourgmont, the Osage post, Fort Orleans, the Kansas post); the Platte River valley (efforts to reach New Mexico; the Comanche barrier; the Mallet brothers, 1739; Chapuis, Satren; the horse trade).

5. The Saskatchewan valley (the "Post of the Western Sea"). The Wisconsin and Minnesota posts reëstablished (1717); Charlevoix's recommendations (1723); new Sioux posts (Fort Beauharnois, 1727); abandoned because of Fox wars; La Vérendrye's trade monopoly; the "Post of the Western Sea" (1731–1747); posts on Rainy Lake, Lake of the Woods, Lake Winnipeg, Assiniboine River, Lake Manitoba; La Vérendrye's expeditions to the southwest (1728, 1742); post on upper Saskatchewan (1752).

6. Permanent French influences in the West. French path-finders; half-breed population; names on the map.

REQUIRED READING

One of the following:

BOLTON, H. E., and MARSHALL, T. M. *The Colonization of North America*, 96–102, 275–288.
BURPEE, L. J. *Historical Atlas of Canada*, maps 19, 20, 26, and accompanying notes.
MUNRO, W. B. *The Crusaders of New France*, chaps. 5, 6, 9.
PARISH, J. C. *The Man with the Iron Hand*, chaps. 26–32.
PRIESTLEY, H. I. *The Coming of the White Man*, 236–258.
THWAITES, R. G. *France in America*, chaps. 4–5.
WRONG, G. M. *The Conquest of New France*, 97–135.

REFERENCES

THE FRENCH IN THE HEART OF THE CONTINENT

ALVORD, C. W. *The Illinois Country, 1673–1818*.
BREBNER, J. B. *The Explorers of North America, 1492–1806*.
BRITTAIN, ALFRED. *Discovery and Exploration*, chap. 14.
BUCK, S. J. "The Story of the Grand Portage," *Minnesota History Bulletin*, Vol. V, No. 1.
BUCK, S. J. and E. H. *Stories of Early Minnesota*.
BURPEE, L. J. (Editor). *Journals and Letters of Pierre Gaultier de Varennes de la Vérendrye and his Sons*.
BURPEE, L. J. *Search for the Western Sea*, 193–284.
CHAMBERS, H. E. *Mississippi Valley Beginnings*, chaps. 1–6.
CHAPAIS, THOMAS. *The Great Intendant* (Talon).
COLBY, C. W. *Canadian Types of the Old Régime*.
CROUSE, N. M. *In Quest of the Western Ocean*.
FINLEY, J. H. *The French in the Heart of America*, 1–216.
FORTIER, ALCÉE. *History of Louisiana*, I, chap. 2.
HAMILTON, P. J. *Colonization of the South*.
HOUCK, LOUIS. *History of Missouri*, I, 149–167.
INNIS, H. A. *The Fur Trade of Canada*.
KELLOGG, L. P. *The French Régime in Wisconsin and the Northwest*.

KENTON, EDNA (Editor). *The Indians of North America,* from "The Jesuit Relations and Allied Documents."

LAUT, A. C. *Cadillac, Knight Errant of the Wilderness.*

LAUT, A. C. *Pathfinders of the West,* 191–237 (Vérendrye).

MOORE, IRENE. *Valiant La Vérendrye.*

MUNRO, W. B. *The Crusaders of New France,* chaps. 6, 9.

OUDARD, GEORGES. *Vieille Amérique: La Louisiane au Temps des Français.*

PARKMAN, FRANCIS. *A Half-Century of Conflict.*

PARKMAN, FRANCIS. *La Salle and the Discovery of the Great West.*

PHELPS, ALBERT. *Louisiana,* I, chaps. 3–4.

REPPLIER, AGNES. *Père Marquette: Priest, Pioneer, and Adventurer.*

RONCIÈRE, CHARLES DE LA. *Une Épopée Canadienne.*

SCHLARMAN, J. H. *From Quebec to New Orleans: the Story of the French in America, Fort de Chartres.*

SHORTT, ADAM, and DOUGHTY, A. G. *Canada and its Provinces,* I, 11–146 ("Pathfinders of the Great West," by L. J. Burpee).

STECK, F. B. *The Jolliet-Marquette Expedition, 1673.*

SURREY, N. M. M. *The Commerce of Louisiana during the French Régime, 1699–1763.*

THWAITES, R. G. *France in America.*

THWAITES, R. G. *Wisconsin,* 1–101.

VILLIERS, BARON MARC DE. *L'Expédition de Cavelier de la Salle dans le Golfe du Mexique, 1684–1687.*

WRONG, G. M. *The Rise and Fall of New France.*

Lecture XIX. The Dutch, Swedish, and Danish Colonies

Introductory. The Dutch, Swedes, and Danes all tried a hand at American trade and colonization. All made contributions and from all we have inherited valuable things. The Dutch colony of New York was but a fragment of a great commercial empire. Dutch voyagers reached the Orient in the wake of the Portuguese. Independence from Spain was followed by an outburst of commercial activity, and the Dutch disputed the high seas with Spaniards. A Dutch East India Company laid the foundations of trade and colonies in the East and in Africa, and a West India Company carried the Dutch flag to North and South America. Dutch corsairs vied with the English in shattering Spain's trade monopoly in America. For a quarter-century a Dutch colony in Brazil threatened Portuguese control there. In Guiana and the Caribbean the Dutch established tropical plantations, trading stations, and buccaneering bases. The New Netherland Company, and then the Dutch West India Company, entered Hudson River valley. From Manhattan Island and Albany trading interests were extended east to the Connecticut, west up the Mohawk, and south to Delaware River. Under the patroon system a feudal landed aristocracy was founded in the Hudson River valley. New Netherland was owned by the trading company and governed by its appointees. The Dutch régime has left deep and permanent marks on New York, some of which Irving has celebrated in *The Knickerbocker History* and *The Sketch Book*. Trade expansion by land and sea involved rivalry with neigh-

93

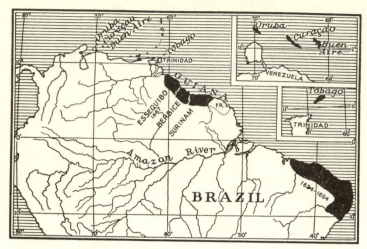

THE DUTCH IN SOUTH AMERICA AND THE CARIBBEAN (MIDDLE OF
SEVENTEENTH CENTURY)

bors. On the Connecticut River Dutch traders competed with
English. New Sweden (the Delaware River valley) was absorbed by New Netherland, and the latter in turn by the English. Late in the seventeenth century the Danes colonized the
Virgin Islands and retained them till 1917, when they sold
them to the United States.

1. The rise of the Netherlands. Revolt from Spain; trade
   expansion; efforts to find Northeast Passage; Mediterranean trade; attacks on Spanish and Portuguese commerce; the Northwest Passage; Hudson.
2. The Dutch in the Far East and in Africa. The East: early
   voyages (Linschoten, Houtman, 1595); East India Company (1602); settlements in Java, Sumatra, etc.; capital at Batavia; trade with China and Japan; discovery
   of the Cape Horn route (Schouten, 1616); attacks on

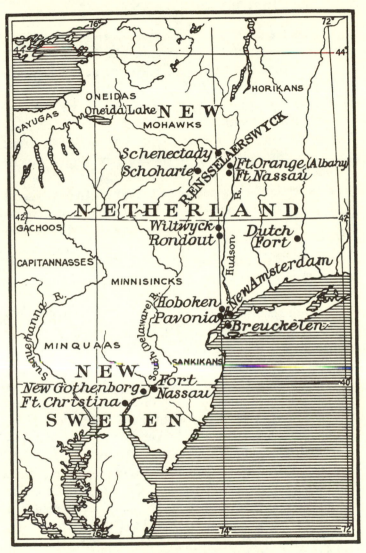

NEW NETHERLAND AND NEW SWEDEN

Portuguese and Spanish commerce; the "Pichilingues" on the California coast (Spillberg). Africa: posts in Sierra Leone and Guinea; settlements at the Cape after 1650; the Boers.

3. The Dutch in Brazil. Early activities of the Dutch on the Atlantic coast; the Dutch West India Company (Usselincx); Piet Heyn; conquests in Brazil (1624–1644); Prince Maurice of Nassau; the Dutch expelled (1661).

4. The Dutch in Guiana and the Caribbean. Guiana: settlements in West Guiana, 1613–1627 (Essequibo, Berbice); in Surinam (1644); sugar and tobacco; English Surinam conquered (1664). The Caribbean Islands (1632–1648): Tobago, St. Eustatius, Curaçao, Buen Aire, Aruba, St. Martin; sugar, tobacco, slave trade; Curaçao the Amsterdam of America.

5. New Netherland and New Sweden. The Dutch on the Hudson, Connecticut, and Delaware rivers; Hudson's discovery (1609) for East India Company; fur trade (1610–1621); the New Netherland Company (Albany, Manhattan); the West India Company (1621); Manhattan Island purchased; the directors-general (Minuit, Van Twiller, Kieft, Stuyvesant); the fur trade; the patroon system (land grants, the Van Rensselaers, Schuylers, etc.); settlements on the Hudson, Connecticut, and Delaware rivers. The Swedes on the Delaware; the expansion of Sweden (Gustavus Adolphus, Oxenstierna); the New Sweden Company (Usselincx, Minuit); settlements on the Delaware; conquered by the Dutch (1655). The English conquest of New Netherland (1664); Surinam held in exchange. Dutch influence in the United States.

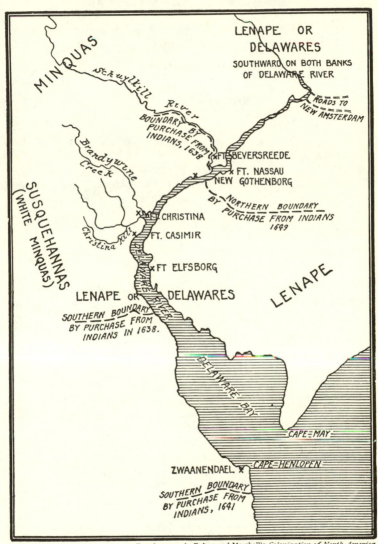

MINQUAS

LENAPE OR DELAWARES

SOUTHWARD ON BOTH BANKS
OF DELAWARE RIVER

Schuylkill River

BOUNDARY BY
PURCHASE FROM
INDIANS, 1638

ROADS TO
NEW AMSTERDAM

Brandywine Creek

× FT. BEVERSREEDE

× FT. NASSAU
NEW GOTHENBORG

SUSQUEHANNAS
(WHITE MINQUAS)

NORTHERN BOUNDARY
BY PURCHASE FROM INDIANS
1649

× FT. CHRISTINA

Christina Kill

FT. CASIMIR

× FT ELFSBORG

LENAPE or DELAWARES

LENAPE

SOUTHERN BOUNDARY
BY PURCHASE FROM
INDIANS IN 1638.

DELAWARE BAY

CAPE MAY

ZWAANENDAEL ×

CAPE HENLOPEN

SOUTHERN BOUNDARY
BY PURCHASE FROM
INDIANS, 1641

Based on map in Bolton and Marshall's *Colonization of North America*

NEW SWEDEN

6. **The Danes in the West Indies.** Danish expansion (Frederick III); Danish West Indies Company; St. Thomas (1671); planting and slave trade.

REQUIRED READING

One of the following:

BOLTON, H. E., and MARSHALL, T. M. *The Colonization of North America*, chap. 9.

FISKE, JOHN. *Dutch and Quaker Colonies in America,* chap. 4.

GOODWIN, M. W. *Dutch and English on the Hudson*, chaps. 1–3 or 4–6.

NEWTON, A. P. *The European Nations in the West Indies, 1493–1688*, chap. 13.

PRIESTLEY, H. I. *The Coming of the White Man* (selections).

REFERENCES

ABBOTT, W. C. *The Expansion of Europe.* (See index and contents.)

ACRELIUS, ISRAEL. *History of New Sweden* (Pennsylvania Historical Society, *Memoirs*, XI).

BLOK, P. J. *History of the State of New York.*

CHANNING, EDWARD. *History of the United States*, I, chaps. 16, 17.

DAWSON, T. C. *South American Republics.*

FISKE, A. K. *The West Indies.*

FISKE, JOHN. *Dutch and Quaker Colonies in America.*

HOLM, T. C. *Description of the Province of New Sweden* (Pennsylvania Historical Society, *Memoirs*, VII).

INNES, J. H. *New Amsterdam and its People.*

JAMESON, J. F. (Editor). *Narratives of New Netherland.*

JANVIER, T. A. *Dutch Founding of New York.*

JOHNSON, AMANDUS. *The Swedish Settlement on the Delaware.*

O'CALLAGHAN, E. B. *History of New Netherland.*

RODWAY, JAMES. *Guiana: British, Dutch, and French.*

SHEPHERD, W. R. *The Story of New Amsterdam.*

TANSILL, C. C. *The Purchase of the Danish West Indies.*

VAN LOON, H. W. *America*, chaps. 11–12.

VAN LOON, H. W. *The Golden Book of the Dutch Navigators.*

VAN LOON, H. W. *Life and Times of Peter Stuyvesant.*

WARD, CHRISTOPHER. *The Dutch and Swedes on the Delaware, 1609-1664.*

WÄTJEN, H. J. E. *Das Holländische Kolonialreich in Brasilien.*

WESTERGAARD, WALDEMAR. *The Danish West Indies.*

WINSOR, JUSTIN. *Narrative and Critical History of America,* II, 468-495; IV, 395-409, 443-488.

Cambridge Modern History, IV, chap. 25 (Transference of Colonial Power to the United Provinces and England).

THE ENGLISH COLONIES

LECTURE XX. THE BEGINNINGS OF ENGLISH EXPANSION

The Sixteenth Century

Introductory. The history of English expansion is an epic story of the growth of commerce, sea power, and self-governing colonies. In the partition of the Americas among the European nations Britain was a late comer, for sixteenth-century England was a comparatively small and weak nation. Nevertheless, that century was a significant era of preparation. Social, economic, and political changes prepared people for enterprise and emigration.

English expansion at first was commercial. With accumulated capital, joint-stock companies sought fresh fields for enterprise and new routes to the Orient. Elizabethan sea-dogs developed fast-sailing ships, engaged in the slave trade of Africa, Brazil, and the Caribbean, smuggled goods into Spanish ports, and plundered Spanish commerce. Of these men Hawkins was the prototype. Drake outdid his master, extended his raids into the Pacific, circumnavigated the globe, and laid the foundations of British commerce in the East. Under Elizabeth, religious hostility supplemented trade rivalry, and the sea-dogs weakened Spanish sea power by the defeat of the Great Armada. The sea war continued, with Spain against the combined Dutch and English fleets. Sixteenth-century English attempts at colonization did not succeed. By the end of the century Englishmen had learned the sea-ways of the Atlantic, and, finding South America preëmpted, had turned their eyes to the unoccupied coasts of North America. The crossing of the Atlantic, the first step in the English westward movement, had been accomplished.

1. The sixteenth century a period of preparation. England a late comer to America. English society in the fifteenth and sixteenth centuries: social and economic changes; the break-up of feudalism; sheep-farming; population freed for emigration and enterprise; rise of a merchant class and of capital; the Reformation; religious unrest and hostilities.

2. Commercial expansion. England's early interest mainly commercial; reflected Spanish and Portuguese activity; the Cabots (Newfoundland fisheries); a way through America (voyages of Thorne, Rut, Hore); William Hawkins's voyages to Africa and Brazil (the slave trade); Henry VIII's interest in the navy (tacking, Fletcher of Rye); commercial companies (the Muscovy, Eastland, Levant, West Africa, and East India companies); Richard Eden's writings (he urges friendly imitation of Spain); Richard Hakluyt's writings (he urges competition with Spain).

3. The search for a Northwest Passage. Richard Willes's *Foure Famous Wayes* to the Orient; Humphrey Gilbert's *Discourse to Prove a North-West Passage to Cathay* (1566); Martin Frobisher's voyages (efforts to obtain royal approval; opposition by the Muscovy Company; voyages of 1576, 1577, 1578; Meta Incognita); John Davis's voyages (1585, 1586, 1587); George Weymouth's voyage (1602); continued interest and later voyages (Knight, Hudson, Button, Bylot, Baffin, Edge, Foxe, James), 1606–1632; geographical results; names on the map.

4. The Elizabethan sea-dogs and England's sea power. John
   Hawkins (the slave trade); attacks on Spanish commerce;
   Drake (early expeditions, voyage around the globe,
   commercial aims; plunder in Spanish ports; capture of

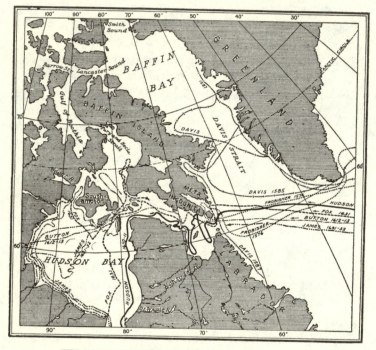

THE EARLY SEARCH FOR THE NORTHWEST PASSAGE

the Manila galleon, New Albion, crowned "Hi-oh,"
knighted); Cavendish; Drake's new raids in the Caribbean (attack on San Agustín). The Elizabethan sea-dogs
and the rise of English sea power: defeat of Spanish
Armada (1588); later sea fights with Spain; Grenville
(Tennyson's *Revenge*).

5. Attempts at colonization. Raleigh's ideas; his colony in North Carolina (Croatan); in Guiana; his search for Manoa.

REQUIRED READING

One of the following:

BOLTON, H. E., and MARSHALL, T. M. *The Colonization of North America*, 104–110.

BURPEE, L. J. *Historical Atlas of Canada*, map 18 and accompanying notes.

HOCKETT, H. C. *Political and Social Growth of the United States, 1492–1852*, chap. 4.

LEACOCK, STEPHEN. *Adventurers of the Far North*, chap. 1.

LUCAS, C. P. *The British Empire*, chap. 50.

TREVELYAN, G. M. *History of England*, 338–356.

WERTENBAKER, T. J. *The First Americans*, 1–22.

WILLIAMSON, J. A. *Short History of British Expansion*, 1922 ed., 92–112, 125–133.

WOOD, WILLIAM. *The Elizabethan Sea-Dogs*, chaps. 1–3, 5–8, or 9–11.

WOODWARD, W. H. *Expansion of the British Empire*, chaps. 1–2.

REFERENCES

THE EUROPEAN BACKGROUND OF ENGLISH EXPANSION

ABBOTT, W. C. *The Expansion of Europe*, I, chaps. 12–16

CHEYNEY, E. P. *European Background of American History*, chaps. 7–16.

CHEYNEY, E. P. *History of England* (1588–1603).

CROSS, A. L. *History of England and Greater Britain*, chaps. 26–35.

GARDINER, S. R. *The Puritan Revolution.*

GREENE, E. B. *Foundations of American Nationality*, chaps. 1, 2.

HAYES, C. J. H. *Political and Social History of Europe*, I.

SEELEY, J. R. *Growth of British Policy*, I.

TAYLOR, E. G. R. *Tudor Geography, 1485–1583*.

Cambridge Modern History, II, chap. 16; III, chaps. 9–10.

THE ELIZABETHAN SEA-DOGS

ANDREWS, C. M. *The Colonial Period of American History*, I.

BENSON, E. R. *Sir Francis Drake.*

BRITTAIN, ALFRED. *Discovery and Exploration.*

BURPEE, L. J. *Search for the Western Sea, 1–63.*
CHIDSEY, D. B. *Sir Humphrey Gilbert, Elizabeth's Racketeer.*
CHIDSEY, D. B. *Sir Walter Raleigh, that Damned Upstart.*
CREIGHTON, LOUISE. *Raleigh.*
CROUSE. N. M. *In Quest of the Western Ocean,* chaps. 1–2.
GOSSE, PHILIP. *Hawkins, Scourge of Spain.*
HARLOW, V. T. (Editor). *Raleigh's Last Voyage.*
McFEE, WILLIAM. *Sir Martin Frobisher.*
MANHART, G. B. *The English Search for a Northwest Passage.*
PARKS, G. B. *Richard Hakluyt and the English Voyages.*
PAYNE, E. J. *Voyages of Elizabethan Seamen.*
STORY, A. T. *The Building of the British Empire.*
TREVES, FREDERICK. *The Cradle of the Deep.*
TYLER, L. G. *England in America, 3–33.*
WAGNER, H. R. *Sir Francis Drake's Voyage around the World.*
WILLIAMSON, J. A. *Maritime Enterprise, 1485–1558.*
WILLIAMSON, J. A. *Sir John Hawkins.*
WILLIAMSON, J. A. *The Voyages of the Cabots and the English Discovery of North America under Henry VII and Henry VIII.*

Lecture XXI. The Swarming of the English

The Seventeenth Century

Introductory. The sixteenth century had been one of preparation. The seventeenth century was one of expansion by emigration. Within that hundred years English colonies and trading stations were founded in America all the way from Guiana to Hudson Bay.

The movement to America reflected periods in English domestic history. Under the early Stuarts a variety of forces operated to send Englishmen to America. Commercial ambition was reflected in the founding of Virginia and the island colonies. Opposition of Catholics, Puritans, and Parliamentarians played a part in the founding of Maryland and New England. Under these impulses the "Great Migration" occurred. During the Revolutionary period there was little emigration to America, but an imperial policy was begun. Jamaica was conquered and the Dutch power challenged. Under the later Stuarts the power of Holland was broken, and the Dutch barrier between New England and the Chesapeake colonies was removed. A new type of commercialism, in which the Western fur trade played a conspicuous part, coupled with the taking over of the Dutch settlements, led to the founding of a line of new colonies, proprietary in form. By the end of the century England had twenty or more colonies on the Atlantic seaboard, with some 200,000 colonists.

The seventeenth-century English colonies generally began as private ventures, designed for trade or other enterprises. Some

began as chartered trading companies and some as proprietary grants. Still others were squatters without legal status.
Most of them were given extravagant "sea to sea" grants,
without regard to the rights of other nations. Toward the
end of the century most of the colonies were taken over by
the government and became royal provinces. However they
began, most of them became commonwealths, with vigorous
popular assemblies.

1. Periods of colony-planting. Mainly in the seventeenth
   century; colonies planted from Guiana to Hudson Bay;
   trading posts in the East; the periods reflect great
   national movements (social, commercial, religious, political). The period of the early Stuarts (1603–1640):
   commercial ambitions (Virginia, the East India Company); religious and political struggle (the Puritans; the
   "Great Migration," 1629–1640); numerous new colonies
   on islands and mainland. The Revolutionary period
   (Civil War, Commonwealth, and Protectorate): little
   colony-planting in America; Cromwell's imperial policy
   (Jamaica conquered, 1655; naval expansion; wars with
   the Dutch begun (Navigation Act of 1651, war of 1652–
   1654)). Period of the later Stuarts (1660–1688): rapid
   expansion; Dutch wars continued (Navigation Acts of
   1660, 1663, 1673; wars of 1665–1667; Holland's sea power
   broken; Dutch barrier of New Netherland removed);
   new proprietary colonies formed; results (more than
   twenty colonies in America by 1689, meaning of "original
   thirteen," 200,000 settlers, islands and tidewater region
   occupied, expansion at the expense of Holland and
   Spain). The eighteenth century: non-English immigration; expansion by conquest; wars with France.

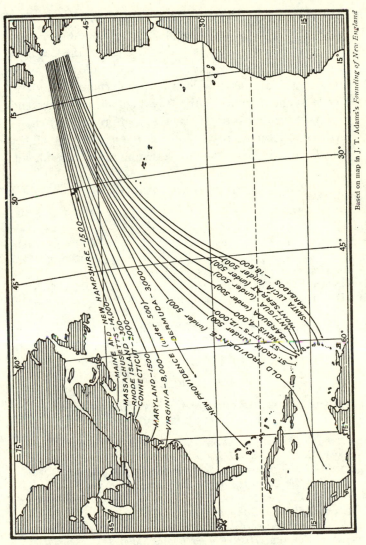

THE SWARMING OF THE ENGLISH

Based on map in J. T. Adams's *Founding of New England*

NEW HAMPSHIRE – 1,500
MAINE AND – 14,000
MASSACHUSETTS – 300
RHODE ISLAND – 2,000
CONNECTICUT – 3,000
(under 500) – 3,000
MARYLAND – 1,500
VIRGINIA – 8,000
BERMUDA (under 500)
NEW PROVIDENCE (under 500)
OLD PROVIDENCE (under 500)
ST. CROIX (under 500)
ST. KITTS – 12,000
NEVIS – 4,000
BARBUDA (under 500)
ANTIGUA (under 500)
MONTSERRAT (under 500)
SANTA LUCIA (under 500)
BARBADOS – 18,600

2. Methods of managing colonies. Chartered companies (some with governing bodies in England, some in America). Proprietors: Gorges, Calvert, Carlisle, the Carolina proprietors, Penn (compare with adelantados and capitanes). Private associations: the Plymouth Colony, Rhode Island, Connecticut. Royal colonies: by the end of the century most of the charter and proprietary rights replaced by direct royal control (governor and higher officials appointed). Popular assemblies the rule for all.

REQUIRED READING

One of the following:

ANDREWS, C. M. *Colonial Folkways*, chap. 1.

ANDREWS, C. M. *The Colonial Period*, chap. 1 or 2.

BOLTON, H. E., and MARSHALL, T. M. *The Colonization of North America*, 112–114, 135–137, 152–153, 179–183.

FORMAN, S. E. *Our Republic*, chap. 2.

MACDONALD, WILLIAM. *Three Centuries of American Democracy*, chap. 1.

MARTIN, A. E. *History of the United States*, Enlarged Edition, I, chap. 2.

WILLIAMSON, J. A. *Short History of British Expansion*, 1922 ed., or 1931 ed., 153–168.

REFERENCES

THE ENGLISH COLONIES IN THE SEVENTEENTH AND EIGHTEENTH CENTURIES

ANDREWS, C. M. *The Colonial Period of American History*, I.

ANDREWS, C. M. *Colonial Self-Government.*

BECKER, C. L. *Beginnings of the American People*, 45–149.

BEER, G. L. *The Origins of the British Colonial System.*

BOLTON, H. E., and MARSHALL, T. M. *The Colonization of North America*, chaps. 6–8, 11–12, 17–19, 22.

BRYCE, GEORGE. *Remarkable History of the Hudson's Bay Company.*

CHANNING, EDWARD. *History of the United States*, I–II.

CHITWOOD, O. P. *A History of Colonial America.*

EDWARDS, BRYAN. *History, Civil and Commercial, of the West Indies.*

FISKE, A. K. *The West Indies,* chaps. 7–8.

GABRIEL, R. H. (Editor). *Pageant of America; a Pictorial History of the United States.* 15 vols.

HOCKETT, H. C. *Political and Social Growth of the United States, 1492–1852,* chaps. 5–8.

INNES, A. D. *The Maritime and Colonial Expansion of England under the Stuarts (1603–1714).*

JERNEGAN, M. W. *Laboring and Dependent Classes in Colonial America, 1607–1783.*

JOSÉ, A. W. *Growth of the Empire,* 16–54.

KERR, P. H. and A. C. *The Growth of the British Empire,* 39–68.

NEWTON, A. P. *Colonizing Activities of the English Puritans,* 13–282.

OSGOOD, H. L. *The American Colonies in the Seventeenth Century.*

The Cambridge History of the British Empire, I. The old Empire from the Beginnings to 1783.

Essays in Colonial History presented to Charles McLean Andrews.

LECTURE XXII. THE ENGLISH COLONIES
IN THE CARIBBEAN

Political, Social, and Economic Characteristics

Introductory. Groups of English colonies in America were distinguished more by geographic and economic differences than by forms of government. The Caribbean area (after Newfoundland) was the earliest center of English economic interest in America, and here England planted a number of colonies. Bermuda was an offshoot of the Jamestown enterprise. In Guiana, Barbados, the Leeward Islands, and Old Providence, English colony-founding was contemporary with the beginnings of New England and represented in part the same movement. The Bahama colonies and the Carolinas were contemporaries and interrelated. Jamaica was conquered from Spain, and most of the Windward Island colonies were won from France. These island colonies were founded in the face of Spanish resistance, and not till 1670 did Spain acknowledge England's right to them.

The Caribbean colonies were tropical plantations, devoted to raising sugar and tobacco. The plantation system was based chiefly on slave labor, and it was in the Caribbean that the slave trade and Negro slavery first assumed large proportions. These colonies were aristocratic, and generally loyalist in politics. The government was proprietary in form, and most of the colonies had representative assemblies. They were buccaneering bases, and from them in the later seventeenth century English freebooters made devastating raids against Spanish towns all round the Caribbean. They were strategic bases

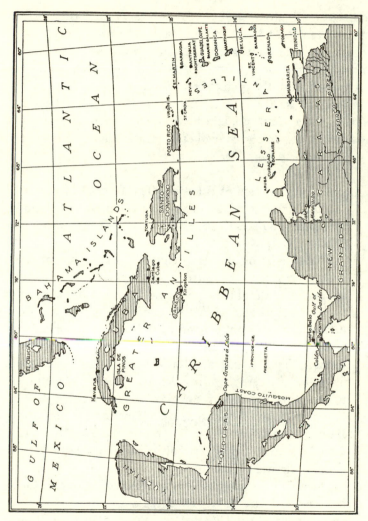

THE CARIBBEAN AREA IN THE SEVENTEENTH CENTURY

and a training ground for the British navy, and they played an important part in all the intercolonial wars. They were a front door to the southern mainland and a base for expansion thither. From them many features of the slave trade, the slave code, and the plantation system were carried to the mainland, especially to South Carolina. Trade with the island colonies was a primary factor in the development of New England, and it was to the control of the Caribbean trade that the Navigation Acts were largely directed.

1. Geographical groups of colonies. The Caribbean area and Guiana; the southern mainland colonies; the middle mainland colonies; the New England colonies; the northern outposts.
2. The Caribbean colonies and Guiana. Principal colonies: Guiana (Surinam conquered by Dutch, later colonies), 1604–1630; Bermudas (Somers Island Company, the "still-vexed Bermoothes" in *The Tempest*), 1609; Barbados (1624) and the Windward Islands (importance of Barbados, large population); Leeward Islands (St. Christopher, Nevis, Antigua, Montserrat, Anguilla, Barbuda, Tortola), 1623–1672; Providence Island (a Puritan experiment, broken up by Spaniards), 1629–1641; Jamaica (conquered by Cromwell, Caymans attached), 1655; Bahamas (New Providence), 1666; the Darién scheme (1695); later British acquisitions (conquests during Napoleonic wars, Honduras).
3. Buccaneering. The buccaneers the successors of the Elizabethan sea-dogs; tacitly encouraged by French and English governments; bases of operations (Tortuga Island, Jamaica, Charleston); Henry Morgan (an indented servant; becomes buccaneer; employed by Governor

Modyford; expeditions against Cuba, Porto Bello, Maracaibo, Panama; knighted for this service; commander and acting governor in Jamaica); other famous buccaneers; raids on the Florida coast; decline of buccaneering (Kidd hanged, not knighted).

4. Characteristics of Caribbean colonies: strategic bases; buccaneering bases; tropical plantations; sugar and tobacco; white servitude and Negro slavery; the slave trade; Royal African Company; aristocratic; loyalist; absenteeism; government (proprietary at first; representative assemblies; struggles with proprietors; an experiment in federal government, 1689); influence on mainland colonies (settlers in the Carolinas, trade with New England); influence on slavery.

REQUIRED READING

One of the following:

BOLTON, H. E., and MARSHALL, T. M. *The Colonization of North America*, 129-134.

NEWTON, A. P. *European Nations in the West Indies*, "Introduction."

ROBINSON, HOWARD. *The Development of the British Empire*, 48-55.

WILLIAMSON, J. A. *Short History of British Expansion*, 1922 ed., or 1931 ed., 207-213, 285-291.

WOODWARD, W. H. *Expansion of the British Empire*, 112-121, 171-176.

REFERENCES

THE BERMUDAS AND THE CARIBBEAN

ANDREWS, C. M. *The Colonial Period of American History*, I.

ANDREWS, C. M. *Our Earliest Colonial Settlements.*

BEER, G. L. *The Origins of the British Colonial System*, 12-20.

BULKELEY, J. P. *The British Empire.*

BURDON, MAJOR SIR J. A. *Archives of British Honduras.*

CHIDSEY, D. B. *Sir Walter Raleigh, that Damned Upstart.*

CUNNINGHAM, WILLIAM. *The Growth of English Industry and Commerce*, I, 331-339.

DONNAN, ELIZABETH. *Documents Illustrative of the Slave Trade to America*. 2 vols.

HARLOW, V. T. (Editor). *Colonising Expeditions to the West Indies and Guiana, 1623–1667*.

HARLOW, V. T. *A History of Barbados, 1625–1685*.

HARLOW, V. T. (Editor). *Raleigh's Last Voyage*.

HART, F. R. *Admirals of the Caribbean*.

HART, F. R. *The Disaster of Darien*.

INMAN, S. G. *Trailing the Conquistadores*.

INSH, G. P. *The Company of Scotland Trading to Africa and the Indies*.

INSH, G. P. *Scottish Colonial Schemes, 1620–1686*.

LUCAS, C. P. *A Historical Geography of the British Colonies*, II, 5–14, 43–50.

NEWTON, A. P. *The Colonizing Activities of the English Puritans*, 13–282.

NEWTON, A. P. *European Nations in the West Indies, 1493–1688*.

PITMAN, F. W. *The Development of the British West Indies, 1700–1763*, 127–333.

RAGATZ, L. J. *The Fall of the Planter Class in the British Caribbean, 1763–1833*.

RODWAY, JAMES. *Guiana: British, Dutch, and French*.

RODWAY, JAMES. *History of British Guiana*.

SCOTT, W. R. *The Constitution and Finance of English, Scottish, and Irish Joint-Stock Companies to 1720*, II, 259–299, 327–337.

TILBY, A. W. *Britain in the Tropics*, 44–50.

WHITSON, A. M. *The Constitutional Development of Jamaica, 1660–1729*.

WILKINSON, HENRY. *The Adventurers of Bermuda: a History of the Island from its Discovery until the Dissolution of the Somers Island Company in 1684*.

WILLIAMSON, J. A. *The Caribbee Islands under the Proprietary Patents*.

WILLIAMSON, J. A. *English Colonies in Guiana and on the Amazon, 1604–1668*.

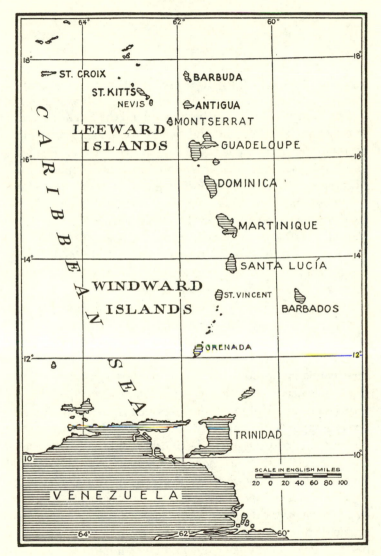

THE LESSER ANTILLES

Lecture XXIII. The Southern Mainland Colonies

Introductory. On the southern mainland the English acquired five colonies by settlement and two by conquest. From threatened failure Virginia was saved by tobacco culture. Beginning as a trading venture it became a self-governing commonwealth. Maryland was an experiment in religious toleration. The Carolina grant embraced a line of Spanish settlements, and in consequence sustained a long border struggle with Florida. North Carolina was a frontier of Virginia, and South Carolina an expansion of Barbados. Georgia was an eighteenth-century buffer against Florida, with which it continued the border contest. The Floridas were conquered from Spain.

The southern mainland colonies were subtropical plantations, based on staple crops. In Virginia and Maryland society was dominated by tobacco; in the Carolinas and Georgia by rice and indigo. In the seventeenth century Negro slavery was relatively unimportant, indentured white servitude being then the rule instead. Most of the servants, after completing their terms, became small planters. In South Carolina Indian slavery was important in the early days. In the eighteenth century Negro slavery spread in all the South, plantations increased in size, and society became more aristocratic. But there was always a back-country democracy which could make itself felt, as in the case of Bacon's Rebellion. Southern life was rural, large towns were few, and the county system of local government prevailed. The Southern frontier was expansive, because soils quickly gave out and new lands were constantly necessary.

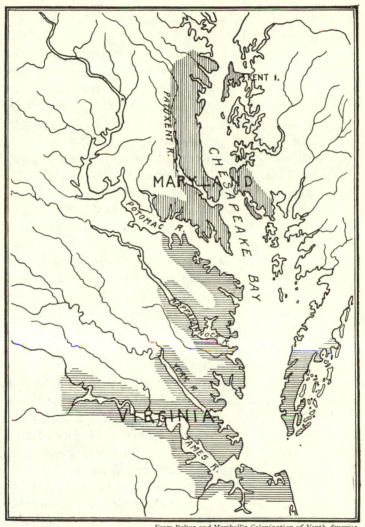

From Bolton and Marshall's *Colonization of North America*

SETTLED AREAS IN VIRGINIA AND MARYLAND (1667)

1. General features. Closely resembled the island colonies:
   five colonies by English settlement; two by conquest.
2. The Chesapeake Bay colonies. The topography; bays and
   estuaries; tidewater lands. Virginia: began as a commercial venture and became a commonwealth; the
   London Company; its charter; pioneer difficulties (due
   to romantic notions, unsuitable colonists, inexperience,
   factional quarrels, communal labor, Indian hostility,
   Spanish hostility); the colony saved by Smith, Poca-
   hontas, Dale, and "King Tobacco" (tobacco the first
   profitable crop, King James's *Counterblast to Tobacco*);
   Virginia becomes a commonwealth (new charters, representative assembly); a royal province; the expulsion of
   Harvey; Berkeley and the Commonwealth; Bacon's
   Rebellion; Virginia and the "Glorious Revolution."
   Maryland: the proprietary grant (the Calverts, the pa-
   latinate of Durham, feudal features); Maryland an experiment in toleration; a tobacco colony; border conflicts
   with Virginia (trade and boundaries, Kent Island,
   Claiborne's post, the outcome); social and religious life;
   the Jesuit missionaries; government.
3. The Carolinas. The proprietary grant; the influence of
   Barbados; first and second charters; Locke's constitutions (feudal, fanciful); settlement (North Carolina a
   frontier of Virginia, South Carolina a frontier of Barbados); rice and indigo; Indian and Negro slavery; the
   Indian trade; Spanish resistance; counter-expeditions
   against Guale and San Agustín; the colony divided.
4. Georgia and the Floridas. Eighteenth-century colonies.
   Georgia a buffer against Spain: Oglethorpe; continued
   struggle with Spain; the Indian trade. The Floridas:
   won by conquest.

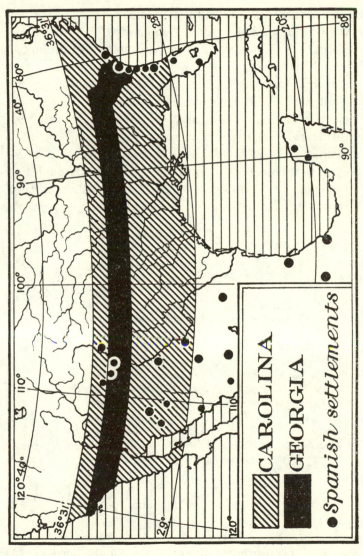

THE CAROLINA AND GEORGIA GRANTS

CAROLINA

GEORGIA

• *Spanish settlements*

5. Characteristics of the southern mainland colonies. Subtropical plantations; society dominated by staple crops
   (tobacco, rice, indigo); the tobacco fleet; plantation life
   (small plantations in the seventeenth century, larger in
   the eighteenth century); dependent labor (indentured
   white servants in the seventeenth century, become sub-
   stantial yeomen, Negro slavery in the eighteenth century); rural life (few towns, sparse population, each large
   plantation its wharf); aristocratic; but always a back-
   country democracy (Bacon's Rebellion); individualistic;
   the county unit of local government; Southern society
   expansive (exhaustion of soils, large areas necessary).

REQUIRED READING

One of the following:

ANDREWS, C. M. *Colonial Folkways*, chap. 2 or 5.
ANDREWS, C. M. *The Colonial Period*, chap. 3 or 4.
BOLTON, H. E., and MARSHALL, T. M. *The Colonization of North
   America*, 112–129, 227–231.
CHITWOOD, O. P. *A History of Colonial America*, 60–107.
GREENE, E. B. *Foundations of American Nationality*, chap. 4.
HOCKETT, H. C. *Political and Social History of the United States,
   1492–1852*, chap. 6.
JERNEGAN, M. W. *The American Colonies*, 47–109.
JOHNSTON, MARY. *Pioneers of the Old South*, chap. 2 or 9.
PEASE, T. C. *The United States*, chap. 2.
WERTENBAKER, T. J. *The First Americans*, 22–48.
WERTENBAKER, T. J. *Virginia under the Stuarts*, chap. 5.
WILLIAMSON, J. A. *Short History of British Expansion*, 1922 ed.,
   or 1931 ed., 169–187, 272–276, 291–298.

REFERENCES

VIRGINIA AND MARYLAND

ANDREWS, M. P. *The Founding of Maryland*.
BECKER, C. L. *Beginnings of the American People*, 65–80.
BEER, G. L. *The Origins of the British Colonial System*, 78–178.

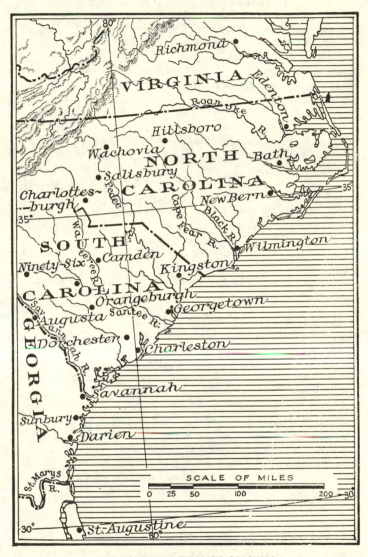

THE SOUTHERN ENGLISH COLONIES

BROWN, ALEXANDER. *The First Republic in America.*
BROWN, ALEXANDER. *Genesis of the United States.*
BROWNE, W. H. *Maryland, 1–50.*
BRUCE, P. A. *Economic History of Virginia in the Seventeenth Century.*
BRUCE, P. A. *Institutional History of Virginia in the Seventeenth Century,* II, 229–262.
CHANNING, EDWARD. *History of the United States,* I, 143–224, 241–268; II, 80–91, 209–213.
CRAVEN, W. F. *Dissolution of the Virginia Company.*
DODSON, LEONIDAS. *Alexander Spotswood, Governor of Colonial Virginia, 1710–1722.*
EGGLESTON, EDWARD. *The Beginners of a Nation,* 25–97, 220–257.
FISKE, JOHN. *Old Virginia and her Neighbors,* I.
FLIPPIN, P. S. *The Royal Government in Virginia, 1624–1775.*
HALL, C. C. (Editor). *Narratives of Early Maryland.*
HAMILTON, P. J. *Colonization of the South,* 55–119.
JERNEGAN, M. W. *Laboring and Dependent Classes in Colonial America, 1607–1783.*
KARRAKER, C. H. *The Seventeenth-Century Sheriff: a Comparative Study of the Sheriff in England and the Chesapeake Colonies, 1607–1689.*
McCORMAC, E. I. *White Servitude in Maryland, 1634–1820.*
MACDONALD, WILLIAM. *Select Charters Illustrative of American History,* 1–23, 53–59.
MERENESS, N. D. *Maryland as a Proprietary Province.*
OSGOOD, H. L. *The American Colonies in the Seventeenth Century.*
SCOTT, A. P. *Criminal Law in Colonial Virginia.*
TYLER, L. G. *England in America,* 34–103, 118–132.
TYLER, L. G. (Editor). *Narratives of Early Virginia.*
WERTENBAKER, T. J. *The First Americans.*
WERTENBAKER, T. J. *Norfolk, Historic Southern Port.*
WERTENBAKER, T. J. *Patrician and Plebeian in Virginia.*
WERTENBAKER, T. J. *The Planters of Colonial Virginia.*
WERTENBAKER, T. J. *Virginia under the Stuarts.*

THE CAROLINAS

ANDREWS, C. M. *Colonial Self-Government,* 129–161.
ANDREWS, C. M. (Editor). *Narratives of the Insurrections,* 143–164.
ASHE, S. A. *North Carolina,* I.

CHANNING, EDWARD. *History of the United States*, II, 13–25.
GREENE, E. B. *Foundations of American Nationality.*
HAMILTON, P. J. *Colonization of the South*, 133–135.
HIRSCH, A. H. *The Huguenots of Colonial South Carolina.*
MCCRADY, EDWARD. *The History of South Carolina under the Proprietary Government*, I, 1–209.
OSGOOD, H. L. *The American Colonies in the Seventeenth Century*, II, 200–225.
RAMSAY, DAVID. *South Carolina.*
SMITH, W. R. *South Carolina as a Royal Province, 1719–1776.*

LECTURE XXIV. THE NORTHERN AND MIDDLE COLONIES

Introductory. The New England colonies in their origin reflected the religious and political aspirations of Separatists, Puritans, and Parliamentarians; but economic motives also played a part. Massachusetts was the "hub" of New England. All earlier colonies (the Maine and New Hampshire settlements and Plymouth) were absorbed by it, and all later ones (Rhode Island, Connecticut, and New Haven) were offshoots from it. The founding of these new colonies on the frontier of Massachusetts was promoted by intolerance, growth of population, land hunger, interest in Indian trade, and Dutch rivalry. Two experiments at colonial union were tried in New England. The New England Confederacy was a voluntary pact designed for defense and to settle boundary disputes, but it had little success. The Dominion of New England was an imperialistic government measure. From this unpopular union New England was released by the "Glorious Revolution." New England society was highly religious in tone. Church and government were controlled by a narrow oligarchy, and suffrage was limited. Life was corporate, most persons being closely associated with their neighbors in church congregation and town. Economic pursuits were dominantly coastwise.

The middle colonies were later-seventeenth-century proprietary foundations based largely on Dutch and Swedish antecedents. They were of mixed social elements and diversified in pursuits. In the Far North fishing and fur-trading

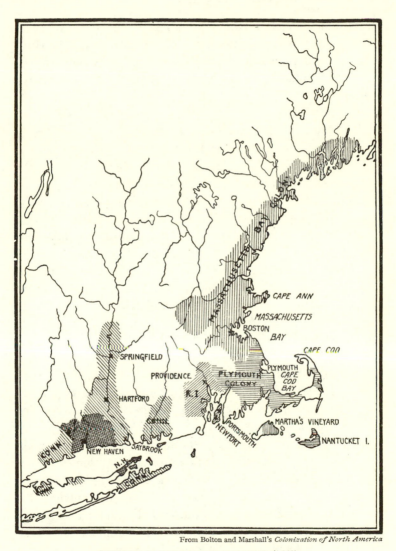

From Bolton and Marshall's *Colonization of North America*

SETTLED AREAS IN NEW ENGLAND (1660)

establishments gave England valuable commerce. Acadia and Newfoundland were disputed with France till 1713. The Hudson's Bay Company, the great fur-trading organization, exerted a powerful influence in British North America for nearly two centuries.

1. The New England colonies. Founding the colonies: early attempts on New England coast; Plymouth (1620); Massachusetts Bay Colony (Salem, Boston), 1629; the "Great Migration" (1629-1640); offshoots from Massachusetts (Rhode Island, Connecticut, New Haven); New Hampshire and Maine (Gorges and Mason grants; absorbed by Massachusetts; New Hampshire independent, 1678). Colonial union (1643-1684), mainly for defense and boundary disputes. The Restoration and the charters: New England practically independent till Restoration; Rhode Island and Connecticut obtain charters (1662-1663); Massachusetts defiant; the Dominion of New England (Andros, 1684-1688); Massachusetts under a royal governor (1691). Characteristics: strong religious and political motives (Separatists, Puritans, Parliamentarians); a narrow church oligarchy; corporate organization (town, congregation); diversified and coastwise pursuits.

2. The middle colonies. The Dutch and Swedish barrier absorbed (1664-1667). New proprietary colonies: New York; the Jerseys; Pennsylvania (1681); Delaware a part of Pennsylvania. Characteristics: intermediate between New England and South; Dutch influence in New York and Delaware; New England influence in East Jersey; Quaker influence in Pennsylvania and West Jersey; diversified life and organization.

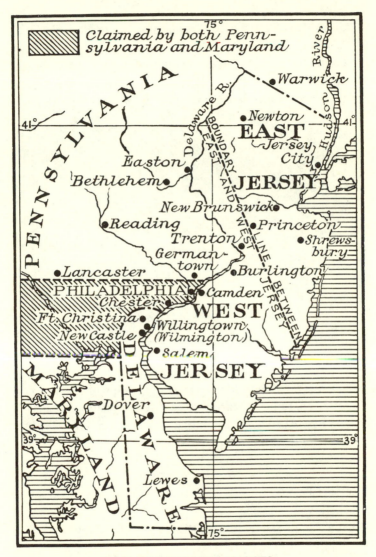

THE MIDDLE ENGLISH COLONIES

3. The northern outposts. Fishing and fur trade; Hudson's Bay Company (Radisson; Gillam; aid in England; Carteret, Prince Rupert, Duke of York; the charter, 1670; privileges; government; importance of Court

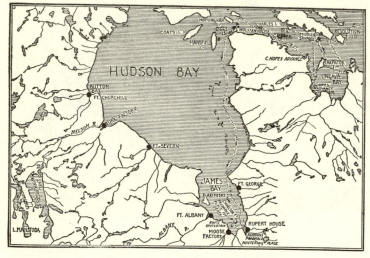

HUDSON'S BAY COMPANY POSTS

patronage); methods (forts, supply ships, markets; conservative policy regarding the interior country); French rivalry. Acadia, Newfoundland, and Labrador; disputed with French; permanently won in 1713.

REQUIRED READING

One of the following:

ANDREWS, C. M. *The Colonial Period*, chap. 4.
BOLTON, H. E., and MARSHALL, T. M. *The Colonization of North America*, chap. 7.
FISHER, S. G. *The Quaker Colonies*, chaps. 1–3 or 8–11.
GOODWIN, M. W. *Dutch and English on the Hudson*, chaps. 8–9.

JERNEGAN, M. W. *The American Colonies*, 114–241.
WILLIAMSON, J. A. *Short History of British Expansion*, 1922 ed., or
1931 ed., 188–207, 233–239, 276–284, 313–317.
WOODWARD, W. H. *Expansion of the British Empire*, 131–146.

REFERENCES

THE BEGINNINGS OF NEW ENGLAND

ADAMS, C. F. *Three Episodes of Massachusetts History*, I, 1–182.
ADAMS, J. T. *The Founding of New England*.
ANDREWS, C. M. *Our Earliest Colonial Settlements*.
ARBER, EDWARD. *The Story of the Pilgrim Fathers*.
BRADFORD, WILLIAM. *History of Plymouth Plantation*.
CALDER, ISABEL. *The New Haven Colony*.
CHANNING, EDWARD. *History of the United States*, I, 271–321, 322–
351, 362–411.
CHEYNEY, E. P. *European Background of American History*, 216–239.
CURTIS, EDITH. *Anne Hutchinson: a Biography*.
DEXTER, H. M. *The England and Holland of the Pilgrims*.
DEXTER, MORTON. *The Story of the Pilgrims*.
DOYLE, J. A. *The Puritan Colonies*.
EGGLESTON, EDWARD. *The Beginners of a Nation*.
ERNST, J. E. *The Political Thought of Roger Williams*.
ERNST, J. E. *Roger Williams, New England Firebrand*.
FISKE, JOHN. *The Beginnings of New England*, 60–111.
GREENE, E. B. *Foundations of American Nationality*.
GRIFFIS, W. E. *The Pilgrims in their Three Homes*.
JOHNSON, EDWARD. *Wonder-Working Providence*.
MILLER, PERRY. *Orthodoxy in Massachusetts, 1630–1650*.
MOLONEY, F. X. *The Fur Trade in New England, 1620–1676*.
MORISON, S. E. *Builders of the Bay Colony*.
NEAL, DANIEL. *History of the Puritans*.
NEWTON, A. P. *Colonizing Activities of the English Puritans*.
PALFREY, J. G. *History of New England*, I, 101–238, 283–405.
PLOOIJ, D. *The Pilgrim Fathers from a Dutch Point of View*.
RICHMAN, I. B. *Rhode Island, a Study in Separatism*.
ROSE-TROUP, FRANCES. *The Massachusetts Bay Company and its Prede-
cessors*.
SLY, J. F. *Town Government in Massachusetts, 1620–1930*.

TYLER, L. G. *England in America.*
USHER, R. G. *The Pilgrims and their History.*
WEEDEN, W. B. *Early Rhode Island.*
WEEDEN, W. B. *Economic and Social History of New England,* I, 8–164.
WINTHROP, JOHN. *Journal.*
YARDLEY, CAPT. J. H. R. *Before the Mayflower.*
YOUNG, ALEXANDER. *Chronicles of the Pilgrim Fathers.*

NEW ENGLAND UNDER THE LATER STUARTS

ADAMS, J. T. *Revolutionary New England.*
ANDREWS, C. M. *Colonial Self-Government,* 51–73, 252–287.
ANDREWS, C. M. *The Fathers of New England.*
ANDREWS, C. M. (Editor). *Narratives of the Insurrections,* 165–207.
BARNES, V. F. *The Dominion of New England.*
CHANNING, EDWARD. *History of the United States,* II, 65–70, 155–203.
DOYLE, J. A. *The Puritan Colonies,* II, 190–276.
ELLIS, G. W., and MORRIS, J. E. *King Philip's War.*
FISKE, JOHN. *The Beginnings of New England,* 199–278.
FRY, W. H. *New Hampshire as a Royal Province.*
GREENE, E. B. *Foundations of American Nationality,* chap. 7.
JAMES, B. B. *The Colonization of New England,* 213–295.
OSGOOD, H. L. *The American Colonies in the Seventeenth Century,* III, 309–335, 378–443.
PALFREY, J. G. *Compendious History of New England,* II, 1–20.
Harvard College Records. 2 vols.

NEW YORK, THE JERSEYS, AND PENNSYLVANIA

ANDREWS, C. M. *Colonial Self-Government.*
ANDREWS, C. M. (Editor). *Narratives of the Insurrections.*
BRAILSFORD, M. R. *The Making of William Penn.*
BRODHEAD, J. R. *History of the State of New York,* II.
CHANNING, EDWARD. *History of the United States,* II, 31–63, 94–130, 203–209.
CLARKSON, THOMAS. *Memoirs of the Private and Public Life of William Penn.*
DOBRÉE, BONAMY. *William Penn, Quaker and Pioneer.*
DOYLE, J. A. *The Middle Colonies,* 78–223, 287–350, 379–410.
FISHER, E. J. *New Jersey as a Royal Province, 1738–1776.*

FISHER, S. G. *The Quaker Colonies.*
FISKE, JOHN. *Dutch and Quaker Colonies in America.*
GREENE, E. B. *Foundations of American Nationality,* chap. 8.
HOLDER, C. F. *The Quakers in Great Britain and America,* 169–217.
JANNEY, S. M. *Life of William Penn.*
JONES, R. M. *The Quakers in the American Colonies,* 357–371, 417–436.
MACDONALD, WILLIAM. *Select Charters,* 139–149, 171–204.
OSGOOD, H. L. *The American Colonies in the Seventeenth Century,* II.
POUND, ARTHUR. *The Penns of Pennsylvania.*
SHARPLESS, ISAAC. *History of Quaker Government in Pennsylvania.*
SHEPHERD, W. R. *History of Proprietary Government in Pennsylvania.*
SMITH, SAMUEL. *History of the Colony of Nova-Cæsaria, or New Jersey,* 35–207.
TANNER, E. P. *The Province of New Jersey,* 1–147.
VULLIAMY, C. E. *William Penn.*
WHITEHEAD, W. A. *East Jersey under the Proprietary Governments.*

NEWFOUNDLAND AND HUDSON'S BAY COMPANY

BODILLY, R. B. *The Voyage of Captain Thomas James for the Discovery of the Northwest Passage, 1631.*
BRYCE, GEORGE. *Remarkable History of the Hudson's Bay Company,* 1–55.
BURPEE, L. J. *Search for the Western Sea,* 64–95.
CROUSE, N. M. *In Quest of the Western Ocean.*
KENNEY, J. F. (Editor). *The Founding of Churchill, being the Journal of Captain James Knight.*
LAUT, A. C. *The Adventurers of England on Hudson Bay.*
LAUT, A. C. *The Conquest of the Great Northwest,* I, 1–225.
LOUNSBERRY, R. G. *The British Fishery at Newfoundland, 1634–1763.*
PINKERTON, R. E. *Hudson's Bay Company.*
TYRELL, J. B. (Editor). *Documents Relating to the Early History of Hudson Bay.*
WALLACE, W. S. (Editor). *John McLean's Notes of a Twenty-five Years' Service in the Hudson's Bay Territory.*
WILSON, BECKLES. *The Great Company,* 1–181.
WINSOR, JUSTIN. *Narrative and Critical History of America,* VIII, 1–34.

LECTURE XXV. EXPANSION OF SETTLEMENT AND OF COLONIAL LIFE

Non-English Immigration; the Westward Movement; the Growth of Democracy

Introductory. English colonization did not end with the founding of Jamestown and Plymouth, but continued across the continent. On the Atlantic seaboard different types of society evolved; each type tended to project itself westward, and on the frontier the streams met and intermingled. Through expansion a part of society was constantly returning to frontier conditions. The frontier was a laboratory for social experimentation and a melting pot for newcome Europeans. An outstanding tendency of the frontier was toward democracy.

By the end of the seventeenth century the northern and middle Tidewater areas had been occupied. During the next half-century the frontier pushed west into the Piedmont and southward into the lower Tidewater. Georgia was founded as a buffer against Spain. The frontier advance was led by Indian traders, cattlemen, and explorers. To prepare the way for white settlement, the Indian frontier was revised by a series of wars and treaties. By 1750 large bands and spurs of settlement had been added beyond the frontier line of 1700. The widest bands were added in the southern Piedmont. To this area settlers went from the Tidewater; a larger stream of Germans and Scotch-Irish pushed south from Pennsylvania up the Shenandoah valley and then east into the uplands of Virginia, North Carolina, and South Carolina.

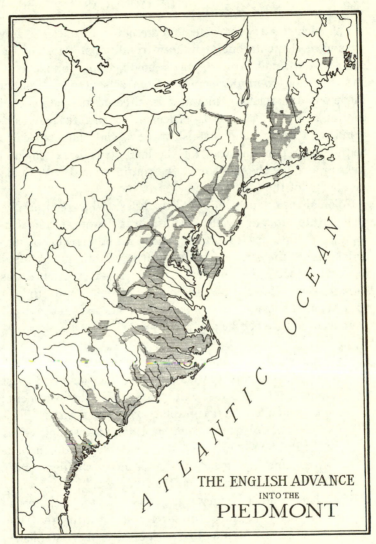

ATLANTIC OCEAN

THE ENGLISH ADVANCE
INTO THE
PIEDMONT

THE ENGLISH ADVANCE INTO THE PIEDMONT (1700–1760)

The back-country settlements represented a frontier society of diverse elements but of uniform conditions. Most of the people were small farmers. Slave-holding was unimportant, and conditions were democratic. Contrasts between frontier Piedmont and settled Tidewater resulted in many sectional contests. Beyond the line of settlement, English fur men competed with French and Spanish traders, and thus expansion helped to prepare the way for the final struggle of England with France for the interior of the continent and with Spain for control of the Gulf.

Colonial society developed culturally as well as territorially. The culture brought by the colonists was European, and Europe long continued to be the model. In the realm of material things the struggle with nature was stimulating, but in many respects the first result of American experience was retrogression. However, by the middle of the eighteenth century colonial society had taken root in the soil, and a truly American culture had begun.

1. The westward movement. The colonization of North America not complete with founding the island and coast colonies; the process continued across the continent; steps coincide with geographic areas (Tidewater, Piedmont, trans-Allegheny country, trans-Mississippi, Great Basin, Pacific slope); each step made a special contribution to American society; significance; the democratic influence of the frontier; a " melting pot."

2. The islands and the Tidewater occupied in the seventeenth century. By the end of the seventeenth century the Tidewater area had been settled; types of society established which projected themselves across the continent, but were modified in the process; New England type (cor-

porate, theocratic, industrial, village life, township system, coastwise pursuits, free labor); the Southern type (individualistic, aristocratic, agricultural, staple crops, dependent labor, county system).

3. The occupation of the Piedmont (1700–1760). Tidewater society largely European in characteristics, but expansion into Piedmont tended to produce an "American"

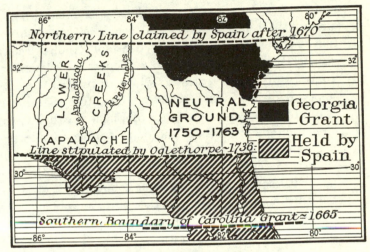

THE DEBATABLE LAND

society. The Piedmont. Factors in eighteenth-century expansion: cheap land and opportunity, growth of population, class conflicts, emancipation of indented servants, land speculation, continued immigration, international rivalry (Georgia). The advance guard: the way led by Indian traders and cattle men (cowpens); official explorations (Knights of Golden Horseshoe); advance made possible by revision of Indian frontier (King Philip's War, Susquehanna War, Tuscarora War, Yamassee War). The Piedmont occupied: New England (narrow band of settlement, spurs up river valleys); New York (not expansive, patroon system); the Southern Piedmont; a double movement (across Tidewater; up the Great Valley from Pennsylvania); the German and Swiss migration (causes, numbers, importance in frontier defense); the Scotch-Irish; names on map.

4. Results. A frontier society of diverse nationalities but uniform in economic and social condition (small farms, slave-holding unimportant), self-reliant (Indian wars), democratic, tolerant; the way prepared for sectional contests of West versus East (over frontier defense, apportionment of taxes, representation, administration); way prepared for final conflict of English with French; similar effects of frontier conditions in other colonies.

5. The expansion of colonial society. Provincial society in the eighteenth century; the structure of society; the economic basis; the aristocrats; the common man; the intellectual outlook; the life of the spirit; new blood; the changing South; the commercialization of the North; the growth of a colonial culture.

REQUIRED READING

One of the following:

ADAMS, J. T. *Provincial Society, 1690–1763*, chap. 5 or 10.

BOLTON, H. E., and MARSHALL, T. M. *The Colonization of North America*, 309–312, 326–328.

GREENE, E. B. *Foundations of American Nationality*, chaps. 12–14.

HOCKETT, H. C. *Political and Social Growth of the United States, 1492–1852*, chap. 9.

JERNEGAN, M. W. *The American Colonies*, 300–352.

MARTIN, A. E. *History of the United States*, Enlarged Edition, I, chap. 3.

SKINNER, C. L. *Pioneers of the Old Southwest*, chap. 1 or 2.

TURNER, F. J. *The Frontier in American History*, chap. 1 or 3.

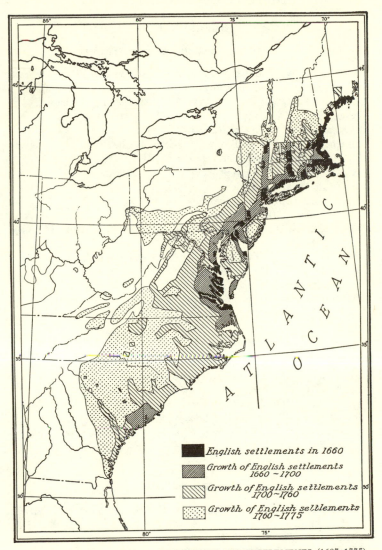

English settlements in 1660

Growth of English settlements
1660~1700

Growth of English settlements
1700~1760

Growth of English settlements
1760~1775

THE EXPANSION OF THE ENGLISH MAINLAND SETTLEMENTS (1607–1775)

REFERENCES

WESTERN EXPLORATION AND SETTLEMENT

ALVORD, C. W., and BIDGOOD, LEE. *First Exploration of the Trans-Alleghany Region, 1650–1674.*

BOLTON, H. E., and ROSS, MARY. *The Debatable Land,* chap. 3.

BOYD, J. P. *The Susquehannah Company Papers.* 2 vols.

COULTER, E. M. *A Short History of Georgia.*

CRANE, V. W. "The Tennessee River as the Road to Carolina," *Mississippi Valley Historical Review,* III, 3–18.

HIGGINS, R. L. *Expansion in New York, with Especial Reference to the Eighteenth Century.*

MATTHEWS, L. K. *The Expansion of New England.*

SAVELLE, MAX. *George Morgan, Colony Builder.*

VOLWILER, A. T. *George Croghan and the Westward Movement, 1741–1782.*

WILLIAMS, S. C. (Editor). *Adair's History of the Indians.*

WILLIAMS, S. C. *The Beginnings of West Tennessee in the Land of the Chickasaws, 1541–1841.*

WILLIAMS, S. C. *Early Travels in the Tennessee Country, 1540–1800.*

THE GERMAN AND SWISS MIGRATION

BERNHEIM, G. D. *German Settlements in North and South Carolina.*

BITTINGER, L. F. *The Germans in Colonial Times,* 11–183.

COBB, S. H. *The Story of the Palatines.*

FAUST, A. B. *The German Element in the United States,* I, 30–262.

JONES, C. C. *The History of Georgia,* I, 163–173, 208–214.

WAYLAND, J. W. *The German Element of the Shenandoah Valley of Virginia.*

THE SCOTCH-IRISH

CAMPBELL, DOUGLAS. *The Puritan in Holland, England, and America,* II, 469–485.

FORD, H. J. *The Scotch-Irish in America,* 1–200.

HANNA, C. A. *The Scotch-Irish,* II, 6–126.

TURNER, F. J. *The Frontier in American History,* chap. 3.

Defense of the Frontiers

Bolton, H. E. *Spain's Title to Georgia.*
Bolton, H. E., and Ross, Mary. *The Debatable Land.*
Channing, Edward. *History of the United States,* II, 341–365.
Crane, V. W. *The Southern Frontier.*
Fiske, John. *Old Virginia and her Neighbors,* II, 383–389.
Greene, E. B. *Provincial America,* 181–184, 249–262.
Hamilton, P. J. *The Colonization of the South,* 291–308.
Henderson, Archibald. *Conquest of the Old Southwest.*
Johnson, Sir William. *The Papers of Sir William Johnson.* (Edited by A. C. Flick.) 8 vols. to 1933.
Jones, C. C. *The History of Georgia,* I, 67–313.
Kingsford, William. *History of Canada,* III, 121–201.
McCain, J. R. *Georgia as a Proprietary Province.*
McCrady, Edward. *The History of South Carolina,* I, 531–680.
Parkman, Francis. *Half-Century of Conflict,* I, 183–271; II, 53–56.
Pound, Arthur. *Johnson of the Mohawks.*
Seymour, F. W. *Lords of the Valley: Sir William Johnson and his Mohawk Brothers.*
Shaw, H. L. *British Administration of the Southern Indians, 1756–1783.*

Lecture XXVI. Imperial Control and the Development of Self-Government

Introductory. Colonial management by the mother country depended upon colonial aims. In the beginning English interest in America was mainly commercial, and colonial administration was chiefly a matter of trade regulation. England's policy was dominated by mercantilist ideas. Colonies were designed to provide raw materials and a market for English goods and to help build up the navy. At first the Navigation Acts were the chief means of control. The later Stuarts developed an imperialistic policy, by which a greater degree of royal authority was exerted.

Before 1689 imperial control was largely personal, and legislation for the colonies was by the King in Council. After 1714 colonial administration was more largely parliamentary. The chief home agencies of colonial administration now were the Secretary for the Southern Department and the Board of Trade and Plantations. In the colonies the home government was represented by governors, judges, and other royal appointees. English colonial administration lacked system and expert service, but before 1763 there was very little oppression.

During the whole colonial period there was a high degree of self-government in the colonies. Isolation and the frontier spirit bred independence. The colonies were self-supporting, and there were many non-English settlers who had little traditional affection for England. As a consequence the colonies were generally ready to assert their rights. They resisted especially the Navigation Acts, proprietary privileges, royal governors, the veto power, and appeals. Inheritance and colonial experience resulted in colonial institutions of a definite type. The colonies were all democratic. They had representative assemblies which controlled the purse. Most of their legislatures were bicameral. Executive, legislative, and judicial departments were sharply separated. All insisted on the supremacy of the Lower House. And written constitutions came to be regarded as normal. Each province had its political parties, but before 1763 no question arose which welded together any group of colonies. Difficulties between provinces over boundaries and trade went far toward counteracting united opposition to imperial authority.

1. English colonial policy. The mercantilist theory; colonies for benefit of mother country through trade and revenue; designed to furnish raw materials and a market (competing industries discouraged, complementary industries encouraged); colonial administration mainly trade regulation.

2. The Navigation Acts and restrictions on manufactures. The Navigation Acts: tobacco regulation (1621); the Ordinance of 1651 (provisions, aimed at Dutch trade); the principle extended to other colonies and other commodities (Acts of 1660, 1663, 1672, 1696); the "enumerated articles" (mainly Southern and island products); trade in them restricted to English ports and English vessels; not rigidly enforced till 1696; the Sugar Act (aimed at French West Indies, effect on New England), 1733. Restrictions on manufactures: woolens, hats, iron, and steel; unimportant compared with Navigation Acts.

3. Agencies of imperial control. Before 1689 control largely
   personal (King in Council); advisory boards; Committee on Trade and Plantations; Lords of Trade; special
   commissioners (Edward Randolph); imperialistic policy
   of later Stuarts. Period of transition (1689–1714). After
   1714 administration parliamentary and departmental;
   more rigid; tendency to unify; colonies become royal
   colonies. Home agencies of control: Parliament (increased authority, statutes instead of orders in council),
   Secretary for Southern Department (virtually colonial
   minister), 1696; Board of Trade and Plantations (becomes chief avenue of communication, without executive
   authority, contrast with Spanish Council of the Indies);
   departments (Treasury, Admiralty, War). Agencies in
   the colonies: royal governors, judges, customs collectors,
   vice-admiralty courts, garrisons (defense more important
   in eighteenth century). Defects of administration: lack
   of system; lack of expert training; inefficiency, graft,
   nepotism; not much fiscal oppression before French and
   Indian War.
4. The development of self-government in the colonies.
   Separatist forces; colonies self-supporting; non-English
   settlers; isolation; independent spirit of frontier.
   Forms of resistance: to Navigation Acts (smuggling,
   hostility to collectors); to quit rents and feudal dues;
   to authority of governors (struggles with assemblies); to
   veto power and appeals (unsuccessfully resisted but
   irritating). Colonial political institutions: democratic;
   written constitutions (the charters were forerunners);
   separation of powers (executive, legislative, judicial);
   supremacy of legislature (control through money power);
   bicameral system.

REQUIRED READING

One of the following:

ANDREWS, C. M. *The Colonial Period*, chap. 5, 7, or 8.
ANDREWS, C. M. *The Fathers of New England*, chap. 6, 7, 9, or 10.
BOLTON, H. E., and MARSHALL, T. M. *The Colonization of North America*, 343–358.
CHITWOOD, O. P. *A History of Colonial America*, 493–515.
GREENE, E. B. *Foundations of American Nationality*, chaps. 9, 11.
JERNEGAN, M. W. *The American Colonies*, 244–297.
WILLIAMSON, J. A. *Short History of British Expansion*, 1922 ed., or 1931 ed., 255–271, 285–302, 325–348.
WITTKE, C. *History of Canada*, chap. 3.

REFERENCES

ANDREWS, C. M. *British Committees, Commissions, and Councils of Trade and Plantations, 1622–1675.*
ANDREWS, C. M. *Colonial Self-Government.*
BARNES, V. F. *The Dominion of New England.*
BASYE, A. H. *The Lords Commissioners of Trade and Plantations, Commonly Known as the Board of Trade, 1748–1782.*
BEER, G. L. *The Commercial Policy of England toward the American Colonies.* (Columbia University Studies in History, Economics, and Public Law, III, No. 2.)
BEER, G. L. *The Old Colonial System*, I, 1–315.
BINGHAM, HIRAM. "Early History of the Scots Darien Company," *Scottish Historical Review*, January, April, July, 1906.
BISHOP, C. F. *History of Elections in the American Colonies.*
BOND, B. W. *The Quit-Rent System in the American Colonies.*
BRISCO, N. A. *The Economic Policy of Robert Walpole.* (Columbia University Studies in History, Economics, and Public Law, XXVII, No. 1.)
CHANNING, EDWARD. *History of the United States*, II, 1–13, 217–281.
CRUMP, H. J. *Colonial Admiralty Jurisdiction in the Seventeenth Century.*
DICKERSON, O. M. *American Colonial Government, 1697–1765.*
EGERTON, H. E. *A Short History of British Colonial Policy*, 66–80, 114–152.

GREENE, E. B. *Provincial America, 166–207.*

GREENE, E. B. *The Provincial Governor in the English Colonies of North America.*

GUTTRIDGE, G. H. *The Colonial Policy of William III.*

KEITH, A. *Constitutional History of the First British Empire.*

LABAREE, L. W. *Royal Government in America: a Study of the British Colonial System before 1783.*

LAUBER, A. W. *Indian Slavery in Colonial Times.*

MORRIS, R. B. *Studies in the History of American Law, with Special Reference to the Seventeenth and Eighteenth Centuries.*

OSGOOD, H. L. *The American Colonies in the Seventeenth Century,* III, 143–241.

PROPER, E. E. *Colonial Immigration Laws.*

ROOT, W. T. *The Relations of Pennsylvania with the British Government, 1696–1795.*

RUSSELL, E. B. *The Review of American Colonial Legislation by the King in Council.*

SMITH, SIR H. L. *The Board of Trade.*

STOCK, L. F. (Editor). *Proceedings and Debates of the British Parliament respecting North America.* 3 vols.

TURNER, E. R. *The Cabinet Council of England in the Seventeenth and Eighteenth Centuries, 1622–1784.* 2 vols.

TURNER, E. R. *The Privy Council,* II.

TURNER, E. R. *The Privy Council of England in the Seventeenth and Eighteenth Centuries.*

WASHBURNE, G. A. *Imperial Control of the Administration of Justice in the Thirteen Colonies, 1684–1776.*

Essays in Colonial History presented to Charles McLean Andrews.

EXPANSION AND INTERNATIONAL RIVALRY

LECTURE XXVII. RIVAL EMPIRES IN SOUTH AMERICA

The Portuguese Drive toward the Andes

Introductory. Colonial expansion involved international rivalry in both South America and North America. Expansion was a result as well as a cause of competition. Local struggles generally reflected European wars, but this was not always the case.

The South American colonies did not stop growing in the sixteenth century. Both Spanish and Portuguese settlements continually expanded. There was steady if slow cultural progress; colleges and universities thrived; scholars wrote important books; beautiful churches, monasteries, and homes were erected. In population, wealth, and commerce Hispanic America still led its rivals in the eighteenth century. Mexico continued to be the first city of America. There was also territorial expansion. New frontiers were occupied; mines, missions, and ranches were opened, and new administrative units were formed.

As the colonies grew, international frontiers clashed. Minor territorial rivalries occurred in Guiana. French and Dutch intruded into Brazil. But the major rivalries in South America were between Brazil and her Spanish neighbors to the west and south. Heedless of papal grant or royal treaties, Brazilians extended their frontiers up the Amazon River and plun-

dered Spanish missions on the Paraguay border. In resisting
the Portuguese advance the Jesuit missionaries played a leading part. Driven from the upper Paraná by Portuguese raids,
farther south they continued their work and held the border
for another century and a quarter. The left bank of the La
Plata, the "Banda Oriental," was another scene of rivalry.
In 1750 by treaty Brazil was given a boundary much like
its present one. Thus the Line of Demarcation was sadly
bent. To restrain the Portuguese (and the British), Spain
founded the Viceroyalty of La Plata. Portugal made serious
inroads in the north, but Spain held the Banda Oriental.

1. General features. Cultural and territorial expansion;
   growth of colonies involved rivalry; intercolonial wars
   reflected European wars; local rivalries.
2. Rivalry in Guiana. English, Dutch, and French collided in
   seventeenth century; English lost possession to Dutch in
   seventeenth century; regained part in eighteenth century.
3 Portuguese expansion. The Line of Demarcation (1493–
   1494). Expansion up north coast (Cape San Roque to
   Amazon River), 1610–1630: sugar, cattle; advance hin-
   dered by Dutch occupation (1630–1661). Up the Amazon; the Jesuits (Father Vieira); Raymundo reaches
   Ecuador (1638); little Spanish resistance; the "Palmares
   Republic" (1647–1697). Expansion of the Paulistas (the
   "backwoodsmen" of Brazil): advance south and northwest; to upper Paraná (slave raids, ranching, hostility
   to Jesuits); to Gozay and Piauhy. The Minas Geraes
   (eighteenth century). The Uruguay border (see below).
   Population of Brazil.
4. Spanish resistance. The Jesuits in Paraguay and the
   struggle with the Portuguese; principal base of Spanish

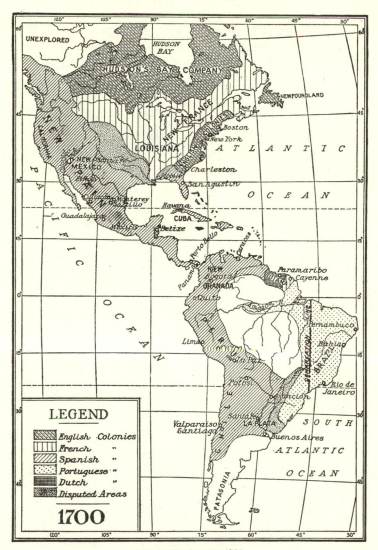

THE AMERICAS IN 1700

expansion; missions in Guayra (on upper Paraná, above cataract); twenty years of prosperity; destroyed by Paulistas (slave raids, hatred for Jesuits, national feeling), 1629–1632; flight of Father Montoya and 12,000 neophytes; below Iguassú River; new Jesuit missions; the Guaraní Indians; across middle Paraná and upper Uruguay rivers; the Seven Missions; the Jesuit republic; headquarters at Candelaria; Paulistas restrained; cattle and agriculture; patriarchal government; Jesuits expelled (1767).

5. Rivalry on the Uruguay border (1680–1776). Uruguay disputed but neglected (Charruas); Colonia founded by Portugal (1680); a smuggling center; series of captures and restorations (captured, 1680; restored, 1683; held by Spain, 1708–1716); Montevideo founded by Spain (Canary Islanders), 1726–1730; the Gauchos in West Uruguay; Rio Grande do Sul founded by Portugal (1735); Colonia exchanged for Seven Missions (1750), then restored; Colonia and Rio Grande captured by Spain (1762), restored (1763); later exchanges.

6. The Viceroyalty of Rio de la Plata (1776). To protect the Portuguese border, stop smuggling, resist England; Zevallos; army of 21,000; Colonia and Rio Grande captured, then restored; summary (Portugal won in the north, Spain in the south).

REQUIRED READING

One of the following:

ABBOTT, W. C. *Expansion of Europe*, I, 239, 310–311; II, 27–28, 105, 167, 200–201.

JAMES, H. G., and MARTIN, P. A. *The Republics of Latin America*, 66–76.

ROBERTSON, W. S. *History of the Latin-American Nations*, 1922 ed., 139–148; 1932 ed., 121–143.

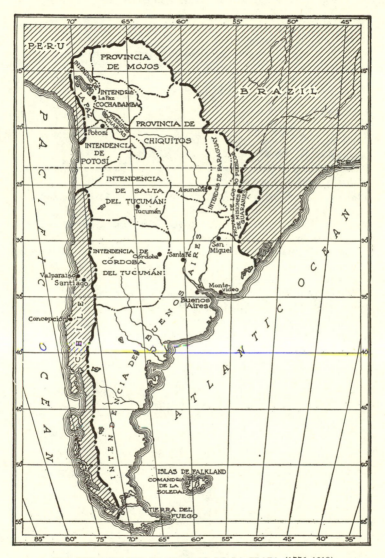

PERU

PROVINCIA
DE MOJOS

BRAZIL

INTEND
La Paz
COCHABAMBA

PRESID
CHARCAS

PROVINCIA DE

Potosí

CHIQUITOS

INTENDENCIA
DE
POTOSÍ

INTENDENCIA
DE SALTA
DEL TUCUMÁN

Asunción

INTEND DE PARAGUAY

PROVA DE MISIONES 30 PUEBLOS
DE LOS GUARANIES

Tucumán

El

San
Miguel

INTENDENCIA DE
CÓRDOBA
DEL TUCUMÁN

Córdoba

Santa Fé

Valparaíso
Santiago

Monte-
video

INTENDENCIA DE BUENOS AIRES

Buenos
Aires

Concepción

EL TUCU

PACIFIC OCEAN

ATLANTIC OCEAN

INTENDENCIA DE

ISLAS DE FALKLAND
COMANDANCIA
DE LA
SOLEDAD

TIERRA DEL
FUEGO

THE VICEROYALTY OF THE RIO DE LA PLATA (1776–1810)

SWEET, W. W. *History of Latin America*, 1919 ed., 27–28, 88–91; 1929 ed., 37–38, 93, 98–102.

WILGUS, A. C. *A History of Hispanic America*, chaps. 11, 14, 15 (selections).

REFERENCES

BULEY, E. C. *North Brazil.*

BULEY, E. C. *South Brazil.*

DAWSON, T. C. *South American Republics.*

ELLIOTT, L. E. *Brazil.*

ESCRAGNOLLE TAUNAY, AFFONSO DE (Editor). *Historia Geral das Bandeiras Paulistas.* 6 vols.

GRAHAM, R. B. C. *A Vanished Arcadia* (the Jesuits in Paraguay).

GRANT, ANDREW. *History of Brazil.*

LUCIO DE AZEVEDO, J. *Os Jesuítas no Grão-Pará: Suas Missões e a Colonização.*

NAVARRO Y LAMARCA. *Compendio de la Historia General de América*, 434–455.

OLIVEIRA LIMA, MANOEL DE. *The Evolution of Brazil.*

O'NEILL, GEORGE, S.J. *Golden Years on the Paraguay*, chaps. 3–7.

RIPPY, J. F. *Historical Evolution of Hispanic America*, chap. 7.

SOUTHEY, ROBERT. *History of Brazil.*

WATSON, R. G. *Spanish and Portuguese South America.*

Lecture XXVIII. Rivalry in the Caribbean and Eastern North America

The Fall of New France

Introductory. Colonial expansion involved territorial rivalry in North America even more than in South America. It began with the first intrusions into Spanish possessions and continued till the middle of the nineteenth century. In the seventeenth century transfers of territory were made in the Caribbean and on the mainland, mainly at the expense of Spain and Holland. By settlement of unoccupied islands, England, France, and Holland absorbed many regions claimed by Spain. England conquered Jamaica, and France took western Haiti. On the mainland Virginia and South Carolina were settled in the face of Spanish resistance, and the Swedish and Dutch colonies were annexed by England. In 1670 Spain first recognized England's title to her American possessions.

Then followed seventy-five years of more militant conflict. In this struggle the fur trade and Indian control played a significant part. Englishmen boldly invaded grounds which the French traders had considered their own preserves. In the West Indies and Georgia the Anglo-Spanish contest still raged. The long struggle was marked by five general European wars. In each of them nearly all frontiers in North America were war zones. England steadily gained ground, just as Portugal earlier had done in South America. In 1713 France gave up her claims to the Hudson Bay region, Newfoundland,

Acadia, and St. Christopher Island. Oglethorpe's colony
and the War of Jenkins's Ear broke Spain's hold on Georgia.
The final clash between France and England came when
English settlers began to threaten the Ohio valley. With
the victory of Wolfe on the Plains of Abraham, France
withdrew from mainland North America. The Mississippi
Valley was divided between Spain and England, and Spain
yielded the Floridas.

1. General features. Expansion in North America, even more
   than in South America, was accompanied by territorial
   rivalries; contiguous borders became war zones; the
   American wars generally reflected European conflicts,
   but not always.
2. Early territorial conquests (before 1689). Mainly at expense
   of Spain and Holland. In the Caribbean: by settlement
   of unoccupied islands (England, France, Holland, and
   Denmark founded their Caribbean settlements in the
   face of Spanish resistance and with much fighting among
   themselves); by conquest of islands already settled (western Santo Domingo by France; Curaçao by the Dutch;
   Jamaica by the English, 1655). On the northern mainland: Virginia and South Carolina settled in the face of
   Spanish protest and menace; in 1670 Spain acknowledged England's title to actual settlements on the mainland and in the Caribbean; by 1686 Spanish settlements
   driven from Santa Elena (Port Royal, South Carolina) and
   from northern Georgia; the Dutch conquered the Swedish
   settlements on the Delaware; New Netherland conquered
   by the English, who lost Surinam to the Dutch.
3. Seventy-five years of conflict (1689–1763). The importance
   of the fur trade and Indian control in the contest for the

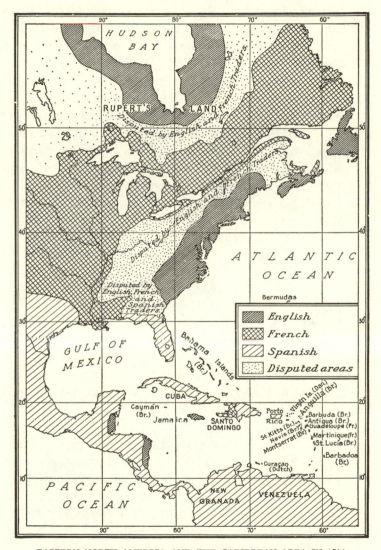

EASTERN NORTH AMERICA AND THE CARIBBEAN AREA IN 1714

interior (Frontenac, Woodward, Cabrera, Moore, Bienville, Oglethorpe, Adair, Priber, and Croghan as representative men of the struggle). Principal wars : War of
English Succession (1689–1697); War of Spanish Succession (1702–1713); War of Jenkins's Ear (1739–
1743); War of the Austrian Succession (1743–1748);
French and Indian War (1754–1763). Chief contestants :
England, France, Spain. War zones : the Caribbean
area; the Florida-Georgia border; the St. Lawrence
border (Acadia, New England, New York); Hudson
Bay; Ohio valley and the Cherokee country.

4. Territorial changes during the wars (gradual English gains).
War of the English Succession : conquests all restored.
War of the Spanish Succession : Acadia, Newfoundland,
and St. Christopher Island ceded to England; Spanish
settlements in southern Georgia and western Florida
largely destroyed. War of Jenkins's Ear (1739–1743) :
English occupation in Georgia extended to St. Mary's
River; other conquests restored. French and Indian
War : clash in the Ohio valley; the final struggle for
Canada (Wolfe and Montcalm); French driven from
mainland; England acquired the Floridas, eastern
Mississippi Valley, Canada, and four Caribbean islands
(Grenada, Dominica, St. Vincent, Tobago); four others
handed back.

5. The new British possessions organized and occupied (1763–
1776). Four new provinces organized (East Florida, West
Florida, Quebec, Grenada); Indian resistance in the Mississippi Valley (Conspiracy of Pontiac, destruction of
British posts, George Croghan's diplomacy); Indian
Reserve created, then opened to settlement; Quebec enlarged to include Ohio country (Quebec Act, 1774).

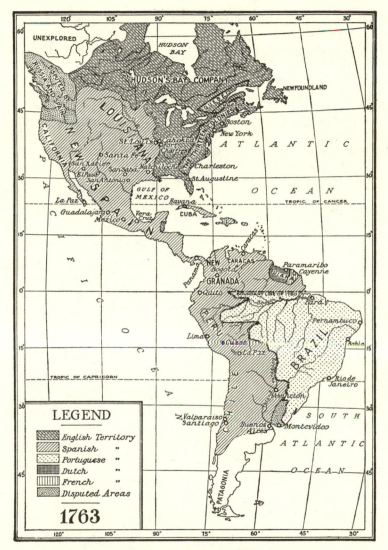

THE AMERICAS IN 1763

REQUIRED READING

One of the following:

BOLTON, H. E., and MARSHALL, T. M. *The Colonization of North America*, chaps. 14, 20.

FORMAN, S. E. *Our Republic*, 40–46.

GREENE, E. B. *Foundations of American Nationality*, chaps. 7, 16.

PRIESTLEY, H. I. *The Coming of the White Man*, chap. 8.

WILLIAMSON, J. A. *Short History of British Expansion*, 1922 ed., or 1931 ed., 333–337, 385–407.

WITTKE, CARL. *A History of Canada*, chap. 3.

WOOD, WILLIAM. *The Winning of Canada*.

WRONG, G. M. *The Conquest of New France*, chap. 8 or 9.

REFERENCES

THE INTERCOLONIAL WARS

General

BOLTON, H. E., and MARSHALL, T. M. *The Colonization of North America*, chap. 20.

CHANNING, EDWARD. *History of the United States*, II, chaps. 18–19.

HOCKETT, H. C. *Political and Social Growth of the United States, 1492–1852*, chap. 10.

THWAITES, R. G. *France in America*, chaps. 5–18.

WINSOR, JUSTIN. *Narrative and Critical History of America*, V, chaps. 1, 7, 8.

Special

ABBOTT, W. C. *Expansion of Europe*, II, chaps. 30, 32.

ANDREWS, C. M. "Anglo-French Rivalry, 1700–1750," *American Historical Review*, XX, 539–556, 761–780.

BAKER-CROTHERS, HAYES. *Virginia and the French and Indian War*.

CASGRAIN, H. R. *Wolfe and Montcalm*. (Written from the French-Canadian point of view.)

CORBETT, J. S. *England in the Seven Years' War*.

COULTER, E. M. *A Short History of Georgia*, chaps. 4–5.

DE FOREST, L. E. *Louisbourg Journals, 1745*.

FORD, W. C. *Washington*, I, chaps. 3–6.

FRANKLIN, BENJAMIN. *Autobiography*, in his *Writings* (edited by A. H. Smyth), I; *Letters*, in his *Writings*, III.

HANOTAUX, GABRIEL, and MARTINEAU, ALFRED (Editors). *Histoire des Colonies Françaises*, I.

HART, F. R. *The Siege of Havana, 1762.*

HOTBLACK, KATE. *Chatham's Colonial Policy*, especially chaps. 7–12.

KIMBALL, G. S. (Editor). *Correspondence of William Pitt with Colonial Governors.*

LINCOLN, C. H. (Editor). *Correspondence of Governors Shirley and Sharpe* (Maryland Archives).

LODGE, H. C. *George Washington*, I, chap. 3.

LONG, J. C. *Lord Jeffrey Amherst, a Soldier of the King.*

LYON, E. W. *Louisiana in French Diplomacy.*

MAHAN, A. T. *Influence of Sea Power upon History, 1660–1783.*

PARGELLIS, S. M. *Lord Loudoun in North America, 1756–1758.*

PARKMAN, FRANCIS. *Montcalm and Wolfe.*

POUND, ARTHUR. *Johnson of the Mohawks.*

ROBERTSON, C. G. *England under the Hanoverians*, chaps. 2–3.

SEYMOUR, F. W. *Lords of the Valley: Sir William Johnson and his Mohawk Brothers.*

VOLWILER, A. T. *George Croghan and the Westward Movement.*

WAUGH, W. T. *James Wolfe, Man and Soldier.*

WEBSTER, J. C. (Editor). *The Journal of Jeffrey Amherst . . . in America from 1758–1763.*

WHITTON, LT. COL. F. E. *Wolfe and North America.*

WRONG, G. M. *The Rise and Fall of New France.* 2 vols.

LECTURE XXIX. WESTERN NORTH AMERICA IN
THE INTERNATIONAL ARENA

Texas, Louisiana, California, and the North Pacific

Introductory. Expansion and rivalry were as much a feature in western as in eastern North America. After the sixteenth century Spanish expansion northward was largely defensive. New Mexico was lost through the uprising of the Pueblo Indians, but after a series of campaigns it was regained and recolonized. Into Texas Spain was forced by French intrusion. La Salle founded his short-lived colony on Matagorda Bay; in reply Spain planted temporary missions in eastern Texas. The French colony of Louisiana split Spain's Gulf possessions in two and threatened the western country. As a counter-stroke Spain permanently occupied Texas. The advance of the French up Platte River was answered by a Spanish gesture toward colonizing eastern Colorado. Louisiana, acquired from France in 1762, was reluctantly occupied and developed by Spain as a means of guarding against English and American intrusions.

Similarly, Spain was forced by foreign danger into Alta California. Jesuit missionaries had carried the northwestern frontier into Pimería Alta (Sonora and Arizona) and Lower California. Then the Russians threatened Alta California. Bering's explorations were followed by the establishment of Russian posts in Alaska. So Spain moved forward. Portolá and Serra planted presidios and missions at San Diego and Monterey. Anza explored an overland route from Sonora

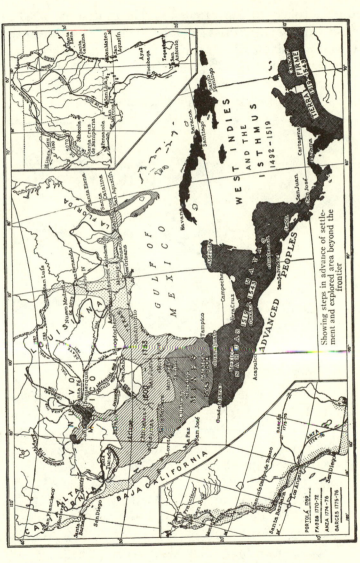

THE EXPANSION OF NEW SPAIN (1492–1800)

Showing steps in advance of settlement and explored area beyond the frontier

and led a colony to San Francisco. The contest extended to British Columbia. British and Russian traders threatened the North Pacific coast. To hold the country Spain built a post at Nootka Sound. England protested and Spain yielded her claim to exclusive sovereignty, but territorial rivalry in the Pacific Northwest continued for another half-century.

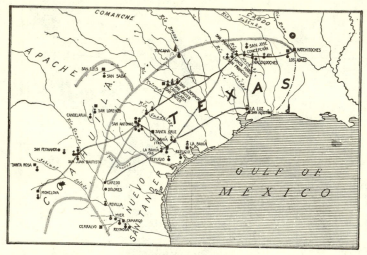

TEXAS UNDER SPAIN

1. Spanish expansion in North America (review). The occupation of the West Indies (1492–1519); the occupation of Central America and southern Mexico (1509–1543); exploration of the northern interior (1513–1543); the occupation of northern Mexico and of Florida (1543–1609). Increased importance of defensive expansion.

2. The revolt and reconquest of New Mexico (1680–1698). Popé, leader of the Pueblos; the massacre (1680); the retreat; beginnings of El Paso. Reconquest of New Mexico: Vargas (1692–1698); new settlements (Albuquerque).

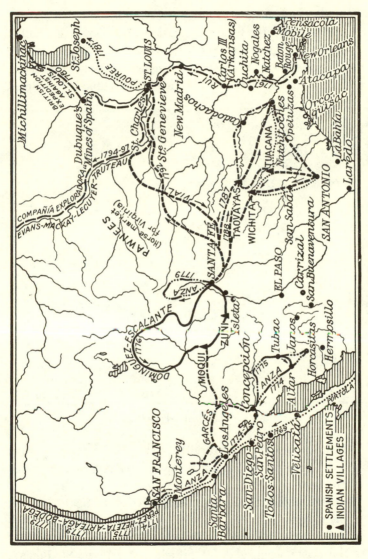

THE NORTHERN FRONTIER OF NEW SPAIN IN THE LATE EIGHTEENTH CENTURY

3. The Texas-Louisiana border. Coahuila founded (1673–1678); the first French intrusion into Texas (La Salle's colony); Texas occupied by Spain (De León, Father Massanet), 1690; second French intrusion (Louisiana, St. Denis in Mexico); Texas reoccupied by Spain

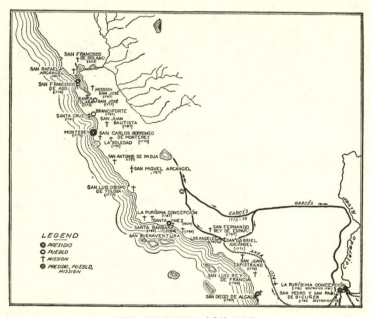

ALTA CALIFORNIA (1769–1823)

(Ramón, Espinosa, Margil), 1716; the Franco-Spanish War (Pensacola, Texas, Platte River), 1719–1720; the Marquis of Aguayo (Texas won for Spain), 1721.

4. Louisiana under Spain. Louisiana ceded to Spain (1762); the English danger; Spain attempts to occupy Louisiana (Ulloa expelled, 1768); "Bloody O'Reilly" (1769); interior posts occupied (Natchitoches, Arkansas, St. Louis);

control by fur trade instead of missions; Bernardo de Gálvez (New Orleans rebuilt).

5. The Jesuits on the Pacific Slope. Sinaloa, Sonora; mining; the Jesuits; Kino in Pimería Alta (1687-1711); Salvatierra in Lower California (1697-1717); the Jesuits expelled (1767); replaced by Franciscans (Serra).

6. The Russian advance and the Spanish occupation of Alta California. Early Spanish plans to occupy (Vizcaíno); eighteenth-century fear of French and English; the Russian advance across Siberia; port at Okhotsk; Bering's discoveries; Russian fur trade on Aleutian Islands; Spanish fears; José de Gálvez, visitor-general of New Spain, decides to occupy Upper California; the Portolá-Serra expedition (San Diego and Monterey founded), 1769; Anza explores overland route from Sonora; Anza's colony; San Francisco founded (1776); advance to British Columbia; the culmination of Spanish expansion in North America.

REQUIRED READING

One of the following:

BOLTON, H. E., and MARSHALL, T. M. *The Colonization of North America*, 237-250, 289-327, 384-403.

BOLTON, H. E. *The Spanish Borderlands*, chap. 8, 9, or 10.

BOLTON, H. E. "Defensive Spanish Expansion and the Significance of the Border Lands," in Willard and Goodykoontz, *The Trans-Mississippi West*, 1-42.

PRIESTLEY, H. I. *The Coming of the White Man*, chap. 10.

REFERENCES

TEXAS

BOLTON, H. E. *Texas in the Middle Eighteenth Century.*

CLARK, R. C. *The Beginnings of Texas.*

DUNN, W. E. *Spanish and French Rivalry in the Gulf Region of the United States.*

GARRISON, G. P. *Texas, a Contest of Civilizations.*
HACKETT, C. W. (Editor). *Pichardo's Treatise on the Limits of Louisiana and Texas.*
HILL, L. F. *José de Escandón and the Founding of Nuevo Santander.*
PARKMAN, FRANCIS. *La Salle and the Discovery of the Great West.*

LOUISIANA

AITON, A. S. "The Diplomacy of the Louisiana Cession," in *American Historical Review*, XXXVI (1931), 701–720.
BARBÉ-MARBOIS, FRANÇOIS. *History of Louisiana.*
BOLTON, H. E. *Athanase de Mézières and the Louisiana-Texas Frontier.*
CAUGHEY, J. W. *Bernardo de Gálvez in Louisiana, 1776–1783.*
CHAMBERS, H. E. *Mississippi Valley Beginnings.*
GAYARRÉ, CHARLES. *History of Louisiana.*
HAMILTON, P. J. *Colonial Mobile.*
HAMILTON, P. J. *The Colonization of the South.*
HOUCK, LOUIS. *History of Missouri.*
LYON, E. W. *Louisiana in French Diplomacy, 1759–1804.*
MARSHALL, T. M. *History of the Western Boundary of the Louisiana Purchase.*
NASATIR, A. P. "The Anglo-Spanish Frontier in the Illinois Country during the American Revolution, 1779–1783," in *Journal of the Illinois State Historical Society*, XXI (1928), 291–358.
NASATIR, A. P. "The Formation of the Missouri Company," in *Missouri Historical Review*, XXV (1930), 10–22.
OGG, F. A. *The Opening of the Mississippi.*
PHELPS, ALBERT. *Louisiana.*
THWAITES, R. G. *France in America.*

NEW MEXICO AND PIMERÍA ALTA

BANCROFT, H. H. *Arizona and New Mexico.*
BOLTON, H. E. (Editor). *Kino's Historical Memoir of Pimería Alta.*
BOLTON, H. E. *The Padre on Horseback.*
FORREST, E. R. *Missions and Pueblos of the Old Southwest.*
HACKETT, C. W. (Editor). *Historical Documents relating to New Mexico, Nueva Vizcaya, and Approaches Thereto, to 1773.*
HACKETT, C.W. *The Revolt of the Pueblo Indians of New Mexico in 1680.*

HAMMOND, G. P. *Don Juan de Oñate and the Founding of New Mexico.*

LOCKWOOD, F. C. *Story of the Spanish Missions of the Middle Southwest.*

LOCKWOOD, F. C. *With Padre Kino on the Trail.*

LUMHOLTZ, CARL. *New Trails in Mexico.*

THOMAS, A. B. (Editor). *Forgotten Frontiers: a Study of the Spanish Indian Policy of Don Juan Bautista de Anza, Governor of New Mexico, 1777–1787.*

VENEGAS, MIGUEL. *Juan María de Salvatierra.* (Translated by M. E. Wilbur.)

CALIFORNIA

BOLTON, H. E. *Anza's California Expeditions.* 5 vols.

BOLTON, H. E. *Outpost of Empire.*

CAUGHEY, J. W. *History of the Pacific Coast.*

CHAPMAN, C. E. *The Founding of Spanish California.*

CHAPMAN, C. E. *A History of California: the Spanish Period.*

COUES, ELLIOTT. *On the Trail of a Spanish Pioneer.*

DENIS, A. J. *Spanish Alta California.*

ELDREDGE, ZOETH. *The Beginnings of San Francisco.*

GHENT, W. J. *The Early Far West: a Narrative Outline, 1540–1850.*

HUNT, R. D. *California the Golden.*

HUNT, R. D., and SÁNCHEZ, NELLIE. *A Short History of California.*

NORTON, H. K. *The Story of California.*

PALÓU, FRANCISCO. *New California.* (H. E. Bolton, Editor.)

PRIESTLEY, H. I. *José de Gálvez.*

REPPLIER, AGNES. *Junípero Serra.*

RICHMAN, I. B. *California under Spain and Mexico.*

SÁNCHEZ, N. V. *California and Californians: the Spanish Period.*

TARAVAL, SIGISMUNDO. *The Indian Uprising in Lower California, 1734–1737.* (M. E. Wilbur, Editor.)

New Spain and the Anglo-American West: Historical Contributions presented to Herbert Eugene Bolton. 2 vols.

PART TWO. THE AMERICAN NATIONS

THE AMERICAS AT THE END OF THE EIGHTEENTH CENTURY
Nearly all the Western Hemisphere was still in the colonial status

THE FOUNDING OF THE UNITED STATES

Lecture XXX. The Parting of the Ways

Introductory. The half-century between 1776 and 1826 witnessed the political separation of most of America from Europe. The event was inevitable. Spain, Portugal, and England founded vigorous colonies. They grew up and asserted their majority. The revolutions were the surest signs that the mother countries had succeeded. Thirteen of the English colonies led the way. Spanish and Portuguese America followed. Throwing off their status as wards, they set themselves up as independent nations.

It is pointless to try to trace the revolt of the English colonies to specific acts of government. The causes were inherent in the situation. English rule in America had not been tyrannical. Her mercantilist policy was selfish in spirit, but in practice it was lightly enforced, and the provincials were in the main self-governing. But the germs of revolution were ever present. England and the colonies had grown apart. The Americans had acquired political experience, they had strength, and they were ready to revolt under pressure. After the French and Indian War that pressure was applied. British colonial policy became increasingly imperialistic. The Stamp Act was but one of many signs of a new spirit. The colonists, fearing the loss of their many liberties, protested. Not the least of their fears was that they would be prevented from extending their settlements unhampered over the mountains. So they adopted slogans and formulated constitutional theories. The home government resorted to coercion and the colonies to armed resistance.

1. England and the colonies before 1763. England not generally tyrannical; colonies self-governed in the main; assemblies in control; the Navigation Acts selfish in purpose but not enforced; smuggling widespread; tendency to closer supervision of colonies in the eighteenth century; form of government unified (crown colonies); more attention to defense; imperial Indian policy, but relations never better than in 1761; the colonies had acquired strength and political experience; disunited but ready to unite under pressure; radical elements in the colonies (immigrants, the frontier).

2. New policy after French and Indian War. Aims (revenue, protection, discipline); Writs of Assistance (smuggling during the war); the Sugar Act and the Stamp Act; other evidences of a new policy; England's policy regarding the West (the Ohio valley temporarily closed to settlement, Western land schemes, land speculation, the Indian Line revised, plans for a new policy); other evidences of a new policy.

3. Colonial protest and the formulation of constitutional doctrines. James Otis, Samuel Adams, and Patrick Henry; "no taxation without representation"; sympathy in England (representation in England, the New Whigs, William Pitt); the Stamp Act Congress; physical resistance; the Stamp Act repealed (1766), but the right to tax maintained; expressions of loyalty.

4. The Townshend Acts and the Boston Tea Party (1767–1773). George III stubborn; duties on glass, paper, tea, etc.; new uses of revenue (officers to be paid by crown);

resistance (boycott associations, Massachusetts Circular); assemblies suspended; efforts to enforce through soldiers; the Boston Massacre (1770); repeal of the Acts, except that on tea (decline of trade, complaint of British

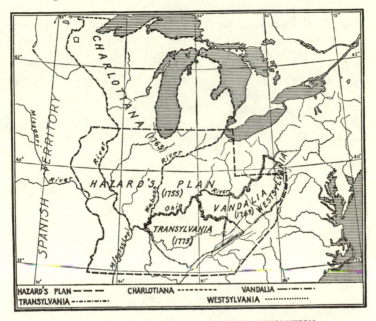

WESTERN LAND SCHEMES BEFORE THE REVOLUTION

merchants); Committees of Correspondence; attempt to relieve East India Company; the Boston Tea Party.
5. Coercion and organized resistance. North's coercive measures (Boston Port Bill, Massachusetts charter annulled; Quartering Act), 1774; Quebec Act (designed to conciliate French colonists, regarded as a blow to westward expansion); First Continental Congress; Declaration of Rights; organization for resistance.

REQUIRED READING

One of the following :

BEARD, C. A. and M. R. *History of the United States*, 1921 ed., chap. 5 : 1929 ed., chap. 6.

BECKER, C. L. *The Eve of the Revolution*, chap. 2, 3, or 4.

BOLTON, H. E., and MARSHALL, T. M. *The Colonization of North America*, chap. 23.

FARRAND, MAX. *The Development of the United States*, 33–44.

FORMAN, S. E. *Our Republic*, 53–62.

HARLOW, R. V. *The Growth of the United States*, 154–170. See also 140–153 (early stages of the Revolution).

MACDONALD, WILLIAM. *Three Centuries of American Democracy*, 26–36.

MARTIN, A. E. *History of the United States*, I, Enlarged Edition, chap. 5.

MORISON, S. E., and COMMAGER, H. S. *Growth of the American Republic*, 1–17 (liberty and empire). See also chaps. 2 and 3.

MUZZEY, D. S. *The United States of America*, I, 55–71, 71–84.

SCHLESINGER, A. M. *New Viewpoints in American History*, chap. 7.

REFERENCES

THE FOUNDING OF THE UNITED STATES

General accounts covering Lectures XXX–XXXVI :

ADAMS, J. T. *Revolutionary New England.*

AVERY, E. M. *The United States and its People.*

BASSETT, J. S. *A Short History of the United States*, 322–357.

CHANNING, EDWARD. *History of the United States.*

CURTIS, G. T. *Constitutional History of the United States.*

DEWEY, D. R. *Financial History of the United States.*

FARRAND, MAX. *The Development of the United States*, 53–125.

FOSTER, J. W. *A Century of American Diplomacy.*

GARNER, J. W., and LODGE, H. C. *The History of the United States*, II.

GORDY, J. P. *Political History of the United States.*

HARLOW, R. V. *Growth of the United States.*

HART, A. B. *Formation of the Union.*

HILDRETH, RICHARD. *History of the United States.*

JOHNSON, ALLEN. *Union and Democracy.*

MCLAUGHLIN, A. C. *The Confederation and the Constitution.*

MCMASTER, J. B. *History of the People of the United States.*

MORAN, T. F. *The Formation and Development of the Constitution.*
MORISON, S. E. *The Oxford History of the United States.*
PEASE, T. C. *The United States.*
SCHOULER, JAMES. *History of the United States under the Constitution.*
TREVELYAN, G. O. *The American Revolution.*
VON HOLST, H. E. *The Constitutional and Political History of the United States.*

WHY THE COLONIES REVOLTED

ADAMS, JOHN. *Works*, II, 337–517.
ADAMS, SAMUEL. *Writings*, II–III.
ALVORD, C. W. *The Mississippi Valley in British Politics.*
ANDREWS, C. M. *The Colonial Background of the American Revolution,* chap. 3.
BALDWIN, A. M. *The New England Clergy and the American Revolution.*
BECKER, C. L. *Beginnings of the American People*, 202–253.
BECKER, C. L. *The Declaration of Independence.*
BECKER, C. L. *The Eve of the Revolution.*
BEER, G. L. *British Colonial Policy, 1754–1763*, 72–355.
BEST, M. A. *Thomas Paine, Prophet and Martyr of Democracy.*
BIGELOW, JOHN (Editor). *The Life of Benjamin Franklin*, II, 7–337.
CARTER, C. E. *The Correspondence of General Thomas Gage with the Secretaries of State, 1763–1775.*
CHANNING, EDWARD. *History of the United States*, III, 29–154.
CLARK, D. M. *British Opinion and the American Revolution.*
CROSS, A. L. *The Anglican Episcopate and the American Revolution.*
COUPLAND, REGINALD. *The Quebec Act.*
DICKINSON, JOHN. *Writings* (edited by P. L. Ford), in Pennsylvania Historical Society, *Memoirs*, XIV, 307–406.
DOYLE, J. A. "The Quarrel with Great Britain, 1761–1776," *Cambridge Modern History*, VII, 148–208.
ECKENRODE, H. J. *The Revolution in Virginia.*
FAŸ, BERNARD. *Franklin, the Apostle of Modern Times.*
FISHER, S. G. *The Struggle for American Independence*, I, 1–300.
FORD, W. C., and HUNT, GAILLARD (Editors). *Journals of the Continental Congress.*
FORTESCUE, SIR JOHN (Editor). *The Correspondence of George III from 1760 to December, 1783.* 6 vols.
FROTHINGHAM, RICHARD. *The Rise of the Republic*, 158–455.

GREENE, E. B. *Foundations of American Nationality*, chaps. 17–18.

GUTTRIDGE, G. H. *The American Correspondence of a Bristol Merchant, 1766–1776. Letters of Richard Champion. Edited with an Introduction.*

GUTTRIDGE, G. H. "English Liberty and the American Revolution," American Historical Association, Pacific Coast Branch, *Proceedings, 1930*, 151–159.

GUTTRIDGE, G. H. "The Whig Opposition in England during the American Revolution," *Journal of Modern History*, VII (1934), 1–13.

HENRY, W. W. *Patrick Henry*, I, 24–357.

HOWARD, G. E. *Preliminaries of the Revolution.*

HUTCHINSON, P. O. *The Diary and Letters of His Excellency Thomas Hutchinson*, I.

JOHNSON, E. R. *History of Domestic and Foreign Commerce of the United States*, I, 84–121.

LECKY, W. E. H. *The American Revolution.*

LINCOLN, C. H. *The Revolutionary Movement in Pennsylvania, 1760–1776.*

MACDONALD, WILLIAM. *Select Charters*, 272–396.

NAMIER, L. B. *England in the Age of the American Revolution.*

SCHLESINGER, A. M. *The Colonial Merchants and the American Revolution, 1763–1776.*

TREVELYAN, G. O. *The American Revolution*, Part I, 1–253.

TYLER, M. C. *Literary History of the American Revolution*, I.

VAN DYKE, PAUL. *George Washington, the Son of his Country, 1732–1775.*

VAN TYNE, C. H. *The American Revolution*, 3–24.

VAN TYNE, C. H. *The Causes of the War of Independence.*

VAN TYNE, C. H. *England and America, Rivals in the American Revolution.*

Lecture XXXI. The Revolutionary War in the English Colonies

Introductory. Protest, disobedience, and coercion gave way to open warfare. The clash at Lexington and Concord made conciliation impossible, although many still hoped for it. When the war began the colonies had little thought of independence; they were struggling for redress of grievances. But soon they began to think of separation. The movement for independence was hastened by harsh British acts, the publication of Paine's *Common Sense*, a desire for foreign aid, and the employment by England of German mercenaries.

The colonists were far from unanimous in their attitude toward the war. Only thirteen of more than twenty colonies joined, though all were urged to do so. In these thirteen probably a third of the people were Loyalists, opposed to the war. The Continental Congress was the great agency of coöperation. It organized the army, issued the Declaration of Independence, and financed the Revolution.

Successes, failures, and valor were probably equal on both sides. American unpreparedness was offset by British lukewarmness. The strategy of the war was relatively simple. An unsuccessful attempt to cut the colonies in two was followed by efforts to defeat them in detail on all frontiers. American privateers won brilliant successes. The back-country people held the Southwest against powerful Indian tribes; Clark won the Illinois country. Gradually the war became international in character. France, Spain, and Holland joined the cause against England. Spain drove the British from the lower

175

Mississippi and recovered the Floridas; in the final victory
the French navy played an important part. The treaty of
peace was a shock to European monarchs. It recognized not
only an American nation, but a nation with a republican form
of government.

1. The war at first one of self-defense and a struggle for redress
   of grievances. Protest, argument, disobedience, and boy-
   cotting give way to open war; Lexington and Concord;
   Crown Point, Ticonderoga; Bunker Hill; the Second
   Continental Congress; appeal to other colonies (Canada
   and West Indies); the country organized for defense;
   Washington in command; the British expelled from
   Boston; Canada invaded.
2. The Declaration of Independence. At first no idea of
   independence; utterances of prominent leaders, colonial
   governments, Continental Congress; mutual illusions;
   effect of Bunker Hill; steps toward the Declaration
   (harsh British acts, Paine's *Common Sense*, the desire for
   a foreign alliance, the employment of German mercenaries); the drafting and adoption of the Declaration; re-
   luctance of some states.
3. Lack of unity in the war. The Loyalists: the Revolution
   organized by a minority; one half to one third of the
   people were Loyalists (classes, distribution, suppression, persecution, emigration). Nonparticipating colonies: Canada (Quebec, Nova Scotia, Newfoundland,
   Hudson's Bay Company); East and West Florida;
   the island colonies (Bermudas, Windward Islands, Leeward Islands, Jamaica, Bahamas, etc.). Lack of political cohesion in these colonies; military suppression;
   aristocracy.

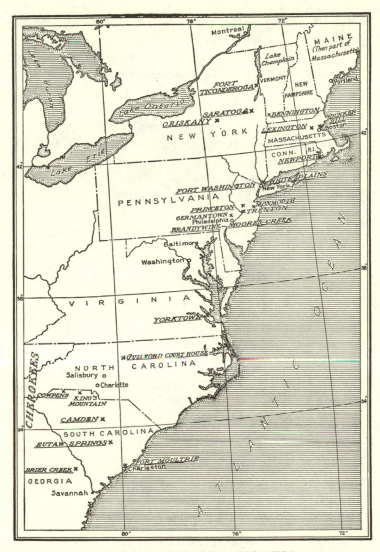

PRINCIPAL BATTLES OF THE REVOLUTION

4. Military history of the war. The effort to cut the colonies in two (the struggle for the middle region); attempt to conquer the colonies in detail; the war as an international contest (the French alliance); Spain and the West in the war (Gálvez, Clark); the war on the sea; the Dutch alliance; Yorktown; the greatness of Washington.

5. The treaty of peace. Foreign interests; the Loyalists; the boundaries; efforts to limit the United States; the Floridas restored to Spain.

REQUIRED READING

One of the following:

BASSETT, J. S. *A Short History of the United States*, chap. 9.

BEARD, C. A. and M. R. *History of the United States*, 1921 ed., chap. 6; 1929 ed., chap. 7.

BOLTON, H. E., and MARSHALL, T. M. *The Colonization of North America*, chap. 24.

FARRAND, MAX. *The Development of the United States*, 44–54.

FORMAN, S. E. *Our Republic*, 65–78 or 78–90.

HARLOW, R. V. *The Growth of the United States*, 181–193 (military operations); 203–215 (foreign relations and the end of the war).

MACDONALD, WILLIAM. *Three Centuries of American Democracy*, 36–49.

MARTIN, A. E. *History of the United States*, I, Enlarged Edition, chap. 6.

MORISON, S. E., and COMMAGER, H. S. *Growth of the American Republic*, 65–88 (the Revolution precipitated); 102–106 (the Peace of Paris). For the military aspects of the war, see 88–102.

MUZZEY, D. S. *The United States of America*, I, 84–103.

REFERENCES

ABBOTT, W. C. *New York in the American Revolution*.

BARCK, O. T. *New York City during the War for Independence, with Special Reference to the Period of British Occupation*.

BECKER, C. L. *The Declaration of Independence*.

BOLTON, C. K. *The Private Soldier under Washington*.

CHANNING, EDWARD. *History of the United States*.

CLOWES, W. L. *The Royal Navy*, III, 354–538.

CORBIN, JOHN. *The Unknown Washington: Biographic Origins of the Republic.*

CORWIN, E. S. *French Policy and the American Alliance of 1778.*

COUPLAND, REGINALD. *The American Revolution and the British Empire.*

CURTIS, E. E. *The Organization of the British Army in the American Revolution.*

EINSTEIN, LEWIS. *Divided Loyalties: Americans in England during the War of Independence.*

FISHER, S. G. *The Struggle for American Independence.*

FISKE, JOHN. *The American Revolution.*

FITZPATRICK, J. C. *George Washington Himself.*

FITZPATRICK, J. C. (Editor). *The Writings of George Washington.*

FORD, W. C., and HUNT, GAILLARD (Editors). *Journals of the Continental Congress.*

FRENCH, ALLEN. *The Taking of Ticonderoga in 1775: the British Story.*

FRIEDENWALD, HERBERT. *The Declaration of Independence.*

GREENE, E. B. *The Foundations of American Nationality*, chaps. 19–23.

GREENE, F. V. *The Revolutionary War.*

GUTTRIDGE, G. H. "Adam Smith on the American Revolution." *American Historical Review*, XXXVIII (1933), 714–720.

GUTTRIDGE, G. H. *David Hartley, M.P., an Advocate of Conciliation, 1774–1783.*

GUTTRIDGE, G. H. "Lord George Germain in Office, 1775–1782." *American Historical Review*, XXXIII (1927), 23–43.

HALE, E. E. *Franklin in France.*

HAMILTON, P. J. *The Colonization of the South*, chap. 23.

HAZELTON, J. H. *The Declaration of Independence.*

JAMES, J. A. (Editor). *George Rogers Clark Papers, 1771–1781*, introduction.

JAMES, J. A. *The Life of George Rogers Clark.*

JAMESON, J. F. "St. Eustatius in the American Revolution." *American Historical Review*, VIII, 683–708.

JONES, E. A. *The Loyalists of Massachusetts: their Memorials, Petitions, and Claims.*

KINNAIRD, LAWRENCE. "The Spanish Expedition against Fort St. Joseph in 1781, a New Interpretation," in *Mississippi Valley Historical Review*, XIX (1932), 173–191.

LECKY, W. E. H. *The American Revolution.*

MACLAY, E. S. *A History of the United States Navy,* I, 34–151.

NASATIR, A. P. "The Anglo-Spanish Frontier in the Illinois Country during the American Revolution, 1779–1783," in *Journal of the Illinois State Historical Society,* XXI (1928), 291–358.

PALMER, FREDERICK. *Clark of the Ohio: a Life of George Rogers Clark.*

PAULLIN, C. O. *The Navy of the American Revolution.*

PERKINS, J. B. *France in the American Revolution.*

PHILLIPS, P. C. *The West in the Diplomacy of the American Revolution.*

ROBERTSON, W. S. (Editor). *The Diary of Francisco de Miranda, Tour of the United States, 1783–1784.*

ROZ, FIRMÍN. *Washington.*

SIEBERT, W. H. *Loyalists in East Florida, 1774 to 1785: the Most Important Documents Pertaining Thereto.*

SMITH, J. H. *Our Struggle for the Fourteenth Colony.*

TRESCOT, W. H. *Diplomacy of the American Revolution.*

TREVELYAN, G. O. *The American Revolution.*

VAN TYNE, C. H. *The American Revolution.*

VAN TYNE, C. H. *England and America, Rivals in the American Revolution.*

VAN TYNE, C. H. *The Loyalists in the American Revolution.*

VAN TYNE, C. H. *The War of Independence.*

WALLACE, W. S. *The United Empire Loyalists.*

WHARTON, FRANCIS. *The Revolutionary Diplomatic Correspondence of the United States,* I.

WHITTON, F. E. *The American War of Independence.*

WILBUR, J. B. *Ira Allen, Founder of Vermont, 1751–1814.*

WOOD, L. A. *The War Chief of the Six Nations.*

LECTURE XXXII. THE STATES, THE UNION, AND
THE NATIONAL DOMAIN

Introductory. The Revolution gave the colonies more than
independence. In the course of the struggle three cornerstones
of the nation were laid. The colonies became states; a union
was formed; and a national domain was created.

The process of state-forming was similar in most cases.
Royal officials were expelled and charters revised or state
constitutions adopted. The constitutions provided for representative government, a sharp separation of legislative, executive, and judicial departments, and unmistakable supremacy
of the legislature over the other branches. The new constitutions showed some steps toward democracy, but they were far
from radical.

The colonies began the Revolution as thirteen separate provinces; in the course of it they formed a union. A frame of
national government was proposed almost simultaneously with
the Declaration of Independence. But so jealous were the
states of their rights and so fearful of a new master that it took
Congress a year to adopt the Articles of Confederation and
the states four years to ratify them.

Scarcely less important than the Union was the national
domain. The country west of the Allegheny Mountains was
won during the war. In the struggle over the ratification
of the Articles it was ceded by the states to the nation.
It was then prepared for settlement. The Ordinance of
1785 outlined a public land system. The Ordinance of 1787
provided a unique system of national expansion — the ulti-

mate admission of colonies on the basis of full equality with the original states.

The Confederation had thus given superb examples of constructive statesmanship. As a frame of government, however, the Articles were defective. A convention called to revise them drew up instead a new Federal Constitution, providing for a carefully devised balance between the states and the nation.

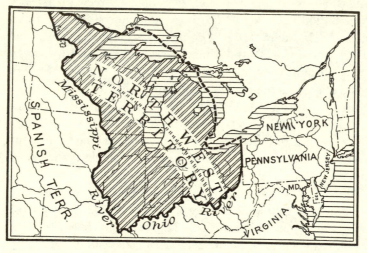

THE NORTHWEST TERRITORY, FORMED IN 1787

1. The formation of state governments. Royal officials expelled; revolutionary committees; charters revised (Rhode Island and Connecticut); eleven states form constitutions; general features (written documents, colonial precedents, bills of rights, representative government, three departments, bicameral legislatures, weak executives, suffrage and office-holding restricted, some steps toward democracy). In the formation of state governments colonial experience served as a guide.

2. **The beginnings of the Union.** Committees of correspondence; boycott associations; achievements of the Continental Congress (organized the army and navy, issued the Declaration of Independence, secured the French alliance, won the Revolution); the Articles of Confederation; Franklin's plan of 1775; Articles reported, July, 1776;

	N							N				
36	30	24	18	12	6		6	5	4	3	2	1
35	29	23	17	11	5		7	8	9	10	11	12
34	28	22	16	10	4		18	17	16	15	14	13
33	27	21	15	9	3		19	20	21	22	23	24
32	26	20	14	8	2		30	29	28	27	26	25
31	25	19	13	7	1		31	32	33	34	35	36

Ordinance of 1785   *Act of 1796*

RECTANGULAR SURVEY SYSTEM ON THE NATIONAL DOMAIN
Old and new methods of numbering the sections of a township

debates lasted over a year; ratification delayed nearly four years (1781); jealousy of states without Western lands.

3. **The winning of the West.** The West organized by England (1763–1774); the Southwest settled by Americans during the war (Boone, Robertson, Sevier, Henderson); the Illinois country conquered by Clark; Lower Mississippi and Florida conquered by Spain (Gálvez); the West in the treaties.

4. **The creation and the organization of the national domain.** Struggle over the Articles of Confederation; small states force large states to cede Western lands to nation; the

domain a bond of union; the Land Ordinance of 1785;
survey before settlement; townships and sections; school
lands; "settlement versus revenue"; territorial governments; the Ordinance of 1787; temporary tutelage of
new colonies (called territories); final admission to equal
statehood; a unique system of expansion.

5. The Federal Constitution. Defects of the Confederation:
a union of states, not a national government; lack of
power to raise revenue and regulate commerce; two-
thirds vote required; difficulty of amending. The
Constitutional Convention (1787): called to amend the
Articles; a new instrument drawn; the Constitution
based on experience of the colonies and the Confederation; "a bundle of compromises"; a national government. Ratification of the Constitution (1788).

REQUIRED READING

One of the following:

BASSETT, J. S. *A Short History of the United States*, 217–237.

BEARD, C. A. and M. R. *History of the United States*, 1921 ed., chap. 7;
1929 ed., chap. 8.

BOLTON, H. E., and MARSHALL, T. M. *The Colonization of North
America*, chap. 28.

FARRAND, MAX. *The Development of the United States*, chap. 3.

HARLOW, R. V. *The Growth of the United States*, 196–199 (formation
of state governments; the Confederation); 216–224 (problems
of the frontier); 233–243 (the Federal Constitution).

MARTIN, A. E. *History of the United States*, I, chaps. 3–5; I, Enlarged
Edition, chaps 8–10. (Selections.)

MORISON, S. E., and COMMAGER, H. S. *Growth of the American Republic*, 107–118 (formation of state governments); 129–149 (the
Confederation); 150–167 (the Federal Constitution); note especially 131–135 on western lands.

MUZZEY, D. S. *The United States of America*, I, chap. 3.

SPARKS, E. E. *The Expansion of the American People*, chap. 10.

REFERENCES

COCHRAN, T. C. *New York in the Confederation: an Economic Study.*
FARRAND, MAX. *The Fathers of the Constitution.*
FARRAND, MAX. *The Framing of the Constitution.*
FISKE, JOHN. *The Critical Period of American History.*
GREENE, E. B. *Foundations of American Nationality,* chaps. 24–28.
HUTCHISON, DAVID. *The Foundations of the Constitution.*
JAMES, J. A. *The Life of George Rogers Clark.*
MCLAUGHLIN, A. C. *The Confederation and the Constitution.*
MCLAUGHLIN, A. C. *The Foundation of American Constitutionalism.*
SCHLESINGER, A. M. *New Viewpoints in American History,* chap. 8.
SPAULDING, E. W. *New York in the Critical Period, 1783–1789.*
TAYLOR, HANNIS. *Origin and Growth of the American Constitution.*
TREAT, P. J. *The National Land System, 1785–1820.*
TURNER, F. J. "Western State-Making in the Revolutionary Era," *American Historical Review,* VII, 271–289.
WARREN, CHARLES. *The Making of the Constitution.*

Lecture XXXIII. The New Government on Trial

Federalists and Republicans

Introductory. Until it was tried, the new Constitution was but a "scrap of paper." Would it work? It did work. Its success was due in part to the fact that it was launched under favorable circumstances. Its adoption was followed by "good times," and it was put into operation by its most ardent supporters — notably Washington and Hamilton.

The first test of the Constitution came with the struggle that raged round Hamilton's financial measures. Adherents and critics represented two opposing views of government, championed respectively by Hamilton and Jefferson. Hamilton favored a strong central government, believed in the rule of the wealthy and intelligent, feared mass rule, and favored a liberal construction of the Constitution. Jefferson feared an overcentralized government, favored rule by the masses and a strict construction of the Constitution.

Hamilton's measures carried, but out of the contest over them arose political parties. Those who followed Hamilton became known as Federalists; those who followed Jefferson, as Republicans. The parties now diverged still further over relations with Europe. Republicans generally were pro-French: they favored a treaty with France and criticized England. Federalists generally were pro-English: they detested the French Revolution, favored a treaty with England, and were angry at French interference in American politics. For twelve years the Federalists had their day. Then arbitrary exercise

186

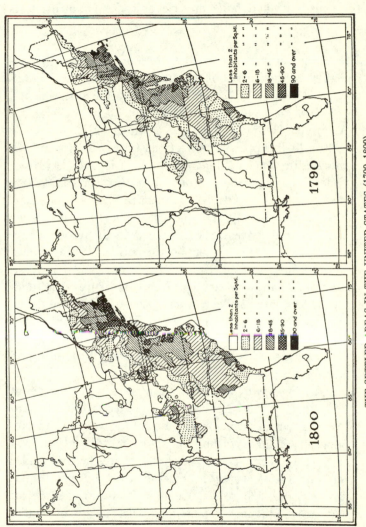

THE SETTLED AREAS IN THE UNITED STATES (1790, 1800)

of their authority and Jefferson's clever leadership of his hosts
brought about their downfall.

1. The new government put into operation; election of Washington; organization of executive departments; Hamilton and Jefferson; the Federal courts; the amendments.
2. Two views of government in conflict. The Federalists: Alexander Hamilton; desired a strong national government; liberal construction of the Constitution; rule of the wealthy and intelligent; aristocratic; conservative; Federalism favored by property-owning class and large trading centers. The Republicans: Thomas Jefferson; believed in rule by the masses; opposed a privileged class; feared concentration of power in the national government; favored "strict construction"; Republican strength lay in rural districts, the South, and the West.
3. Hamilton's financial measures. Aims; measures (the funding of the national debt, assumption of the state debts, the establishment of the National Bank, the excise tax); opposition to Hamilton's measures; the Whisky Insurrection in Pennsylvania (1794); the rise of Federalist and Republican parties.
4. Party divergence over European politics. Inclination of Federalists toward England, of the Republicans toward France; enthusiasm for the French Revolution in Republican circles; Washington's Neutrality Proclamation (1793); English violation of United States neutral trade; the Jay Treaty (1794); criticism led by Republicans; Monroe's mission to France brought out the same divergence; Pinckney rejected by Directory; Federalist anger; French restrictions on neutral trade; the XYZ episode.

5. Overconfidence and downfall of the Federalists. Unpopular acts of Adams; the Naturalization Act; the Alien Laws; the Sedition Law; emigration of Frenchmen; Republican opposition organized by Jefferson; the Virginia and Kentucky Resolutions; the "compact" theory of government; the "nullification" doctrine (a political measure); division among the Federalists (Hamilton versus Adams); victory for the Republicans (Jefferson elected president); "the first of several great periodic popular upheavals by which the people have shown that they mean the government to rest on the will of all the people."

6. Nationalistic tendencies under the Republican administrations; liberal construction in actual practice (the Louisiana Purchase, building the national road, etc.; Marshall's judicial decisions).

REQUIRED READING

One of the following:

BEARD, C. A. and M. R. *History of the United States*, 1921 ed., chaps. 8, 9; 1929 ed., chaps. 9, 10.

CORWIN, E. S. *The Constitution and What it Means Today* (selections).

FARRAND, MAX. *The Development of the United States*, chap. 4.

FORD, H. J. *Washington and his Colleagues*, chap. 3 or 8.

FORMAN, S. E. *Our Republic*, chap. 8.

HARLOW, R. V. *The Growth of the United States*, 244–265.

MACDONALD, WILLIAM. *Three Centuries of American Democracy*, chap. 4.

MARTIN, A. E. *History of the United States*, I, chaps. 5–9; I, Enlarged Edition, chaps. 11–14. (Selections.)

MORISON, S. E., and COMMAGER, H. S. *Growth of the American Republic*, 191–194 (the prospect); 201–215 (Hamilton and Jefferson).

MUZZEY, D. S. *The United States of America*, I, chap. 4.

REFERENCES

ATHERTON, GERTRUDE. *The Conqueror*. (A novel.)

BASSETT, J. S. *The Federalist System*.

BEARD, C. A. *An Economic Interpretation of the Constitution*.

BEARD, C. A. *Economic Origins of Jeffersonian Democracy*.

BEVERIDGE, A. J. *The Life of John Marshall*. 4 vols.

BOWERS, C. G. *Jefferson and Hamilton; the Struggle for Democracy in America*.

CHINARD, GILBERT. *Honest John Adams*.

CHINARD, GILBERT. *Thomas Jefferson, the Apostle of Americanism*.

CRAIGMYLE, LORD. *John Marshall in Diplomacy and in Law*.

FAŸ, BERNARD. *George Washington, Republican Aristocrat*.

LODGE, H. C. *Alexander Hamilton*.

LYNCH, W. O. *Fifty Years of Party Warfare*.

MCLAUGHLIN, A. C. *The Courts, the Constitution, and the Parties*.

MORISON, S. E. *The Oxford History of the United States*.

MORSE, J. T., JR. *Thomas Jefferson*.

ROBINSON, E. E. *The Evolution of American Political Parties: a Sketch of Party Development*.

SEARS, L. M. *George Washington*.

TRESCOT, W. H. *Diplomatic History under Washington and Adams*.

WARREN, CHARLES. *The Supreme Court in United States History*.

LECTURE XXXIV. THE SHADOW OF EUROPE IN THE
WEST (1783–1819)

The Acquisition of Louisiana and Florida

Introductory. For thirty years European interests in the
Mississippi Valley were a menace to the independence and
growth of the United States. The infant nation was not born
a giant, and many people even thought it would fail. European
nations looked on with interest. If the young upstart ceased
to exist they would share in the estate; if it survived they
wished to check its growth or dominate its fortunes. The
danger was averted by jealousy and conflict among the European nations themselves, and by the vigor of American growth.

Spain threatened the development of the Southwest. The
Anglo-American treaty of 1782 fixed the Florida boundary at
31 degrees and granted Americans free use of the Mississippi.
Spain objected, and for twelve years her policy was to hold on
to the disputed area and keep the Americans out. Finally in
1795 she yielded to the United States on both points.

In the Northwest England occupied an analogous position.
For thirteen years she maintained military posts on United
States soil, hoping that by some turn in politics she might
regain the area. Jay negotiated a treaty by whose terms
England gave up her posts, but British traders continued to
operate in the Northwest and to exert a dominating influence
over the Indians there. England hoped to recover the region
in the War of 1812, but failed. The English menace in the
Northwest now passed.

France was even more dangerous in the West than either Spain or England. She hoped to dominate the Ohio valley, or even to separate it from the United States. In this she failed, but by browbeating Spain Napoleon secured the retrocession of Louisiana. Then suddenly, his colonial plans having failed, he ceded it to the United States. The shadow of France had been dispelled. Later, by the acquisition of Florida, the United States acquired a frontage on the Gulf of Mexico.

1. Spain in the Southwest. Questions at issue (the treaty of 1783, the West Florida boundary, the navigation of the Mississippi); Spain's policy; control of the Indians (Alexander McGillivray); intrigues with the Southwestern settlers; separatist feeling in the Southwest (James Wilkinson, Brown, O'Fallon); Spain's demands in negotiation; counter colonization (Loyalists, Acadians, Canary Islanders, Americans); British interests (Bowles); the Pinckney Treaty of 1795 (boundary, navigation of the Mississippi, right of deposit); delay in delivery of posts; United States efforts to purchase West Florida.

2. England in the Northwest. Retention of the Western posts; British traders among the Indians; Wayne's victory at Fallen Timbers (1794); the Jay Treaty (1794); the English posts withdrawn (1796); Blount's conspiracy (British plan to lead Western settlers against Louisiana and Florida), 1796-1797; English traders continue to operate in Northwest; efforts to reconquer Northwest in War of 1812; demand of traders for the Ohio-Missouri boundary (1814).

3. French intrigues in the West and the retrocession of Louisiana. Fear of English influence; desire to regain

AREAS IN DISPUTE
AFTER 1783

with England

with Spain

AREAS IN DISPUTE IN EASTERN NORTH AMERICA AFTER 1783

Louisiana; Genêt's plans to conquer Louisiana and Florida; three expeditions proposed; George Rogers Clark joins in the plan; Jefferson favors "a little explosion on the Mississippi" to induce Spain to negotiate; Washington interferes; Genêt recalled; expedition collapses; the Jay Treaty with England turns France to the recovery of Louisiana (Fauchet's report); intrigues in the West (Fulton, Milhet, Collot); spread of separatist ideas; the retrocession (1800).

4. The Louisiana Purchase. Jefferson's alarm; justified by closing of the Mississippi (1802); Monroe sent to try to purchase New Orleans or Florida; failure of Napoleon's colonial plans; Louisiana sold to the United States.

5. Boundary questions and the acquisition of Florida. Uncertainty of the boundaries; efforts to negotiate; border disorders during the Spanish-American Revolution; West Florida seized; East Florida occupied by Jackson; purchased (1819); Texas relinquished.

6. Significance. Foreign danger in the West removed; vast area for expansion acquired; constitutional significance (a blow at strict construction).

REQUIRED READING

One of the following:

BASSETT, J. S. *A Short History of the United States*, 261–266, 296–300, 303–306.

FARRAND, MAX. *The Development of the United States*, 98–104.

FORMAN, S. E. *Our Republic*, 191–197, 247–248.

HARLOW, R. V. *The Growth of the United States*, 271–277 (the Louisiana Purchase); 328–330 (Florida).

MACDONALD, WILLIAM. *Three Centuries of American Democracy*, 107–115.

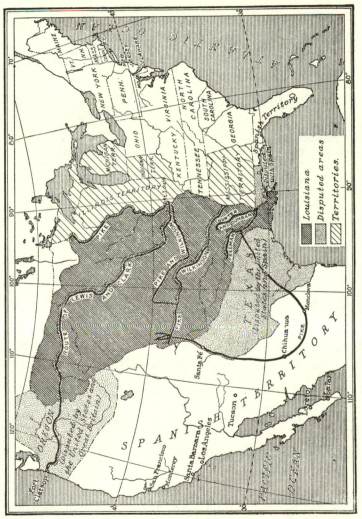

THE LOUISIANA PURCHASE AND DISPUTED BOUNDARIES

MARTIN, A. E. *History of the United States*, I, chaps. 7, 10; I, Enlarged Edition, chaps. 13, 16. (Selections.)

MORISON, S. E. *The Oxford History of the United States*, chap. 5.

MORISON, S. E., and COMMAGER, H. S. *Growth of the American Republic*, 222–231 (France); 232–241 (England); 241–242, 282–284 (Spain); 272–276 (the Louisiana Purchase).

MUZZEY, D. S. *The United States of America*, I, 204–223.

REFERENCES

(For general accounts consult preceding list.)

ADAMS, HENRY. *History of the United States.*

ADAMS, R. G. *History of the Foreign Policy of the United States.*

BEARD, C. A. *The Supreme Court and the Constitution.*

BEMIS, S. F. *Jay's Treaty.*

BEMIS, S. F. *Pinckney's Treaty.*

BROOKS, P. C. "The Pacific Coast's First International Boundary Delineation, 1816–1819," in *Pacific Historical Review*, III (1934), 62–79.

CHANNING, EDWARD. *History of the United States.*

CHANNING, EDWARD. *The Jeffersonian System.*

COX, I. J. *The West Florida Controversy, 1798–1813.*

DAVIDSON, G. C. *The North West Company*, Appendix N.

FISH, C. R. *American Diplomacy.*

FOREMAN, GRANT. *Indians and Pioneers: the Story of the American Southwest before 1830.*

FULLER, H. B. *The Purchase of Florida.*

GAYARRÉ, CHARLES. *History of Louisiana*, III (The Spanish Domination).

GEER, C. M. *The Louisiana Purchase and the Westward Movement.*

HACKETT, C. W. (Editor). *Pichardo's Treatise on the Limits of Louisiana and Texas.*

HASKINS, C. H. *Yazoo Land Companies.*

HENDERSON, ARCHIBALD. *Conquest of the Old Southwest.*

JAMES, J. A. *The Life of George Rogers Clark.*

KINNAIRD, LAWRENCE. "International Rivalry in the Creek Country," in *Florida Historical Society Quarterly*, X (1931), 59–85.

KINNAIRD, LAWRENCE. "The Significance of William Augustus Bowles' Seizure of Panton's Apalachee Store in 1792," in *Florida Historical Society Quarterly*, IX (1931), 156–192.

LYON, E. W. *Louisiana in French Diplomacy, 1759-1804.*

MCMASTER, J. B. *History of the People of the United States.*

MARSHALL, T. M. *History of the Western Boundary of the Louisiana Purchase, 1-70.*

MATTHEWS, J. M. *American Foreign Relations: Conduct and Policies.*

MORSE, J. T., JR. *Thomas Jefferson.*

NASATIR, A. P. "The Anglo-Spanish Frontier on the Upper Mississippi, 1786-1796," in *Iowa Journal of History and Politics*, XXIX (1931), 155-232.

PALMER, FREDERICK. *Clark of the Ohio: a Life of George Rogers Clark.*

PICKETT, A. J. *History of Alabama.*

POUND, ARTHUR. *Johnson of the Mohawks.*

ROBERTSON, J. A. (Editor). *Louisiana under the Rule of Spain, France, and the United States.*

SEARS, L. M. *A History of American Foreign Relations.*

STEVENS, W. E. *The Northwest Fur Trade, 1763-1800.*

TURNER, F. J. "The Policy of France toward the Mississippi Valley," *American Historical Review*, X, 249.

WHITAKER, A. P. *The Mississippi Question, 1795-1803.*

WHITAKER, A. P. *The Spanish American Frontier, 1783-1795.*

Lecture XXXV. The Great Trek over the Mountains

The Crossing

Introductory. " Going West " is our national epic. Every region has had its trappers, surveyors, speculators, miners, settlers, and town-builders, its romance of adventure, its struggle with Indian and forest. The Mississippi Valley is no exception.

While diplomats were arguing over western boundaries, pioneers were crossing the mountains into the disputed areas. They first entered the Old Southwest. This region was occupied by American settlers a whole generation earlier than the Old Northwest. The pioneers, among whom Scotch-Irish from the Piedmont were conspicuous, went ahead of the government. They settled in the face of Indian resistance and of Spanish opposition. Finding themselves isolated, they took government into their own hands. Distant and neglected, they often considered separatist projects, but these were only temporary. The Watauga Association, the Nashborough Association, Transylvania, and the State of Franklin all soon gave way to state jurisdiction. The tide of settlement pushed on into Mississippi and Alabama. In the eighteenth century many Americans had crossed the Mississippi and become citizens of Spain. After the Louisiana Purchase the movement across the river was greatly accelerated.

In contrast with the Old Southwest, the settlement of the Old Northwest was a paternalistic movement. Settlement there was on the national domain. The Federal government

198

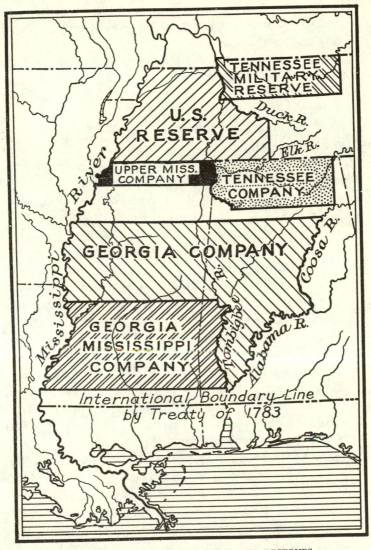

SOUTHWESTERN LAND SCHEMES AND RESERVES

removed the Indians, and provided a land system, a territorial government, and defense. The government partly defeated its plans for systematic development by making special grants to companies, on whose lands most of the first settlements were made. Before 1820 the South sent a strong tide of migration across the Ohio; thereafter New England and New York furnished the dominant stream.

Growth of population led logically to a demand for self-government in the West, and by 1820 eight states and several territories had been erected beyond the mountains. The new constitutions reflected the democratic effects of frontier experience.

1. The settlement of Transappalachia (1763–1820). (a) The Old Southwest: priority; "the crossing" (hunters, prospectors, settlers); the trails; a squatter movement; separatist governments; the beginnings of Tennessee (Robertson, Sevier, the Watauga Association, Nashborough); the beginnings of Kentucky (Boone, Henderson, the Wilderness Trail, Transylvania); land companies and speculation; the struggle for statehood (back lands ceded; territory south of the Ohio, 1790), Kentucky admitted (1792), Tennessee (1796); Mississippi Territory (1799–1804); Mississippi (1817); Alabama (1819). (b) The Old Northwest: preparation for settlement (land ordinance, 1785; Ordinance of 1787, posts, Indian cessions); settlement by companies and on special grants; the Ohio Company (Marietta); Symmes's Tract ("Losantiville," Cincinnati); Scioto Company (Gallipolis); Virginia Military Reserve (Chillicothe); Connecticut Reserve (Cleveland); settlement checked by Indian wars (Wayne's victory; Treaty of Greenville, 1795); political organization

(Indiana Territory, 1800; Ohio admitted, 1802; Michigan
Territory, 1805; Illinois Territory, 1809; Indiana admitted, 1816; Illinois admitted, 1818); Southern influence in the Northwest; the Hoosiers.

2. Opening the Louisiana Purchase, and the fixing of boundaries (1803–1819). The official explorers (Lewis and

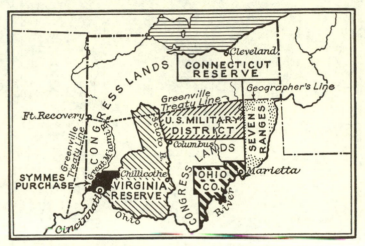

OHIO GRANTS AND RESERVES

Clark; claim to Oregon; Pike, Long, Cass); the fur-
traders (Lisa, Chouteau, Missouri Fur Company, Southwestern traders); the settlers (immigration before 1803,
the rush after 1803); political organization; Territory of
Orleans (1804); Louisiana Territory (1804–1805); Louisiana state admitted (part of Florida annexed); Missouri
Territory (1812); Arkansas Territory (1819); Missouri
admitted (1821). Fixing the boundaries: the Florida
boundary (West Florida seized; East Florida occupied
to keep order, and purchased, 1819); Texas-Louisiana

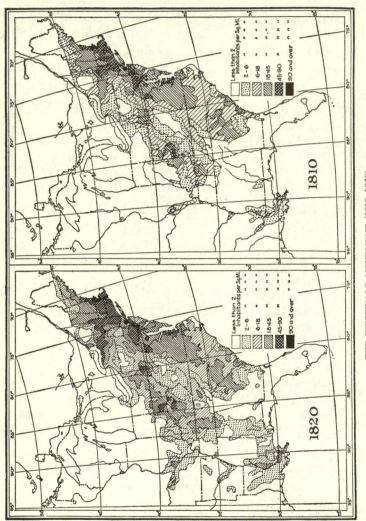

THE WESTWARD MOVEMENT (1810–1820)

boundary (Texas yielded for claims to Oregon, 1819);
the Northwest boundary (agreement of 1818, joint occupation in Oregon).
3. Significance of expansion. Political, social, economic, constitutional, international.

REQUIRED READING
One of the following:

BASSETT, J. S. *A Short History of the United States*, chap. 16.
BOLTON, H. E., and MARSHALL, T. M. *The Colonization of North
America*, chap. 22.
FARRAND, MAX. *The Development of the United States*, chap. 6 or 7.
FORMAN, S. E. *Our Republic*, 160–166, 218–234.
MARTIN, A. E. *History of the United States*, I, chap. 2; I, Enlarged
Edition, chap. 8.
MUZZEY, D. S. *The United States of America*, I, 283–309.
OGG, F. A. *The Old Northwest*.
SKINNER, C. L. *Pioneers of the Old Southwest*.
SPARKS, E. E. *The Expansion of the American People*, chap. 11 or 12.

REFERENCES

THE SETTLEMENT OF TRANSAPPALACHIA (1763–1820)

ALVORD, C. W., and BIDGOOD, LEE. *First Explorations of the Trans-
Alleghany Region by the Virginians, 1650–1674*.
AMBLER, C. H. *A History of Transportation in the Ohio Valley, with
Special Reference to its Waterways, Trade and Commerce from the
Earliest Period to the Present Time*.
BOND, B. W. *The Civilization of the Old Northwest: a Study of Political,
Social, and Economic Development, 1788–1812*.
CHURCHILL, WINSTON. *The Crossing*. (A novel.)
COMAN, KATHARINE. *Economic Beginnings of the Far West*.
COX, I. J. *Early Exploration of Louisiana*.
DRIVER, C. S. *John Sevier, Pioneer of the Old Southwest*.
HAMILTON, P. J. *The Colonization of the South*, 409–457.
HENDERSON, ARCHIBALD. *The Conquest of the Old Southwest*.
HINSDALE, B. A. *The Old Northwest*, 247–380.

HULBERT, A. B. *The Cumberland Road.*
JAMES, J. A. *The Life of George Rogers Clark.*
JILSON, W. R. *The Kentuckie Country: an Historical Exposition of Land Interest in Kentucky Prior to 1790.*
MATTHEWS, L. K. *The Expansion of New England.*
MOHR, W. H. *Federal Indian Relations, 1774–1788.*
MORISON, S. E. *The Oxford History of the United States,* chaps. 13–14.
OGG, F. A. *The Opening of the Mississippi,* 539–658.
PALMER, FREDERICK. *Clark of the Ohio: a Life of George Rogers Clark.*
PAXSON, F. L. *History of the American Frontier.*
PEASE, T. C. *The United States.*
ROOSEVELT, THEODORE. *Winning of the West.*
STEVENS, W. E. *The Northwest Fur Trade, 1763–1800.*
TURNER, F. J. *Rise of the New West,* chaps. 5–7.
VANDIVEER, C. A. *The Fur-trade and Early Western Exploration.*
WINSOR, JUSTIN. *The Westward Movement.*

Lecture XXXVI. Rights of Neutrals and Ambitions of the "War Hawks"

Introductory. The shadow of Europe was cast on the sea as well as on the land. For two decades the United States was in danger of being involved in the European struggles of England and France, and at last this calamity fell. When England and France went to war, Washington declared for neutrality. But this was a difficult position to maintain. Each combatant tried to injure the other by cutting off neutral commerce, in which Americans played a large part. War with England was averted by the Jay Treaty, and with France by temporary peace in Europe. War broke out again and aggressions on neutral commerce were renewed. Both nations seized American vessels, and England impressed American seamen. For this there was a good excuse, as many of the sailors were deserters from the English navy. Jefferson tried peaceful coercion without avail.

The victory at Trafalgar left England mistress of the waves, and she proceeded to sweep neutral commerce from the sea. Napoleon retaliated in kind. American commerce was now between the upper and the nether millstone. The United States was in doubt which aggressor to strike, if either. The seizure of the *Chesapeake* prepared American sentiment for war with England, but Madison tried an embargo instead. Europeans smiled.

Madison was finally forced into war. British traders were still active in the Old Northwest and on the Florida border. Western "War Hawks" protested, and urged the conquest of Canada. Thus driven, Congress declared war when it was too late. The United States was unprepared, and the war was badly handled. All along the northern frontier American interests suffered disaster. But American failures on land were offset by brilliant victories at sea. In the peace conference British diplomats tried to obtain the cession of a vast portion

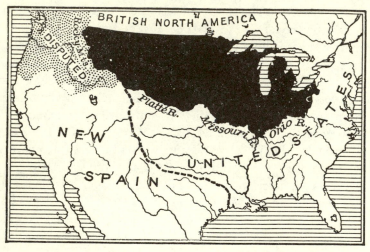

CESSION PROPOSED BY BRITISH FUR-TRADERS IN 1814

of the upper Mississippi Valley, but without avail. The war was far from glorious, but it was not a disgrace. It secured the Northwestern frontier, and it won respect for American seamen and soldiers.

1. Early struggles for neutrality. Neutrality declared: the French Revolution; sympathy in the United States; treaty obligations (1778); the European war; Washington's neutrality proclamation (1793); Genêt's violation of neutrality. On the verge of war with England (1794):

the neutral trade of the United States; seizures by both England and France; impressment by England; war averted by the Jay Treaty (1794). French insults and the naval war with France (1796–1800) : French resentment of English treaty; American vessels seized; Pinckney ordered from France; the X Y Z episode; naval warfare without declaration (privateering, sea fights); Napoleon favors peace; Convention (1800).

2. The crisis in American trade (1803–1809). War in Europe renewed (1803); renewed attack by England on neutral trade (impressments, desertions from English navy, the press gang, renewed seizures, the Rule of 1756); commercial interests opposed to war; Jefferson adopts policy of "gunboats" and nonimportation (1804). Between England and France: the Continental system, Orders in Council, Berlin and Milan Decrees (1806–1807). Peaceful coercion tried by the United States: the *Chesapeake* affair; the embargo (1807–1809) against both England and France; smuggling; outcry of shippers; repeal of the embargo.

3. The War of 1812. The West and the "War Hawks"; fear of English designs on Florida; Indian war in the Northwest; Henry Clay; war declared against England (1812). Mismanagement of the war: Madison's weak military policy; lack of preparation and discipline; partisan opposition; New England recalcitrant. The war on the Canadian frontier: Detroit, Niagara, Lakes Erie and Ontario, Lake Champlain. Naval warfare: initial American victories (the *United States*, the *Constitution*, the *Hornet*, and the *Wasp*); final triumph of English navy. The blockade of the American coast; defeat of Napoleon; the attack on Washington and Baltimore;

Plattsburg and New Orleans; the Oregon country (Astoria seized); the Hartford Convention.
4. The results of the war. Direct, few; indirect, many; the Treaty of Ghent (British boundary proposals rejected).

REQUIRED READING

One of the following:

BASSETT, J. S. *A Short History of the United States*, 306–338.
FARRAND, MAX. *The Development of the United States*, 105–123.
FORMAN, S. E. *Our Republic*, 153–160, 175–182, or chap. 11.
HARLOW, R. V. *The Growth of the United States*, 278–301.
JOHNSON, ALLEN. *Jefferson and his Colleagues*, chap. 7 or 8.
MACDONALD, WILLIAM. *Three Centuries of American Democracy*, 115–126.
MARTIN, A. E. *History of the United States*, I, chaps. 11–12; I, Enlarged Edition, chaps. 17–18.
MORISON, S. E., and COMMAGER, H. S. *Growth of the American Republic*, 284–288 (impressment); 288–291 (embargo); 292–315 (War of 1812).
MUZZEY, D. S. *The United States of America*, I, 224–282.
ROBINSON, H. *The Development of the British Empire*, 212–229.
WILLIAMSON, J. A. *A Short History of British Expansion*, 1922 ed., 484–499; 1930 ed., II, 60–76.

REFERENCES

ADAMS, HENRY. *History of the United States.*
BABCOCK, K. C. *Rise of American Nationality.*
BABCOCK, L. L. *The War of 1812 on the Niagara Frontier.*
CHANNING, EDWARD. *The Jeffersonian System*, 169–270.
GURD, N. S. *The Story of Tecumseh.*
INGERSOLL, C. J. *Second War between the United States and Great Britain.*
IRWIN, R. W. *The Diplomatic Relations of the United States with the Barbary Powers, 1776–1816.*
MACLAY, E. S. *History of American Privateers.*
MACLAY, E. S. *History of the United States Navy from 1775 to 1902.*
MCMASTER, J. B. *History of the People of the United States.*

MAHAN, A. T. *Sea Power in its Relations to the War of 1812.*
MEYER, LELAND. *The Life and Times of Colonel Richard M. Johnson of Kentucky.*
PAINE, R. D. *The Fight for a Free Sea.*
PRATT, J. W. *Expansionists of 1812.*
RAYMOND, E. T. *Tecumseh.*
ROOSEVELT, THEODORE. *Naval War of 1812.*
ROOSEVELT, THEODORE. *The Winning of the West.*
SEARS, L. M. *Jefferson and the Embargo.*
SMITH, T. C. *Wars between England and America.*
THOMAS, C. M. *American Neutrality in 1793: a Study in Cabinet Government.*
UPDYKE, F. A. *The Diplomacy of the War of 1812.*
WOOD, WILLIAM. *The War with the United States.*
ZIMMERMAN, J. F. *Impressment of American Seamen.*
Cambridge Modern History, VII, 331–348.

THE FOUNDING OF BRITISH CANADA AND THE OPENING OF THE FAR NORTHWEST

Lecture XXXVII. The Loyalists found Another Nation

Introductory. The revolt of thirteen of the British colonies laid the foundations not of one but of two English-speaking nations in North America. One was the United States; the other was the Dominion of Canada.

Before 1776 Canada was mainly French in race stock. There were a few English settlers at the Hudson's Bay Company posts, a few Scotch people in Nova Scotia and Newfoundland, and a few British soldiers who had remained as settlers and fur-traders in the St. Lawrence valley. The Loyalists, who now came, made up the first large English-speaking element in Canada. Under harsh treatment in the colonies, thousands of them emigrated during or after the Revolution. Some settled in the older Maritime Provinces and in New Brunswick. Still other thousands settled in Upper Canada — the Ontario of today. As a mark of honor the early immigrants from the Thirteen Colonies were officially designated as United-Empire Loyalists. These United-Empire Loyalists were Canada's Pilgrim Fathers. The western Loyalists found themselves a part of Quebec, where French institutions had been left intact. They were dissatisfied; they desired representative government, such as was enjoyed by the Maritime Provinces. So in 1791 Upper Canada was separated from Quebec, or Lower Canada, and both were given assemblies. Other Americans

followed the United-Empire Loyalists, and for many years
English-speaking Canada continued to be largely American
in origin. But the War of 1812 checked this migration, and
accentuated the sentiment of Canadian solidarity and of loyalty to England. After the war a heavy tide of British immigration set in, and American influence was consequently lessened.

BRITISH NORTH AMERICA IN 1763 (NORTHERN PORTION)

England did not completely learn her lesson from the revolt
of the Thirteen Colonies, and in British North America she
continued her old methods of government. The colonies there
were still royal provinces of the old type. Governors and
other high officials were appointed by the crown. In Upper
Canada government was in the hands of a conservative clique
known as the "Family Compact." But Canada was a frontier,
stirred by the same influences that gave the United States a
Jacksonian Democracy. The mass of people became dissatisfied. They saw a liberal movement under way in England and

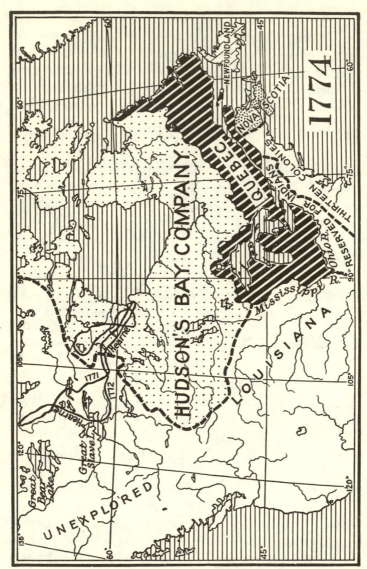

BRITISH NORTH AMERICA IN 1774 (NORTHERN PORTION)

observed the democratic methods of their cousins to the south. The radicals demanded reforms. Agitation being suppressed by force, the outcome was revolution in both Upper and Lower Canada. The home government could delay no longer, and Lord Durham was sent to investigate. He recommended re-uniting Upper and Lower Canada and the granting of responsible government. Similar struggles took place in the Maritime Provinces, and by 1849 most of these also had achieved responsible government. But Canada was still colonial and was still composed of separate provinces.

The treatment of the French people by England had been liberal. By the Quebec Act they were permitted to retain French civil law and the old Church privileges. In 1791 the same rights were confirmed. This liberal policy made for French loyalty, but it was an obstacle to assimilation.

1. Canada before 1774. Usage of the word "Canada"; the French in Canada; Hudson's Bay Company; British settlement in Nova Scotia and Newfoundland before 1763; the conquest of Canada (1760); military rule (1760–1763); the Proclamation of 1763 (Quebec organized); the Quebec Act; the Scotch traders in Montreal; Canada mainly French till 1776.

2. The United-Empire Loyalists (founders of British Canada). American efforts to conquer Canada (1775); the Loyalists in the Revolution; persecution; emigration to Canada; the Maritime Provinces (Nova Scotia, New Brunswick, Prince Edward Island); Upper Canada (Kingston, Niagara, York); government aid; settlement by regiment and sect; land grants; subsequent immigration from the United States; the United-Empire Loyalists (Order in Council, 1789; the list, 1796).

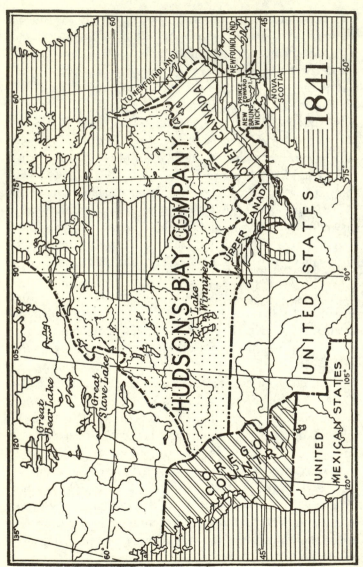

BRITISH NORTH AMERICA IN 1841

3. Separation of Upper and Lower Canada. The Loyalists under the Quebec Act; hostility of French and English; petitions for representative government; the Constitutional Act of 1791; Upper and Lower Canada separated; each given an assembly; assemblies in the Maritime Provinces; privileges of the French confirmed.

4. The war with the United States (1812-1814). Continued American immigration (Simcoe's immigration propaganda, speculation and land-grabbing); Canada largely American and French till after War of 1812; the war regarded in Canada as a war of conquest; the French loyal, recent Americans neutral; Isaac Brock, the national hero; defense against odds; Loyalism accentuated by the war.

5. British immigration after the war. Hard times in Europe; the Industrial Revolution; land bounties for disbanded soldiers; immigration societies and land companies; the tide of British immigration.

6. The struggle for self-government. Defects of the constitution (irresponsible government); the lesson not learned from the American Revolution; the Family Compact (aristocracy, conservatism, fear of American and French ideas, United-Empire Loyalism); clique control of government, land, and patronage; the opposition (American settlers, supported by newcome Europeans on the frontier; the Methodists); influence of the frontier.

7. Revolution, union, and responsible government (1837-1849). Demand for reform and responsible government; agitation suppressed; the revolution in Upper Canada (Mackenzie); the revolution in Lower Canada (Papineau); United States filibusters ("Hunters' Lodges"); Lord Durham's report (1839); union of Upper and Lower Canada (1841); responsible government by 1849.

8. British expansion in the Caribbean. Losses during American Revolution; Rodney; gains during Napoleonic wars (St. Lucia, Trinidad, Tobago, Guiana, Honduras), 1793–1815; decline of West Indian interests; revived by Panama Canal.

REQUIRED READING

One of the following:

BOLTON, H. E., and MARSHALL, T. M. *The Colonization of North America*, 212–214, 374, 404, 419–424.

BRADLEY, A. G. *Canada*, chap. 3.

WALLACE, W. S. *United Empire Loyalists*, chap. 2 or 6.

WITTKE, C. *A History of Canada*, chaps. 5–12 (selections).

WOOD, WILLIAM. *The Father of British Canada*.

WOODWARD, W. H. *Expansion of the British Empire*, chap. 8.

REFERENCES

GENERAL WORKS

BOURINOT, J. G. *Canada*, chaps. 19–24.

BRADLEY, A. G. *Canada*.

BRYCE, GEORGE. *A Short History of the Canadian People*, chaps. 6–11.

BURPEE, L. J. *An Historical Atlas of Canada*.

EGERTON, H. E. *Canada*, Part II, 1–185.

KINGSFORD, WILLIAM. *History of Canada*. 10 vols.

MUNRO, W. B. *Canada and British North America*.

MURRAY, HUGH. *Historical and Descriptive Account of British America*.

ROBERTS, C. G. D. *A History of Canada*, chaps. 13–20.

SHORTT, ADAM, and DOUGHTY, A. G. (Editors). *Canada and its Provinces*, III–IV.

TROTTER, R. G. *Canadian History: Syllabus and Guide to Reading*.

BEGINNINGS OF BRITISH CANADA

BRADLEY, A. G. *The Making of Canada.*
BRADLEY, A. G. *The United Empire Loyalists; Founders of British Canada.*
BREBNER, J. B. *New England's Outpost: Acadia before the Conquest of Canada.*
BUCKINGHAM, J. S. *Canada, Nova Scotia, New Brunswick, and the Other British Provinces in North America.*
BURT, A. L. *The Old Province of Quebec.*
COWAN, H. I. *British Emigration to British North America, 1783–1837.*
GRAHAM, G. S. *British Policy and Canada, 1774–1791.*
KENNEDY, W. P. M., and LANCTOT, GUSTAVE. *Reports on the Laws of Quebec, 1767–1770.*
NEWTON, A. P., and EWING, J. *The British Empire since 1783.*
PIERCE, LORNE. *William Kirby: the Portrait of a Tory Loyalist.*
PROWSE, D. W. *A History of Newfoundland.*
WALLACE, W. S. *The Family Compact.*
WALLACE, W. S. *United Empire Loyalists.*
WOOD, WILLIAM. *The Father of British Canada.*

THE WAR OF 1812

READ, D. B. *Life and Times of Major-General Sir Isaac Brock.*
SMITH, T. C. *The Wars between England and America.*
WOOD, WILLIAM. *The War with the United States.*

SOCIAL AND ECONOMIC LIFE

GUILLET, E. C. *Early Life in Upper Canada.*
HARRINGTON, W. S. *Pioneer Life among the Loyalists in Upper Canada.*
HIND, H. Y. *Eighty Years' Progress of British North America.*
INNIS, H. A., and LOWER, A. R. M. *Select Documents in Canadian Economic History, 1703–1885.*
MOODIE, SUSANNAH (STRICKLAND). *Roughing it in the Bush: or Life in Canada.*
SHORTT, ADAM, and DOUGHTY, A. G. (Editors). *Canada and its Provinces.*

SKELTON, ISABEL. *The Backwoodswoman: a Chronicle of Pioneer Home Life in Upper and Lower Canada.*

SMITH, W. L. *The Pioneers of Old Ontario.*

WOOD, W. C. H. *All Afloat.*

POLITICS AND GOVERNMENT

BELL, K. N., and MORRELL, W. P. *Select Documents on British Colonial Policy, 1830–1860.*

BRADSHAW, FREDERICK. *Self-Government in Canada and How it was Achieved: the Story of Lord Durham's Report.*

BRYCE, GEORGE. *A Short History of the Canadian People.*

DECELLES, A. D. *The Patriotes of '37.*

DENT, J. C. *The Story of the Upper Canadian Rebellion.*

KENNEDY, W. P. M. *The Constitution of Canada.*

KENNEDY, W. P. M. *Statutes, Treaties and Documents of the Canadian Constitution, 1713–1929.*

LANGSTONE, R. W. *Responsible Government in Canada.*

LIVINGSTON, W. R. *Responsible Government in Nova Scotia.*

LIVINGSTON, W. R. *Responsible Government in Prince Edward Island.*

MACMECHAN, ARCHIBALD. *The Winning of Popular Government.*

MIDDLETON, J. E., and LANDON, FRED. *The Province of Ontario: a History, 1615–1927.* 4 vols.

MORISON, J. L. *The Eighth Earl of Elgin: a Chapter in Nineteenth-Century Imperial History.*

MUNRO, W. B. *American Influences on Canadian Government.*

MUNRO, W. B. *Canada and British North America.*

NEW, C. W. *Lord Durham: a Biography of John George Lambton, First Earl of Durham.*

READ, D. B. *The Canadian Rebellion of 1837.*

ROBERTS, C. G. D. *A History of Canada.*

SCOTT, D. C. *John Graves Simcoe.*

SKELTON, O. D. *The Canadian Dominion.*

WHITELAW, W. M. *The Maritimes and Canada before Confederation.*

WILSON, G. E. *The Life of Robert Baldwin: a Study in the Struggle for Responsible Government.*

Cambridge History of the British Empire, VI (Canada and Newfoundland).

LECTURE XXXVIII. THE BRITISH FUR MEN
IN THE WEST

Introductory. The same half-century that saw the laying of the foundations of British Canada witnessed also the advance of British and Americans across the continent into the Pacific Northwest. These "splendid wayfarers" profited by the commerce in furs, marked out spheres of influence for the two expanding neighbor peoples, prepared the way for diplomats in fixing boundaries, and led the way for permanent civilization.

The British traders moved west from two eastern bases and represented two competing organizations. Hudson's Bay Company at first had held close to the eastern shores. From this policy it had been forced inland by French rivalry in the back country and by British criticism at home. Now it found a hardier rival in the St. Lawrence valley. Scotch settlers entered the fur trade at Montreal, formed the Northwest Company, and boldly pushed west. South of the Great Lakes they competed with American traders, and west of the Mississippi they invaded Spanish territory. In the Canadian prairies they engaged in a vigorous competition with the Hudson's Bay Company. Rival posts were planted on every important stream. Price wars and bloodshed ensued, and Indian tribal relations were sadly disturbed. But important exploration resulted; the Rocky Mountains were soon reached, and Mackenzie descended the Mackenzie River to the Arctic Ocean.

The next step was across the Rockies. Bold Mackenzie led the way and rivals followed. Spaniards from St. Louis ascended the Missouri, and Lewis and Clark crossed the Rockies.

For the "Nor'westers" Simon Fraser established the fur trade in Fraser River valley and David Thompson on the upper Columbia. Close behind went Astor's men to the lower Columbia. This region, too, soon fell to the British fur men, for Astoria was sold to the "Nor'westers" as an incident of the War of 1812. The British overland traders had clearly outdistanced their American rivals. England and the United States now agreed on joint occupation of the Oregon country. Legally the rights of the two nations were equal. But in fact the advantage was with the British. In 1821 the Northwest Company and the Hudson's Bay Company consolidated. A western capital was established at Fort Vancouver, and for nearly two decades, under the direction of picturesque Dr. John McLoughlin, the Hudson's Bay Company controlled most of the fur trade of the Northwest, all the way from central California to the borders of Alaska.

1. Hudson's Bay Company. Origin (commercial expansion of England; Radisson, Gillam); aid in England (Carteret, Prince Rupert, Duke of York); the charter (privileges, government); importance of court patronage; methods (forts, markets, exclusive policy); forced inland by rivalry and criticism; French rivalry (La Vérendrye, Hendry); Arthur Dobbs (new efforts to find the Northwest Passage); explorations by Hearne (1769–1772).
2. The Northwest Company. The independent Scotch traders at Montreal; rival companies; the Northwest Company (1787); posts, partners; Fort William.
3. Rival traders in the Great Lakes region and the upper Mississippi; international aspects (Spanish, American, British); the treaties of 1783 and 1794; Northwest Company posts (La Pointe, Fort William, Fond du Lac,

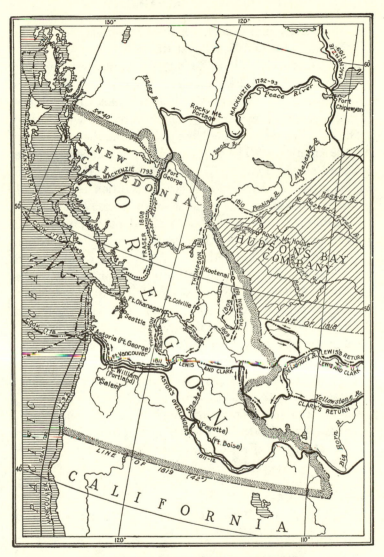

THE OPENING OF THE PACIFIC NORTHWEST

Sandy Lake, and others); David Thompson; British influence in the Old Northwest till 1814.
4. Rivalry in the Canadian interior. The Northwest Company versus Hudson's Bay Company; rival posts on Rainy, Winnipeg, Red, Assiniboine, Saskatchewan, Churchill, and Athabasca rivers; discovery of Mackenzie River (1789).
5. The "Nor'westers" on the Pacific Slope, and the conflict with the Americans. The mountain passes; Mackenzie crosses the Rockies (1792–1793); his proposal for the fur trade; effect of the Lewis and Clark expedition (1803–1806); occupation of the Fraser River valley (Simon Fraser; posts established, 1806–1808); New Caledonia; occupation of the upper Columbia River valley (1807–1811); David Thompson; posts in Idaho and Montana (1809); American traders on the upper Missouri; Astoria on the lower Columbia (1811); Astoria sold out during War of 1812; joint occupation of Oregon with England (1818); boundary settled at 49 degrees to the "Stony Mountains."
6. The union of the rival companies. Warfare in the interior; Lord Selkirk's Pembina colony; war; consolidation (Simpson, Hudson's Bay Company's trading privileges extended to the Pacific), 1821.
7. The Hudson's Bay Company's régime in the Pacific Northwest (1824–1846). Dr. McLoughlin; posts; the brigades; in California; effect on ownership of the country.

REQUIRED READING

One of the following:

BOLTON, H. E., and MARSHALL, T. M. *The Colonization of North America*, 213–214, 257–261, 423–424.
LAUT, A. C. *The Adventurers of England on Hudson Bay*, chap. 4.
LAUT, A. C. *Pioneers of the Pacific Coast*, chap. 5, 6, or 7.
SCHAFER, JOSEPH. *History of the Pacific Northwest*, chap. 6.

REFERENCES

ANSTEY, ARTHUR. *The Romance of British Columbia.*

BANCROFT, H. H. *History of British Columbia.*

BRYCE, GEORGE. *Mackenzie, Selkirk, Simpson.*

BRYCE, GEORGE. *The Remarkable History of the Hudson's Bay Company.*

BRYCE, GEORGE. *The Romantic Settlement of Lord Selkirk's Colonists.*

BURPEE, L. J. *The Search for the Western Sea.*

COATS, R. H., and GOSNELL, R. E. *Sir James Douglas.*

COCHRANE, C. N. *David Thompson, the Explorer.*

DAVIDSON, G. C. *The North West Company.*

GARVIN, J. W. (Editor). *Voyages of Alexander Mackenzie.*

GRAHAM, G. S. *British Policy and Canada, 1774-1791: a Study in 18th Century Trade Policy.*

GREENBIE, SYDNEY. *Frontiers and the Fur Trade.*

GUILLET, E. C. *Early Life in Upper Canada.*

HAWORTH, P. L. *Trailmakers of the Northwest.*

HEARNE, SAMUEL. *A Journey from Prince of Wales Fort to the Northern Ocean in the Years 1769, 1770, 1771, and 1772.*

HOWAY, F. W. "Early Days of the Maritime Fur Trade on the Northwest Coast," *Canadian Historical Review*, March, 1923.

INNIS, H. A. *The Fur Trade in Canada: an Introduction to Canadian Economic History.*

INNIS, H. A. *Peter Pond, Fur Trader and Adventurer.*

IRVING, WASHINGTON. *Astoria.*

LAUT, A. C. *The Conquest of the Great Northwest.* 2 vols.

LAUT, A. C. *Fur Trade of America.*

LAUT, A. C. *Pathfinders of the West.*

LAUT, A. C. *Pioneers of the Pacific Coast.*

MACKENZIE, ALEXANDER. *Voyages from Montreal through the Continent of North America to the Frozen and Pacific Oceans in 1789 and 1793.*

MERK, FREDERICK (Editor). *Fur Trade and Empire.*

SAGE, W. N. *Sir James Douglas.*

SCHOLEFIELD, E. O. S., and HOWAY, F. W. *British Columbia from the Earliest Times to the Present.*

TROTTER, R. G. *Canadian History: Syllabus and Guide to Reading.*

WALLACE, J. N. *The Wintering Partners on Peace River.*

WILLSON, BECKLES. *The Great Company.*

WOOD, L. A. *The Red River Colony.*

WRONG, HUME. *Sir Alexander Mackenzie, Explorer and Fur-Trader.*

Lecture XXXIX. Trade and Empire in the North Pacific

Introductory. On the shores of the North Pacific overland fur men met traders who had come by water. Indeed, the latter arrived first. The sea traders, like the others, were empire-builders. They too helped to carve out spheres of national influence and led the way for civilization.

In the sixteenth century the Pacific Ocean had been a Spanish lake, whose commerce was carried in galleons from the Philippines to Mexico. Dutch and English intruded in the seventeenth century; Russians and Americans in the eighteenth. The clash that came in the North Pacific has well been called the "swirl of the nations."

The Russians led the way. Bering's explorations were followed by feverish hunting of the sea otter on the Aleutian Islands. As a counter move Spain colonized Alta California and sent explorers to the northern waters. British traders came next. Cook's voyage to Nootka Sound was followed by a fleet of British merchant craft. Again Spain resisted. She captured British vessels, fortified Nootka Sound, and established missions. England threatened war and Spain withdrew her posts and her claims to exclusive sovereignty.

American traders too now swarmed the North Pacific, and for a time they nearly monopolized the sea trade there. Gray explored the Columbia River, which Spaniards had previously discovered. At the same time the Russians advanced southward. Sitka became the capital of the Russian-American Fur Company. At St. Petersburg there was talk of occupying the

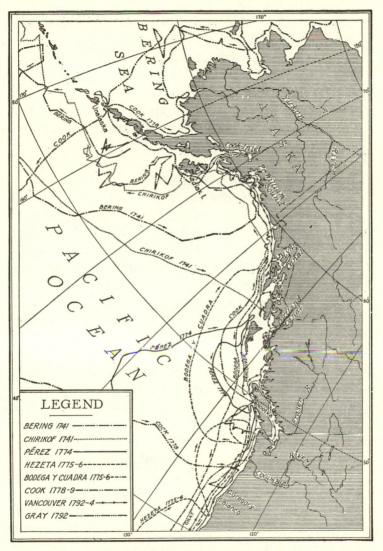

THE OPENING OF THE NORTH PACIFIC

mouth of the Columbia River, and Fort Ross was built by Russians on Spanish soil just north of San Francisco. For a time Russian commerce flourished all down the Pacific shores. The medley of traders gave four nations conflicting claims to dominion on the Pacific coast. Diplomats argued. Spain withdrew to 42° and Russia to 54° 40′. This left a thousand miles of American coast to the joint occupation of England and the United States.

1. European interest in the Pacific Ocean. Spain and Portugal in the sixteenth century; English and Dutch intrusions in the seventeenth; Russian, French, and English in the eighteenth; the clash of interests in the North Pacific (East and West, Russian, Spanish, English, Americans); the "swirl of the nations"; relation to ownership.
2. Early Russian trade in Alaska. Russian advance across Siberia (seventeenth century); a port on the Pacific; Bering's explorations (1728–1741); rise of fur trade on Aleutian Islands (1745); the "outlaw hunters" (sea otter, oppression of natives); posts (Bering Island, Unalaska, Kadiak); government regulation results; Spain advances into Alta California.
3. Cook's voyage and the English on the North Pacific. Cook's voyage (1778); Nootka Sound; the rush of traders; English traders (Hanna, Meares, Colnett, etc.); American traders.
4. Spanish resistance and the Nootka Sound controversy. Renewed Spanish exploration (Arteaga, Bodega, Martínez, 1779–1788); Martínez sent to fortify Nootka (1789); seizure of English vessels; England and Spain on the verge of war; the Treaty of 1790 (Spain yields exclusive claim); both parties withdraw posts (1795); Bodega and Vancouver; new explorations of Northwest coast.

5. Rise of American coast trade and claims. Rise of New England merchant fleet; Kendrick and Gray (1787); Gray's "discovery" of the Columbia (1792); American traders on the Pacific (numbers, combination with Russians at first; contraband in California); Astoria, 1811; sold to Northwest Company during War of 1812; hide-and-tallow trade in California; *Two Years before the Mast.*
6. The Russian advance southward. The Russian-American Fur Company (1798); monopoly for twenty years; Baranoff; capital at Sitka, combination with Americans at first; southward advance; claim to the Columbia (1806); Rezanoff in California (1806); Doña Concepción; Fort Ross (1812); fur trade on the coast.
7. Withdrawal of Spain and Russia. Spain's claims ceded to United States (1819); Russian claim to exclusive jurisdiction above 51° (1821); Monroe Doctrine (1823); Russia withdraws to 54° 40'; treaty with United States (1824) and England (1825); Fort Ross sold to Sutter (1841); Alaska sold to United States (1867); Pacific Northwest divided between Canada and United States.

REQUIRED READING

One of the following:

LAUT, A. C. *Pioneers of the Pacific Coast*, chaps. 2, 3, 4.
SCHAFER, JOSEPH. *History of the Pacific Northwest*, chaps. 1, 2, 5, 6.

REFERENCES

BANCROFT, H. H. *History of Alaska.*
BANCROFT, H. H. *History of British Columbia.*
BANCROFT, H. H. *History of the Northwest Coast.*
CAUGHEY, J. W. *History of the Pacific Coast.*
CLARK, H. W. *History of Alaska.*
CLARK, R. C. *History of the Willamette Valley, Oregon.*

COMAN, KATHERINE. *Economic Beginnings of the Far West.*

FULLER, G. W. *A History of the Pacific Northwest.*

GODWIN, G. S. *Vancouver, a Life.*

GOLDER, F. A. *Russian Expansion on the Pacific.*

HOWAY, F. W. *British Columbia: the Making of a Province.*

HOWAY, F. W. *The Dixon-Meares Controversy.*

KERNER, R. J. "Russian Expansion to America: its Bibliographical Foundations," in *Papers of the Bibliographical Society of America*, XXV (1931), 111–129.

KITSON, ARTHUR. *Captain James Cook, R.N.*

LYMAN, H. S. *History of Oregon.*

MANNING, W. R. *The Nootka Sound Controversy.*

MORISON, S. E. *The Maritime History of Massachusetts.*

OGDEN, ADELE. "The Californias in Spain's Pacific Otter Trade, 1775–1795," in *Pacific Historical Review*, I (1932), 444–469.

PORTER, K. W. *John Jacob Astor, Business Man.* 2 vols.

SCHAFER, JOSEPH. *History of the Pacific Northwest.*

SCHAFER, JOSEPH. *The Pacific Slope and Alaska.*

SMITH, A. D. H. *John Jacob Astor.*

THOMAS, B. P. *Russo-American Relations, 1815–1867.*

WAGNER, H. R. *Spanish Explorations in the Strait of Juan de Fuca.*

THE FOUNDING OF THE HISPANIC–AMERICAN NATIONS

Lecture XL. Napoleon shakes the Tree of Independence

Causes and General Features of the Hispanic-American Revolution

Introductory. A third of a century behind the English colonies, those of Spain and Portugal rose in revolt. In the two cases there were various similarities and many contrasts. The causes were in many respects alike. In both cases independence was achieved through outside aid. The area and population involved in the latter case were many times larger than in the former. In Hispanic America there were vastly greater obstacles to united action than in English America. Mountains and distance gave much greater isolation. There was lack of political experience and of social solidarity. As a consequence there were separate revolutionary movements in the various areas, and several nations resulted.

The causes of the Spanish-American revolution were both internal and external. Within there were grave economic restrictions; taxation was burdensome; great landed estates were confined to the few. Worst of all was class favoritism. The eighteenth century gave evidence of growing restlessness and disrespect for authority, and the Creole class gradually rose to a place where it provided agitators. Charles III made many reforms, but they were royalist in aim, and they came too late.

External influence played a prominent part in bringing the revolution about. English and French trade rivals plotted the liberation of Spain's colonies. French philosophy penetrated Spanish America in spite of efforts to keep it out. Young Creoles were educated in Europe. English and American contact through trade and smuggling spread liberal ideas. The example of the revolt of English colonies, the French Revolution, and the independence of Santo Domingo stimulated discontent.

The Spanish-American revolution went through several general phases. There were preliminary movements which did not succeed. A general uprising was precipitated by Napoleon's invasion of Spain and the seating of his brother Joseph on the Spanish throne. Everywhere in Spanish America juntas were formed to resist Napoleon, but the movement soon took the form of a struggle for independence instead. The cabildos became centers for organized resistance. The leaders were mainly Creoles or mestizos. The higher clergy were quite generally loyalists, but many of the lesser clergy took part with the revolutionists. There were three main regional movements — in northern South America, in southern South America, and in North America.

1. Comparison with Anglo-American revolution. Area involved; number of people involved; greater obstacles to united action (geographic isolation, lack of political experience, loyalists versus patriots); outside aid in both cases; separate movements in Hispanic America; numerous separate nations resulting.
2. Causes of the Spanish-American revolution. Evils of the colonial system: economic (trade monopoly, industrial monopolies, great landed estates, taxation); class dis-

tinctions and political favoritism (Peninsulars, or Gachu-
pines, Creoles, mestizos, Indians, Negroes); growth of
disrespect for authority (smuggling, corruption); early
uprisings (Tupac Amarú); Bourbon reforms (in commerce, mining, administration, defense of the realm);
results ineffectual. External influences: example of the
Anglo-American revolution; French liberal ideas
(Rousseau, the French Revolution); contact with English and Anglo-Americans through trade; the English
conquest of Trinidad (1797); the revolution in Santo
Domingo.

3. Preliminary movements. Miranda's efforts; the English
occupation of Buenos Aires and Montevideo (1806–1808);
the conquest of Spain by Napoleon (Joseph Bonaparte
crowned), 1808; "legitimate" governments erected in
Spain and Spanish America (juntas, congresses, trium-
virates).

4. General phases of the revolution. Preliminary efforts;
the struggle for Ferdinand VII ("Old king or none");
the struggle for independence; three main regional movements; outstanding leaders (nearly all Creoles or
mestizos); Northern South America (Miranda, Bolívar);
the La Plata region (Artigas, Francia, San Martín);
Chile (O'Higgins); Mexico (Hidalgo, Morelos, Mina,
Iturbide); the cabildos as revolutionary centers.

REQUIRED READING

One of the following:

García Calderón, F. *Latin America*, 58–85 (the struggle for independence).

James, H. G., and Martin, P. A. *The Republics of Latin America*,
79–85.

Priestley, H. I. *The Mexican Nation*, chap. 11.

RIPPY, J. F. *Historical Evolution of Hispanic America*, 133–141.
ROBERTSON, W. S. *History of the Latin-American Nations*, 1922 ed., chap. 6; 1932 ed., 207–215.
ROBERTSON, W. S. *Rise of the Spanish-American Republics*, chaps. 1, 2.
SHEPHERD, W. R. *Hispanic Nations of the New World*, chaps. 1, 2.
SWEET, W. W. *History of Latin America*, chap. 12.
WEBSTER, HUTTON. *History of Latin America*, 116–120.
WILGUS, A. C. *A History of Hispanic America*, chap. 16.
WILLIAMS, M. W. *People and Politics of Latin America*, 228–236 (colonial social classes); 287–294 (causes of the revolutions, and preliminary movements).

REFERENCES

THE REVOLUTION IN HISPANIC AMERICA AND THE FOUNDING
OF THE HISPANIC-AMERICAN STATES

ALTAMIRA Y CREVEA, RAFAEL. *Resumen Histórico de la Independencia de la América Española.*
ÁLVAREZ, JUAN. *Estudio sobre las Guerras Civiles Argentinas.*
AMUNÁTEGUI, G. V. *Camilo Henríquez.*
ANDRADE, M. DE JERÓNIMO. *Ecuador: Próceres de la Independencia.*
ARENALES, J. I. *Segunda Campaña á la Sierra del Perú.*
BANCROFT, H. H. *History of Mexico*, IV.
BECKER, JERÓNIMO. *Historia de las Relaciones Exteriores de España durante el Siglo XIX*, I.
BINGHAM, HIRAM. *Across South America*, chap. 4.
BRYCE, JAMES. *Modern Democracies*, I, chap. 17.
BULNES, FRANCISCO. *La Guerra de Independencia: Hidalgo–Iturbide.*
CHISHOLM, A. S. M. *The Independence of Chile.*
CLEVEN, N. A. N. *Readings in Hispanic American History*, 373–458.
DAWSON, T. C. *South American Republics*, I, 80–114 (Argentine), 188–198 (Francia in Paraguay), 247–264 (Uruguay), 401–420 (Brazil); II, 74–97 (Peru), 156–188 (Chile), 255–265 (Bolivia), 311–329 (Ecuador), 357–383 (Venezuela), 430–446 (Colombia).
ESPEJO, JERÓNIMO. *Recuerdos Históricos; San Martín y Bolívar.*
FISHER, L. E. *The Background of the Revolution for Mexican Independence.*
FORTIER, ALCÉE, and FICKLEN, J. R. *Central America and Mexico*, 121–130, 275–313.

GARAY, BLAS. *Historia de la Revolución del Paraguay.*

GARCÍA, GENARO. *El Plan de la Independencia de la Nueva España en 1808.*

GARCÍA CALDERÓN, FRANCISCO. *Latin America, its Rise and Progress,* Books I–IV, 29–231.

GROUSSAC, PAUL. *Santiago de Liniers, Conde de Buenos Aires, 1753–1810.*

HALE, SUSAN. *The Story of Mexico,* chaps. 24–27 (pp. 233–271) (to the death of Iturbide).

HEREDIA Y MIESES, J. F. *Memorias sobre las Revoluciones de Venezuela.*

KOEBEL, W. H. *South America,* chaps. 15, 19, 22 (pp. 151–210, 228–236).

LARRAZÁBAL, FELIPE. *The Life of Simón Bolívar, Liberator of Colombia and Perú, Father and Founder of Bolivia.*

MACY, JESSE, and GANNAWAY, J. W. *Comparative Free Government,* chaps. 5, 7.

MAESO, JUSTO. *El General Artigas y su Época.*

MARKHAM, CLEMENTS. "Colonial History of South America, and the Wars of Independence," in Winsor's *Narrative and Critical History of America,* VIII, 323–341.

MARKHAM, CLEMENTS. *History of Peru,* chaps. 9–12 (pp. 215–289).

MEHEGAN, J. J. *O'Higgins of Chile.*

MITRE, BARTOLOMÉ. *The Emancipation of South America.* (William Pilling, translator.)

MITRE, BARTOLOMÉ. *Historia de Belgrano.*

NAVARRO Y LAMARCA, CARLOS. *Compendio de la Historia General de América.*

NOLL, A. H. *From Empire to Republic,* chaps. 1–5 (pp. 1–108, Mexico).

NOLL, A. H., and MCMAHON, A. P. *The Life and Times of Miguel Hidalgo y Costilla.*

OLIVEIRA LIMA, MANOEL DE. *The Evolution of Brazil compared with that of Spanish and Anglo-Saxon America.*

PAXSON, F. L. *The Independence of the South American Republics.*

PEREYRA, CARLOS. *Bolívar y Washington, un Paralelo Imposible.*

PESADO, J. J. *El Libertador de México, D. Agustín de Iturbide.*

RESTREPO, J. M. *Historia de la Revolución de la República de Colombia.*

ROBERTSON, W. S. "Francisco de Miranda," Annual Report of the American Historical Association, I (1907), 189–490.

ROBERTSON, W. S. *Hispanic-American Relations with the United States,* chap. 1.

ROBERTSON, W. S. *The Life of Miranda.* 2 vols.

RYDJORD, JOHN. "The French Revolution and Mexico," in *Hispanic-American Historical Review*, IX (1929), 60–98.

SAMPER, J. M. *Juicio sobre Bolívar.*

SHEPHERD, W. R. *Hispanic Nations of the New World.*

SHEPHERD, W. R. *Latin America.*

WASHBURN, C. A. *History of Paraguay.*

WAXMAN, PERCY. *The Black Napoleon: the Story of Toussaint L'Ouverture.*

For the European background of the revolutions consult histories of Spain by Chapman, Hume, Merriman, and others, and general histories of Europe, especially of the eighteenth century and the revolutionary and Napoleonic periods.

Lecture XLI. Miranda, Bolívar, and Greater Colombia

The War of Independence in Northern South America

Introductory. The War of Independence in South America was a great military drama. It consisted of two main movements, starting in opposite ends of the continent, and coming together in Peru for the final overthrow of Spanish rule. In the north Caracas and Bogotá were the chief centers of revolution. In the south Buenos Aires and Santiago were the principal foci. Peru was the bulwark of royalist power, against which the final blow was aimed.

Miranda the "Precursor" led the way in the north. His two expeditions against Caracas were premature, but Napoleon's invasion of Spain was a signal for a new assault. Juntas were formed to resist French rule, but the movement quickly became a struggle for independence. Miranda led in the formation of a republic at Caracas, but when it was crushed he fell. Bolívar the "Liberator" now assumed Miranda's mantle, and became the moving spirit of the revolution in the north. For fifteen years this brilliant figure moved back and forth across the continent, defeated here, winning victories there. His Second Republic of Venezuela was crushed, but undaunted he headed another at Bogotá. Then for a time revolution was nearly stamped out. Napoleon was overthrown and Ferdinand VII restored. With veterans from Spain royalists won victories everywhere. But Bolívar had a habit of "coming back." With a fleet and a new army he set up a third Venezuelan republic.

235

Then, aided by British volunteers, he ascended the Orinoco, crossed the Andes, routed royalists in New Granada, recrossed the Andes, and completed the revolution in Venezuela. Aided by the indomitable Sucre, he now annexed Ecuador to his conquests and united them all into Greater Colombia. This Washington of South America merited his title of "Liberator."

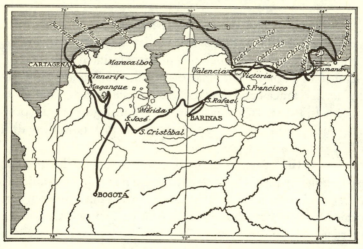

CAMPAIGNS OF BOLÍVAR AND MORILLO

1. Uprisings in New Granada and Venezuela (1808–1809). Napoleon's invasion of Spain (1808); divided opinion in America; provincial juntas in New Granada (local character of movements there, rivalries between cities); the Junta Central recognized in Caracas (1809); opposition of the "patriots."

2. Miranda and the First Republic of Venezuela. The junta at Caracas (April 19, 1810); Bolívar in Europe; Miranda at the head in Caracas; declaration of independence by seven eastern provinces (July 5, 1811); the republican

constitution; the earthquake of 1812; decline of revolutionary cause; reconquest by Monteverde; imprisonment and death of Miranda.

3. The rise of Bolívar, and the Second Republic of Venezuela. Simón Bolívar; part in Miranda's downfall; recapture of Caracas with force from New Granada (1814); new republic established; defeat by Boves and Indian cavalry (the Llaneros).

4. Morillo and the temporary crushing of the revolution. Bolívar again in New Granada; rival centers united; the new royal army (Morillo); rebellion in New Granada and Venezuela subdued (1814).

5. Bolívar's Orinoco campaign (1817–1818). Fleet organized in West Indies; British sailors; campaign on the Orinoco (1817); new capital at Angostura; defeat by Morillo.

6. British aid and the founding of the Republic of Colombia. The British volunteers; Bolívar's expedition up the Orinoco and across the Andes; the victory at Boyacá (1819); Bolívar enters Bogotá; victory at Carabobo (1821); the Republic of Colombia (Venezuela and New Granada united, capital at Cúcuta); the Constitution of 1821; Quito incorporated (royalist control at Quito since 1812; Sucre's victory at Pichincha, 1822).

REQUIRED READING

One of the following:

JAMES, H. G., and MARTIN, P. A. *The Republics of Latin America*, 86–88, 98–101.

RIPPY, J. F. *Historical Evolution of Hispanic America*, 156–159.

ROBERTSON, W. S. *History of the Latin-American Nations*, 1922 ed., chap. 6; 1932 ed., 218–221, 232–234.

ROBERTSON, W. S. *Rise of the Spanish-American Republics*, chap. 7.

SHEPHERD, W. R. *Hispanic Nations of the New World*, chap. 3.

Sweet, W. W. *History of Latin America*, 1919 ed., 148–156; 1929 ed., 165–174.

Wilgus, A. C. *A History of Hispanic America*, chap. 18.

Williams, M. W. *People and Politics of Latin America*, 294–302 (Miranda, Bolívar).

REFERENCES

Chisholm, A. S. M. *The Independence of Chile.*

Hasbrouck, Alfred. *Foreign Legionaries in the Liberation of Spanish South America.*

Lecuna, Vicente. *Cartas del Libertador.*

Maeso, Justo. *El General Artigas y su Época.*

Mehegan, J. J. *O'Higgins of Chile.*

Mitre, Bartolomé. *The Emancipation of South America.*

See also the list of References at the end of Lecture XL.

LECTURE XLII. THE WAR IN THE SOUTH AND THE
UNION OF FORCES

Introductory. In the north the dominating figures of Miranda and Bolívar gave unity to the War of Independence. In the south there was less cohesion. The British intrusion stirred up a spirit of self-determination in Argentina and gave the people there a taste of free commerce. Napoleon's invasion of Spain was followed by uprisings in Buenos Aires, Santiago, and elsewhere. Inspired at first by resistance to France, the movement soon became a struggle for independence.

In Argentina the war was marred by factional struggles, but by 1816 the republic of the United Provinces was firmly established. Buenos Aires attempted to direct the course of the revolution in the whole La Plata valley. With this in view Belgrano marched north with an army, but he found the other provinces ambitious to liberate themselves. In Paraguay Dr. Francia expelled the royalists and made himself dictator. In Charcas (Bolivia) Belgrano was defeated by royalist forces. The Banda Oriental produced Artigas, the picturesque Gaucho chieftain. He successfully coped with Argentinians and royalists; but he could not withstand the Brazilians, who took this chance to recover the region. Brazil held the district for several years, but it was finally released and became the Republic of Uruguay.

In Chile the first revolutionary movements were crushed. But stubborn independents, led by O'Higgins, fled across the Andes to reorganize at Mendoza. Now arose San Martín, veteran of European wars, and the greatest leader of the South.

He forged a new army at Mendoza, made an heroic march over the mountains, and completed the revolution in Chile. Then with fresh forces, carried north by the British Admiral Cochrane's fleet, San Martín defeated the royalists at Lima and set up a republic in Peru.

Now the armies of the north and south were united. Meeting reverses, San Martín patriotically resigned in favor of Bolívar. Quickly the combined army recovered Lima, ascended the Andes, created the Republic of Bolivia, and ended the wars for independence in South America.

1. The beginnings of the revolution. The English invasion: English interest in South Africa and South America; capture of the Cape (1805); capture of Buenos Aires (1806); Beresford; expelled by the inhabitants; Liniers chosen viceroy; the second English expedition (Whitelocke, 1807); Montevideo taken; failure at Buenos Aires; commercial and political stimulus. The revolt against the French: invasion of Spain; viceroy of La Plata deposed (May, 1810); Cisneros; junta formed at Buenos Aires; class hostility at Buenos Aires; the young Creole leaders (Belgrano, Moreno).

2. Separate movements in the La Plata country (four main currents). Civil war in Argentina (between leaders and between provinces and the capital): talk of sending to Europe for a king; triumph of republican ideas; declaration of independence (1816); the United Provinces of South America (Argentina); effort of Buenos Aires to direct the provinces. Charcas (Bolivia) conquered by royalists from Peru: Belgrano's victory at Tucumán (1812); his defeat at Vilcapujio and Ayohuma (1813); San Martín in command. Paraguay: failure of Bel-

THE WARS OF INDEPENDENCE IN SPANISH SOUTH AMERICA

The union of northern and southern forces

grano's campaign; Dr. Francia dictator (El Supremo); resists both Spain and Buenos Aires; policy of isolation. The Banda Oriental (Uruguay): Montevideo a royalist center; subdued by Buenos Aires; Artigas and his Gaucho cavalry; breach with Buenos Aires; "Protector of Free Peoples"; the Portuguese conquest (1817).

3. The liberation of Chile. The revolution in Chile (1810); separate movements at Santiago and Concepción (Carrera and Rosas); royalist invasion from Peru; O'Higgins; flight of the patriots to Mendoza; San Martín's plan to liberate Chile and Peru; army organized at Mendoza (1816–1817); the march over the mountains; victories at Chacabuco and Maipú (February, May, 1818); Chilean independence won.

4. The liberation of Peru. Conjunction of the forces from the north and the south: new army organized by San Martín; Lord Cochrane's fleet; the expedition of 1820; San Martín enters Lima; a republic proclaimed (1821); San Martín "Protector"; revival of royalist cause (1822); meeting of San Martín and Bolívar at Guayaquil; San Martín resigns; Bolívar Director of Peru; Sucre's victory at Ayacucho (1824); the fall of Callao (1826).

5. The Republic of Bolivia. Charcas still held by royalists; defeated by Sucre; declaration of independence (1825); the Republic of Bolivia (Sucre); Bolívar's triumphal tour.

REQUIRED READING

One of the following:

ROBERTSON, W. S. *Rise of the Spanish-American Republics*, chaps. 5, 6.
SHEPHERD, W. R. *Hispanic Nations of the New World*, 20–47.
SWEET, W. W. *History of Latin America*, 1919 ed., 156–163; 1929 ed., 174–181.
WILLIAMS, M. W. *People and Politics of Latin America*, 302–311.

Lecture XLIII. The Liberation of Spanish North America

Introductory. In North America the Spanish War of Independence went through the same general stages as that in South America. The overthrow of Ferdinand VII was followed by disturbances in Mexico and Valladolid (Morelia), but the revolution proper began in 1810 with the "Grito de Dolores." At the head of an armed mob, Miguel Hidalgo marched against the royalists at Guanajuato and captured the royal storehouses there. As he continued south his army grew. Turning aside from Mexico City, he set up his capital at Guadalajara. Defeated there by royalist forces, he fled north, was captured, and with several leaders was executed at Chihuahua. Rayón assembled a new revolutionary army and continued the struggle. Then arose Morelos, the chief military figure in the war. Astounding victories were followed by a declaration of independence.

The revolt spread to the northern provinces, where it was given special character by the proximity of the United States. The American people favored the revolution. They were interested in democracy, Mexican commerce, and Mexican land. There were boundary disputes with Spain, and this was a good time to settle them. President Madison encouraged a revolution at Baton Rouge, but when a republic was erected there he seized West Florida to keep order and prevent England from taking it. In East Florida he fostered another short-lived revolt, with similar purposes in view. Texas was "liberated" by an army raised in the United States, but was reconquered.

Meanwhile the revolutionary congress fled from place to place. Heroic Morelos was captured and executed. The revolt was now stamped out in the center, but was kept alive on the frontiers. Mina revived the spark by a raid from Texas.

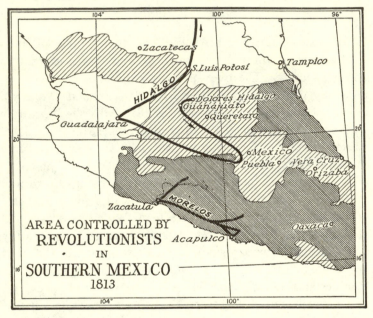

AREA CONTROLLED BY REVOLUTIONISTS IN SOUTHERN MEXICO (1813)

Bouchard tried in vain to liberate California. Jackson embarrassed Spain by invading and holding East Florida. Long led two more dangerous expeditions from the United States into Texas, and Galveston Island continued to be a base for proclamations and raids. In the south Guerrero kept up guerrilla warfare.

Iturbide now brought the struggle to a climax. Sent by royalists to crush Guerrero, he joined hands with him instead, and by the Plan of Iguala he ended the rule of the viceroys. Then making himself emperor, he annexed Central America. He in turn was soon overthrown, and the Republic of Mexico was established, though shorn of Central America, eastern Texas, and both Floridas.

1. The junta of 1808. Talmantes; the viceroy implicated; deposed by conservatives; the movement at Valladolid (1809).
2. Hidalgo and the revolution of 1810. The curate of Dolores; conspiracy (Allende, Aldama); the outbreak (September 16, 1810); the "Grito de Dolores"; the march of the mob to Celaya and Guanajuato; advance toward Mexico; defeat by Calleja at Las Cruces; retreat to Guadalajara; government established; defeat (January, 1811); flight and capture of Hidalgo and associates; execution as a warning to rebels (Chihuahua, 1811).
3. Rayón and Morelos. The spread of the revolt, north and south; Rayón's campaign, and efforts to establish liberal government; brilliant victories of Morelos around Acapulco (Bravo and Victoria), 1812–1813; the Congress of Chilpancingo (1813); declaration of independence (1813); wanderings of the Congress; execution of Morelos (1815); decline of insurgent cause; Guerrero continues guerrilla warfare.
4. The revolt in the northern provinces, and the American filibusters. Spread of the revolt in the north: United States interest; the Burr expedition; Pike in Chihuahua. West Florida: United States desire to obtain West Florida; the movement for independence at Baton Rouge (1808–1810); United States fear of English designs; West Florida annexed. The revolt in East Florida; in

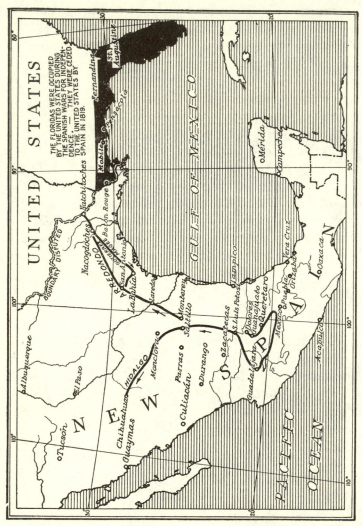

Texas (Casas); republican movement at San Antonio crushed; expedition from United States led by Gutiérrez and Magee (1812); the "liberation" of Texas; reconquest by Arredondo (1813).

5. The expedition of Mina (1817). Mina's defense of Spain against Napoleon; revolt against Ferdinand; expedition to America (1816); at Galveston Island; union with Aury and Perry (1817); the "Relief Army of the Mexican Republic"; defection of Aury and Perry; the bold march to interior; capture near Guanajuato; execution of Mina. The revolutionary cause now crushed in the center; sparks kept alive on the borders (Guerrero in the south; Long in Texas; Lafitte on the Gulf; Bouchard in California; East Florida disturbances (American filibusters at Amelia Island)).

6. Iturbide and the independence of Mexico. Iturbide (a royalist soldier, brilliant services in early wars, relieved of command, 1816); appointed to subdue Guerrero (1820); combination with Guerrero; the plan of Iguala (the three guarantees: union, independence, religion), 1821; factions united; viceroy deposed; O'Donojú and the Treaty of Córdova; refusal of Spain to recognize independence; Iturbide elected emperor (1822); struggle with congress; revolt led by Santa Anna; Iturbide abdicates (1823); exiled; return, capture, and execution; the Constitution of 1824.

7. The independence of Central America. A bloodless revolution; the captaincy general of Guatemala; follows neighbors; declarations of independence by Central American States (1821); annexed to Mexico by Iturbide; revolt against Mexico (1823); the United Provinces of Central America.

REQUIRED READING

One of the following:

JAMES, H. G., and MARTIN, P. A. *The Republics of Latin America*, 334–336.

PRIESTLEY, H. I. *The Mexican Nation*, chap. 12 ("El Grito de Dolores"), chap. 13 (Morelos), chap. 14 (Iturbide).

ROBERTSON, W. S. *History of the Latin-American Nations*, 1922 ed., chap. 6; 1932 ed., chaps. 3–4.

ROBERTSON, W. S. *Rise of the Spanish-American Republics*, chaps. 3, 4.

SWEET, W. W. *History of Latin America*, 1919 ed., chap. 14; 1929 ed., 186–192.

WEBSTER, HUTTON. *History of Latin America*, 123–127.

WILGUS, A. C. *A History of Hispanic America*, chap. 20.

WILLIAMS, M. W. *People and Politics of Latin America*, 311–317.

REFERENCES

BANCROFT, H. H. *History of Mexico*, IV, chaps. 1, 2, 5–19, 39–41.

BULNES, FRANCISCO. *La Guerra de Independencia: Hidalgo–Iturbide*.

BUSTAMANTE, C. M. DE. *Cuadro Histórico de la Revolución Mexicana*.

CLEVEN, N. A. N. *Readings in Hispanic American History*, 421–422.

FORTIER, ALCÉE, and FICKLEN, J. R. *Central America and Mexico*, chap. 7.

GARCÍA, GENARO. *El Clero de México y la Guerra de Independencia: Documentos del Arzobispado de México*.

GARCÍA, GENARO. *El Plan de Independencia de la Nueva España en 1808*.

HUMBOLDT, ALEXANDER VON. *Political Essay on the Kingdom of New Spain*.

MAYER, BRANTZ. *Mexico*, I, Book III, chap. 1.

MORA, J. M. L. *Méjico y sus Revoluciones*.

NOLL, A. H. *From Empire to Republic*, chaps. 1–2.

NOLL, A. H., and McMAHON, A. P. *The Life and Times of Miguel Hidalgo y Costilla*.

PESADO, J. J. *El Libertador de México, D. Agustín de Iturbide*.

RIVES, G. L. *The United States and Mexico*, I.

ROBERTSON, W. S. *Rise of the Spanish-American Republics*.

ROBINSON, FAYETTE. *Mexico and her Military Chieftains*.

ROBINSON, W. D. *Memoirs of the Mexican Revolution*.

YOUNG, PHILIP. *History of Mexico*.

Lecture XLIV. Neutrality, Recognition, and the Monroe Doctrine

Introductory. The Spanish-American Revolution raised many difficulties for other nations. The United States and England were the only countries that looked on with any high degree of sympathy. For these, and especially the former, it was not easy to maintain a correct position in the course of the long struggle.

Appeals for help and recognition were made at once, but the United States government declared itself neutral and denied recognition until de facto governments should be established. However, unofficial agents were sent and received. It was one thing to declare neutrality, and quite another to maintain it. The cause of "liberty" was popular in the United States. Filibustering and privateering expeditions were organized in various ports, and President Madison himself encouraged the revolts in Florida. Spain of course complained. Privateers were tried in the courts, but juries would not convict. A part of the trouble was due to defects of the United States neutrality law, and as a result a new one was passed.

The question of recognition of the new republics raised a vigorous contest in the United States. After the establishment of the United Provinces of South America in 1816, the question was urgent. Argentina clamored, and agents were sent from Washington to inquire. Clay led the fight for recognition in Congress; Adams opposed, and there was delay. Recognition was complicated by the Florida question. During Spain's troubles both Floridas had been seized by the United States.

Helpless, Spain ceded both provinces for a price, and then delayed ratification of the treaty, to prevent recognition of her revolted colonies. But she yielded, without obtaining a promise, and some of the republics were recognized.

European monarchs looked askance at the large crop of young American republics. After the overthrow of Napoleon a mutual insurance society called the Holy Alliance and including nearly all the European countries, was formed to restore legitimate sovereigns. It essayed this task in Spain and Italy and then discussed the reconquest of Spanish America. England now withdrew from the alliance. At the same time Russia took an aggressive attitude regarding northwestern America. In reply Monroe issued his famous dictum, denouncing further colonization of America by Europe or the effort to restore monarchy here. Russia now withdrew all claims below 54° 40′, and the allies gave up their plans to restore Spanish rule in America. England, led by Canning and inspired by commercial interests, soon recognized the Hispanic American republics. Other nations followed; Spain, naturally, was slowest of all.

1. The policy of neutrality declared by the United States. Appeals for help and recognition by the insurgents; agents sent to the United States; the question of de facto independence; neutrality declared; United States agents in Spanish America ("unofficial but accredited"); Poinsett.

2. Difficulty of maintaining neutrality. Enthusiasm in the United States for "liberty"; official interest in Spain's border provinces (Florida, Texas, Oregon); West Florida seized; commercial interest (better prospects if Spanish America independent); filibustering and privateering expeditions fitted out in the United States; protests by Onís; difficulty of getting a jury verdict against fili-

busters; defect in United States neutrality laws (not designed for conflict between a nation and her colonies); new Neutrality Act (1817).

3. The struggle in the United States over recognition. A question of de facto independence; prominent after 1816 (declaration of independence by the La Plata provinces); clamor of South American agents and of newspapers in the United States (Lautaro); commissioners sent for information; conflicting reports; Clay's factional fight for recognition; genuine enthusiasm and desire to discredit the administration; the balance held by John Quincy Adams; the question complicated by the boundary treaty of 1819; Spain demands nonrecognition as a price of ratification; Monroe's protest; Spain ratifies (October, 1819); recognition granted (ministers exchanged, treaties made, etc.), 1822.

4. Recognition of Hispanic America by European states. England: changes in England's attitude toward Spain (hostility at first, friendly aid against Napoleon, hostility to restored Ferdinand VII); British aid to revolutionists; conflict of policy toward recognition after 1815 (obligations toward European powers, commercial interests in South America); Canning and the commercial interests; reports on America called for (1823); recognition accorded (La Plata, Colombia, Mexico), 1825; protests by allies; English loans to Hispanic America (£22,000,000 by 1833); financial dependence on England. Recognition by Spain delayed till 1836–1895. Other countries.

5. The Holy Alliance, Russian pretensions, and the Monroe Doctrine. The Holy Alliance; mutual insurance against revolution; intervention in Spanish America proposed; Russian claim to northwest coast of America to 51 degrees;

Canning's suggestion of a joint protest; the United States cabinet decides to act alone; Monroe's famous message (colonization, intervention, extension of European political system), December 2, 1823. Results: plans for intervention given up; Russia withdraws to 54° 40' (treaties with United States and England).

6. The United States and the Panama Congress. Bolívar's idea; his desire to obtain aid from United States to revolutionize Cuba; invitation accepted; slavery interests; delegates arrive too late; opportunity for United States leadership lost.

REQUIRED READING

One of the following:

FORMAN, S. E.   *Our Republic*, 249–254.

GARCÍA CALDERÓN, F.   *Latin America*, 298–312 (the North American Peril).

HARLOW, R. V.   *The Growth of the United States*, 326–335.

JAMES, H. G., and MARTIN, P. A.   *The Republics of Latin America*, 447–454.

LATANÉ, J. H.   *From Isolation to Leadership*, chap. 2.

MARTIN, A. E.   *History of the United States*, I, 324–332; I, Enlarged Edition, chap. 21.

RIPPY, J. F.   *Historical Evolution of Hispanic America*, chap. 6.

ROBERTSON, W. S.   *Hispanic-American Relations with the United States*, chaps. 2, 4.

STUART, G. H.   *Latin America and the United States*, chap. 2 (the Monroe Doctrine).

WILGUS, A. C.   *A History of Hispanic America*, chap. 41.

WILLIAMS, M. W.   *People and Politics of Latin America*, 338–347 (neutrality, recognition, Monroe Doctrine).

REFERENCES

ADAMS, R. G.   *History of the Foreign Policy of the United States.*

ÁLVAREZ, ALEJANDRO.   *Le Droit international américain.*

BEAUMARCHAIS, M. P. J. D. DE.   *La Doctrine de Monroë.*

BINGHAM, HIRAM.   *The Monroe Doctrine, an Obsolete Shibboleth.*

BRYCE, JAMES. *South America; Observations and Impressions.*

CAPELLA Y PONS, F. *Monroïsme?*

CÁRDENAS Y ECHARTE, RAÚL DE. *La Política de los Estados Unidos en el Continente Americano,* 89–186.

CLARK, B. C. *John Quincy Adams, "Old Man Eloquent."*

EDINGTON, T. B. *The Monroe Doctrine.*

HALL, A. B. *The Monroe Doctrine and the Great War.*

HART, A. B. *The Monroe Doctrine.*

KLEIN, JULIUS. "The Monroe Doctrine as a Regional Understanding," *Hispanic American Historical Review,* IV, No. 2, May, 1921.

KRAUS, HERBERT. *Die Monroedoktrin.*

LATANÉ, J. H. *History of American Foreign Policy.*

LOCKEY, JOSEPH. *Pan-Americanism: its Beginning.*

MAHONEY, T. H. *The Monroe Doctrine.*

MANNING, W. R. *Early Diplomatic Relations between the United States and Mexico.*

MOORE, J. B. *A Digest of International Law.*

PAXSON, F. L. *The Independence of the South American Republics.*

PEREYRA, CARLOS. *La Doctrina de Monroe.*

PEREYRA, CARLOS. *El Mito de Monroe.*

PERKINS, DEXTER. *The Monroe Doctrine, 1823–1826.*

PERKINS, DEXTER. *The Monroe Doctrine, 1826–1867.*

PETIN, HECTOR. *Les États-Unis et la Doctrine de Monroe.*

QUESADA, ERNESTO. *La Doctrina Monroe, su Evolución Histórica.*

REDDAWAY, W. F. *The Monroe Doctrine.*

RIPPY, J. F. *Latin America in World Politics.*

RIPPY, J. F. *The United States and Mexico.*

ROBERTSON, W. S. *Hispanic-American Relations with the United States.*

SHEPHERD, W. R. "Bolívar and the United States," *Hispanic American Historical Review,* III, No. 3, August, 1918.

SHERRILL, C. H. *Modernizing the Monroe Doctrine.*

STUART, G. H. *Latin America and the United States.*

TEMPERLEY, H. W. V. *The Foreign Policy of Canning, 1822–1827.*

THOMAS, D. Y. *One Hundred Years of the Monroe Doctrine,* chaps. 1–4.

VILLANUEVA, C. A. *Historia y Diplomacia: Napoleón y la Independencia de América.*

WEBSTER, C. K. *The Foreign Policy of Castlereagh, 1815–1822.*

ZUBIETA, P. A. *Congresos de Panamá y Tacubaya.*

Lecture XLV. Independence and the Empire in Brazil

Introductory. Independence came to Brazil without bloodshed. Here, as in Spanish America, Napoleon started the ball a rolling. When he threatened to depose the Braganzas in Portugal, John, Prince Regent, fled with his court to Brazil. By his liberal and enlightened policy he stirred new life in the quiescent colony. In 1815 Brazil was raised to the rank of a kingdom. Six years later John returned to Portugal, leaving his son Pedro as regent. Brazil and Portugal now grew apart, and there was talk of separation. Ordered home, Pedro refused to go, declared for independence, and became emperor (1822).

Pedro began to rule brilliantly, but his light soon waned. He accepted a liberal constitution (1824), but he quarreled with Parliament, became arbitrary and unpopular, lost the Banda Oriental, and finally abdicated, leaving his five-year-old son on the throne (1831). The ten years' regency that followed was a time of turbulence. Monarchists struggled with Federalists and Conservatives. Provinces threatened to secede. But wisdom came with experience, and patriotism won. Dom Pedro II became a rallying point for a new nationalism, and in 1840 his majority was proclaimed.

For half a century now Pedro ruled, a modest, democratic philosopher, though an emperor. The liberal Constitution of 1824 continued in force, but under it Pedro exercised the "moderative power," which made him almost a dictator. His rule was progressive. He respected freedom of speech, the press, and religion. A healthy political life was fostered. Con-

servatives tempered the haste of Liberal reformers, who sometimes resorted to revolution. To gain enlightenment, Dom
Pedro II visited Europe and the United States. In his reign

THE EMPIRE OF BRAZIL, SHOWING NAMES OF PROVINCES AND
CLIMATIC ZONES

railroads were built, industries stimulated, and immigration
encouraged. In the affairs of her turbulent Spanish neighbors
Brazil took an aggressive interest. She intervened in Uruguay,
assisted in the overthrow of Rosas in Argentina, and waged

fierce war against the Paraguayan dictator López. In Brazil slavery held on with unusual tenacity. Pressed by England, Pedro II championed the abolition of the slave trade. Two decades later a law provided for gradual emancipation (1871), but nearly twenty more years went by before slavery was totally abolished.

1. Brazil in transition. Napoleon and Portugal; flight of the royal family to Brazil (Prince John), 1807–1808; results of the transfer (administrative reforms, free trade, a national bank, immigration, other economic changes, printing press, educational institutions). Brazil a kingdom (King John), 1815. Brazil and the Spanish American wars of independence : Princess Carlota ; policy regarding Uruguay and Paraguay.

2. The establishment of the empire. Anti-Portuguese sentiment (uprising in Pernambuco); the revolution in Portugal (recall of John), 1820; the regency of Pedro; anti-Brazilian legislation of the Cortes; growth of sentiment for independence; the "Grito de Ypiranga" (September 7, 1822); expulsion of Portuguese garrisons; British aid (Lord Cochrane, restraining influence of Britain on Portugal). Brazil independent; recognized.

3. Pedro I (1822–1831). The Constitution of 1824 (moderative powers of the crown, absolutist tendencies, parliamentary opposition) ; foreign relations (withdrawal from Uruguay, war with Argentina); demand for federation; opposition to Pedro I; his abdication, 1831.

4. The Regency (1831–1840). Political disorders (Liberal Monarchists, Conservatives, Federalists); amendment of the Constitution (1834); the Liberalist victory (Vasconcellos and the Andradas).

5. Pedro II (1840–1889). Establishment of order (revolutions suppressed); rivalries of Conservatives and Liberals; relations with neighbors (hostility toward Argentina, intervention in Uruguay, war with Paraguay, opening the Amazon to commerce); economic and cultural progress; the antislavery movement (antislavery sentiment; abolition of the slave trade; influence of Great Britain; gradual abolition of slavery, 1871–1888).

REQUIRED READING
One of the following:

GARCÍA CALDERÓN, F. *Latin America*, 180–190.
JAMES, H. G., and MARTIN, P. A. *The Republics of Latin America*, 110–126.
ROBERTSON, W. S. *History of the Latin-American Nations*, 1922 ed., 153–161, 191–205; 1932 ed., 207–209, 238–245, 253–269.
SWEET, W. W. *History of Latin America*, 1919 ed., 165–168, 196–201; 1929 ed., 183–186, 233–238.
WILLIAMS, M. W. *People and Politics of Latin America*, 269–271 (colonial society); 319–323 (independence); 686–710 (empire).

REFERENCES

ARMITAGE, JOHN. *The History of Brazil.*
BALDRICH, J. A. *Historia de la Guerra del Brasil.*
BENNETT, FRANK. *Forty Years in Brazil.*
CLEVEN, N. A. N. *Readings in Hispanic American History.*
DENIS, PIERRE. *Brazil.*
DOMVILLE-FIFE, C. W. *The United States of Brazil.*
ELLIOTT, L. E. *Brazil, To-day and To-morrow.*
FLETCHER, J. C. *Brazil and the Brazilians.*
HARING, C. H. *The Germans in South America.*
JAMES, H. G. *Brazil after a Century of Independence.*
MARTIN, P. A. "Causes of the Collapse of the Brazilian Empire," *Hispanic American Historical Review*, February, 1921.
MOSSÉ, BENJAMIN. *Dom Pedro II, Empereur du Brésil.*
NABUCO, JOAQUIM. *The Spirit of Nationality in the History of Brazil.*
OLIVEIRA LIMA, MANOEL DE. *The Evolution of Brazil.*

LECTURE XLVI. RISE OF THE DICTATORS IN SPANISH SOUTH AMERICA

Introductory. After the wars of independence Spanish America, like the United States somewhat earlier, underwent a long struggle for stability, national solidarity, and economic prosperity, a struggle which in some regions has not even yet been brought to a successful culmination.

During the Revolution the leaders planned large nations, even dreaming of a state or federation embracing all of Spanish America. This large-state idea won partial success at first. Bolívar united his five republics into Greater Colombia; Uruguay was annexed to Brazil, and Central America to Mexico. Some leaders proposed constitutional monarchies, with native or European princes; others favored republics. Monarchies were tried in Mexico and Brazil for a time, but the republican idea triumphed. The large units fell apart, however, and the outcome is nineteen Hispanic American republics. Some of these are centralized republics, like France; others federal republics, like the United States.

In most of the new states independence was followed by disorder. The turbulence was due to lack of national cohesion. This in turn was caused by want of political experience, social and racial antipathies, geographical barriers, and sectional and personal ambitions. But the struggle was not meaningless chaos. In the long period of strife, soiled by personal ambition, cleavage in politics usually centered on fundamental issues: centralism versus federalism; conservatism versus liberalism; civilian rule versus militarism; privilege versus opportunity.

THE AMERICAS AFTER HISPANIC-AMERICAN INDEPENDENCE (1826)

Disorder led inevitably to one-man power. In most of the uprisings there was a typical succession of events. Liberators headed revolutions, issued pronunciamentos, by the use of soldiery became provisional presidents, and then, having vanquished their opponents, were "elected" constitutional presidents, after which they became in fact dictators or presidential despots. Some of these dictators were benevolent despots; others selfish. Typical dictators were Francia and López in Paraguay, Rosas in Argentina, Santa Anna in Mexico.

1. Disintegration of the large revolutionary states. Ideas of the leaders: Miranda in 1790 proposed one state from Canada to Patagonia, and in 1808, four great states; Moreno (1810), a great La Plata state, including Brazil; Pueyrredón, one Spanish American nation; Bolívar, a great federation; plans of Panama Congress. Partial success at first: Bolívar's conquests united; Brazil and Uruguay; Mexico and Central America. Disintegration: Uruguay separated from Brazil; Paraguay and Bolivia from Argentina; Bolívar's conquests into Venezuela, Colombia, Ecuador; Central America from Mexico.

2. Formation of the republics. Proposals of the revolutionary leaders regarding the governments of the large states: constitutional monarchies, ruled by Incas or European princes; large republics (breach between San Martín and Bolívar over this point); small republics. Triumph of the small-republic idea; the temporary empires (Mexico, Brazil); the republics (federal republics, centralized republics). Influence of the United States.

3. Disorders in the new republics: lack of political cohesion; lack of experience; ambition of cabildos; ambition of caudillos. Lines of cleavage in the struggles: Centralists

versus Federalists (city versus country); Conservatives versus Liberals (church and secular landholders versus non-landholders); the question of education; militarists versus civilians; personal followings (caudillos).

4. The presidential despots. Disorder leads to one-man power, revolutions, liberators, pronunciamentos, provisional presidents, constitutional presidents. Some typical dictators: Rosas in Argentina, Francia and López in Paraguay, Moreno in Ecuador, Páez and Castro in Venezuela, Díaz in Mexico.

REQUIRED READING

One of the following:

GARCÍA CALDERÓN, F. *Latin America*, 86–98 (military anarchy and the industrial period); 365–377 (the political problem).

JAMES, H. G., and MARTIN, P. A. *The Republics of Latin America*, 104, 109, 157–161, 195–197, 268–269, 304–305, 324–326.

RIPPY, J. F. *Historical Evolution of Hispanic America*, chap. 9.

ROBERTSON, W. S. *History of the Latin-American Nations* (selections).

SHEPHERD, W. R. *Hispanic Nations of the New World*, chap. 5.

SHEPHERD, W. R. *Latin America*, chap. 8.

SWEET, W. W. *History of Latin America*, chaps. 15–16 (selections).

WEBSTER, HUTTON. *History of Latin America*, 130–133.

WILGUS, A. C. *A History of Hispanic America*, chaps. 23–38 (selections).

WILLIAMS, M. W. *People and Politics of Latin America*, 347–356 (problems of self-government); 496–499 (disruption of Greater Colombia). One of the following: 523–525 (Páez); 537–545 (García Moreno); 584–588 (O'Higgins); 617–627 (Francia and López); 648–660 (Rosas).

REFERENCES

AKERS, C. E. *A History of South America.*

ALBERDI, J. B. *Las Bases y Puntos de Partida para la Organización Política de la República Argentina.*

ÁLVAREZ, AGUSTÍN. *South America, Ensayo de Psicología Política.*

AYARRAGARAY, LUCAS. *La Anarquía Argentina y el Caudillismo.*
DAWSON, T. C. *South American Republics.*
GARCÍA CALDERÓN, FRANCISCO. *Latin America, its Rise and Progress.*
GUERRA, J. G. *Sarmiento, su Vida y sus Obras.*
HERRERA, JULIO. *Anarquismo y Defensa Social.*
KOEBEL, W. H. *Central America.*
MECHAM, J. L. *Church and State in Latin America.*
OLIVEIRA LIMA, MANOEL DE. *The Evolution of Brazil.*
RIPPY, J. F. *Historical Evolution of Hispanic America,* chaps. 10–11.
ROBERTSON, W. S. *Hispanic-American Relations with the United States,* chap. 3.

See other references at the end of Lecture XL.

Lecture XLVII. The Struggle for Nationality in Mexico

Domestic Disorder, the "Colossus of the North," and French Dreams of Empire

Introductory. The struggle for nationality in the Spanish American countries during the first half-century is typified by the fortunes of Mexico. There disorder and inexperience led not only to dictatorship, but also to foreign invasion and loss of territory. Mexico's career after independence, as before, was given special character by its nearness to the United States. For thirty years struggles went on around centralism versus federalism, conservatism versus liberalism, privilege versus democracy, militarism versus civilian rule, personal ambition versus the commonweal.

The Constitution of 1824 embodied the federal principle. It was launched by well-meaning but simple presidents, former military heroes, whose policies were dictated largely by Lucas Alamán, a brilliant man inspired by hatred for republicanism. Presidents followed each other in rapid succession. In thirty years Mexico had fifty rulers. Centralists replaced Federalists; monarchism again raised its head; then Santa Anna, with his bravado and his corrupting hold on the army, became dictator. A foreign war called forth patriotism unexcelled. Santa Anna fell, discredited by his own selfishness and by the loss of Texas and California. The republican constitution was now restored and the Indian Juárez arose to shame selfish politicians. If Santa Anna reeked with greed, Juárez bled for

his people. With grim purpose he attacked privilege, championed law, and drove through La Reforma, a landmark in
Mexican history.

In the midst of his domestic tasks Juárez was confronted
with foreign intervention. Monarchism was not dead in
Mexico. Napoleon III dreamed of a new colonial empire
for France. Mexico looked inviting, and an excuse was easy
to find. Archduke Maximilian of Austria was a cat's-paw
ready at hand. Civil war in the United States made the
time opportune. Mexico was invaded, and an empire proclaimed. Juárez struggled manfully but against odds, till
Grant's victory at Appomattox. The United States then
issued a protest and the French army withdrew, leaving
Maximilian to his tragic fate. Mexico at awful cost had
preserved her nationality.

1. The empire of Iturbide. Causes of Iturbide's failure:
   personal vanity, race antagonism, political ingratitude,
   cynical disregard for the adopted forms of government.
2. The period of military anarchy (1823–1855). Struggle
   between actual law and living custom; tradition and
   progress; privilege and equality; central rule and local
   rule; clergy and military against the "people." Anarchy
   advancing to tyranny.
   a. The test of federalism. Adopted in an exigency; conflict between center and the provinces; between old
   Spanish-French ideas of government and the system
   of the United States; the Constitution of 1824 (its
   provisions); the fallacy of federation; chief enemies
   (colonial ideal of military dictator, lack of political understanding among people, mutual jealousies of local
   celebrities); opposition of the clergy and military.

b. The test of centralism. Influence of Alamán ; his attitude
   toward the United States ; clerical use of Santa Anna ;
   the parliamentary coup d'état ; the Constitution of
   1836 ; it relegated the legislative, judicial, and executive

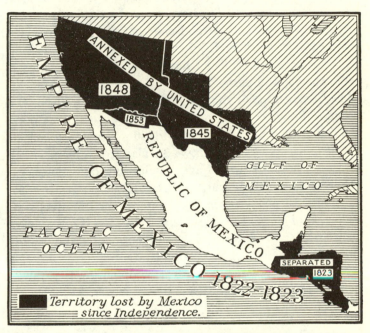

MEXICO AFTER INDEPENDENCE

   powers to impotence through the "Poder Conservador,"
   a committee of supermen to register the "will of the
   nation," removed by Plan de Tacubaya (1842).
c. The test of personalism. The "Bases Orgánicas Políticas"
   of 1843, an alleged popular government which made
   Santa Anna, militarism, and the Church triumphant and
   supreme ; Santa Anna's expulsion ; restoration of the

Constitution of 1824; the return of Santa Anna, the war with the United States, the dictatorship (1853); exile (1855).
d. The revolution under Plan de Ayutla. The rise of Comonfort and Juárez. The Ley Juárez (November 23, 1855): suppressed military and church jurisdiction over civil cases at law. The Ley Lerdo (June 25, 1856): provided for disentailment of Church property; opposition by the Clerical party.
3. The Constitution of 1857 and the War of the Reform. The cry "Religión y Fueros," opposed by the Juárez party. The Leyes de Reforma: provided for religious toleration, curtailed power of clergy, secularized convent lands, provided for civil marriage, secularized the cemeteries.
4. French intervention and the Second Empire (1863–1867). Juárez suspends payment of interest on the debt; the plans of Napoleon III; aided by the Conservative-Clericals; the failure of the intervention and the triumph of Juárez; influence of the United States; death of Juárez; rule of Lerdo de Tejada, preparing the way for the "reign" of Porfirio Díaz.

REQUIRED READING
One of the following:

BANCROFT, H. H. *History of Mexico*, 400–514. 1 vol.
GARCÍA CALDERÓN, F. *Latin America*, 149–163 (Mexico: the two empires, the dictators).
JAMES, H. G., and MARTIN, P. A. *The Republics of Latin America*, 336–343.
NOLL, A. H. *A Short History of Mexico*, 188–295.
PRIESTLEY, H. I. *The Mexican Nation*, chap. 15 (military anarchy), chap. 17 (centralism at its height), chaps. 19–20 (reform), chap. 21 (Maximilian).
RIPPY, J. F. *Historical Evolution of Hispanic America*, pp. 226–233.

ROBERTSON, W. S. *History of the Latin-American Nations*, 1922 ed., 478–495; 1932 ed., 636–654.
SWEET, W. W. *History of Latin America*, 1919 ed., 202–208; 1929 ed., 257–265.
WEBSTER, HUTTON. *History of Latin America*, 150–156.
WILGUS, A. C. *A History of Hispanic America*, chap. 25.
WILLIAMS, M. W. *People and Politics of Latin America*, 443–470 (Empire and Republic).

REFERENCES

ADAMS, E. D. *British Interests and Activities in Texas.*
ALAMÁN, LUCAS. *Historia de Méjico.*
BANCROFT, H. H. *History of Mexico*, V, chaps. 1–6, 11–13.
BARBER, A. W. *The Benevolent Raid of General Lew Wallace.*
BEALS, CARLETON. *Porfirio Díaz.*
BISHOP, FARNHAM. *Our First War with Mexico.*
BURKE, U. R. *Life of Juárez.*
CAESAR, COUNT CORTI EGON. *Maximilian and Charlotte of Mexico.*
CALDERÓN DE LA BARCA, F. E. *Life in Mexico.*
CALLAHAN, J. M. *American Foreign Policy in Mexican Relations.*
CALLCOTT, W. H. *Church and State in Mexico, 1822–1857.*
CALLCOTT, W. H. *Liberalism in Mexico, 1857–1929.*
CASTAÑEDA, C. E. (Editor). *La guerra de Reforma según el archivo del General D. Manuel Doblado, 1857–1860.*
CASTAÑEDA, C. E. (Editor). *The Mexican Side of the Texan Revolution* [1836]. *By the Chief Mexican Participants.*
CHYNOWETH, W. H. *The Fall of Maximilian.*
CREEL, GEORGE. *The People Next Door.*
FOLSOM, C. J. *Mexico in 1842.*
GARCÍA, GENARO. *Los Gobiernos de Álvarez y Comonfort.*
GARRISON, G. P. *Westward Extension.*
GRUENING, E. H. *Mexico and its Heritage.*
HALE, SUSAN. *The Story of Mexico.*
HALL, FREDERICK. *The Invasion of Mexico by the French.*
HASBROUCK, L. S. *Mexico from Cortés to Carranza*, chaps. 16–17.
HÉRICAULT, CHARLES DE. *Maximilien et le Mexique.*
KENDALL, J. J. *Mexico under Maximilian.*
LAFRAGUA, J. M. *Historia de la Revolución contra la Dictadura del General Santa Anna.*

LALLY, F. E. *French Opposition to the Mexican Policy of the Second Empire.*

LEÓN, NICOLÁS. *Compendio de la Historia General de México.*

MARTIN, P. F. *Mexico under Maximilian.*

MAYER, BRANTZ. *Mexico as it Was and Is.*

NOLL, A. H. *From Empire to Republic*, chaps. 4–5, 6, 7.

PEREYRA, CARLOS. *Historia del Pueblo Mejicano.*

PERKINS, DEXTER. *The Monroe Doctrine, 1826–1867.*

POINSETT, JOEL. *Notes on Mexico.*

RIPPY, J. F. *The United States and Mexico.*

RIVES, G. L. *The United States and Mexico.*

ROBINSON, FAYETTE. *Mexico and her Military Chieftains.*

ROMERO, MATÍAS. *Mexico and the United States.*

SIERRA, JUSTO. *Benito Juárez, su Obra y su Tiempo.*

SMITH, J. H. *The Annexation of Texas.*

SMITH, J. H. *The War with Mexico.*

VERDÍA, L. P. *Historia de México.*

YOUNG, PHILIP. *History of Mexico.*

THE EXPANSION AND CONSOLIDATION OF THE UNITED STATES

Lecture XLVIII. The Middle West and Jacksonian Democracy

Introductory. By 1820 the United States had achieved stability and confirmed its independence from Europe. In the next two decades the most significant development of the nation was the growth of the Middle West. The westward movement during this period was promoted by both propulsive and attractive forces. Hard times in Europe and on the Atlantic coast after the Napoleonic wars, drove people to America and to the free lands of the West. New machinery and the growth of manufactures increased the demand for raw materials. Migration was facilitated by better ocean vessels, turnpike roads, canals, river steamboats, and railroads. It was encouraged by a liberal land policy and by internal improvements at government expense. By wars and treaties the Indians were moved farther west and the way opened for white settlers. Beyond the 95th meridian a vast area was set aside for the red man, and many tribes were removed thither, with promises that they never more would be disturbed.

Under these conditions there was a rush of settlers to the West. The craze for land became a veritable mania. Crowds thronged the National Pike, the Erie Canal boats, Cumberland Gap, the roads through Georgia, and the Gulf and Ohio River steamers. Into the Northwest the settlers went to raise pork, wool, and grain; into the Southwest to produce cotton, corn.

and tobacco. When the Indian line was reached, the tide of settlement swung sharply northeast into Wisconsin and Michigan, or crossed the international boundary into the Mexican province of Texas.

By 1840 one third of the population of the United States lived west of the Allegheny Mountains. There twelve states

INDIAN LAND CESSIONS (1816–1850)

had been erected out of a total of twenty-six, thus shifting the balance of the nation. The growth of the West notably increased the country's economic strength. Settlement on the public domain was a nationalizing force. On the other hand, the new demand **for slaves** revived moribund slavery in the Old South. The **great migration** wrought many less obvious but equally significant changes. Western society took on a peculiar character, the result of frontier experience. In the Mississippi Valley there developed a Western democracy that has indelibly stamped our social and political life. There belief in the "common man" was rampant. It was typified in the election of Andrew Jackson, a Western hero and a man of the people. His slogan, "Let the people rule," was not a mere campaign phrase; it voiced a deep-seated article of faith. Western democracy found expression in legislation, party politics, and party machinery. The new state constitutions generally abolished religious and property qualifications for voting and for office-holding. Offices once appointive were made elective. Conventions replaced caucuses; the "spoils system" became generally accepted in practice. Legislation and party platforms reflected hostility to aristocracy and to vested interest. Provisions for public schools expressed the belief in the capacity as well as the rights of the "common man." Foreigners laughed at Western crudity; but they recognized also self-reliance, adaptability, and idealism. For years to come many of the nation's great problems — Indian troubles, internal improvements, disposition of public lands, slavery extension — arose out of the West.

1. The growth of the Middle West. Conditions of expansion: hard times after War of 1812; renewed immigration after 1830; improved means of communication (turnpikes, canals, the Erie Canal, steamboats on Western rivers, railroads after 1830); demand for cotton lands; the American System (internal improvements, protective tariffs); liberalized land policy (small tract, low price, credit, speculation, relief acts, preëmption laws); revision of Indian frontier; Creek and Seminole wars; Black Hawk War; removal of Indians west of 95th meridian (Indian country). Settlement in the West: in the Northwest (influence of Erie Canal, conflict of

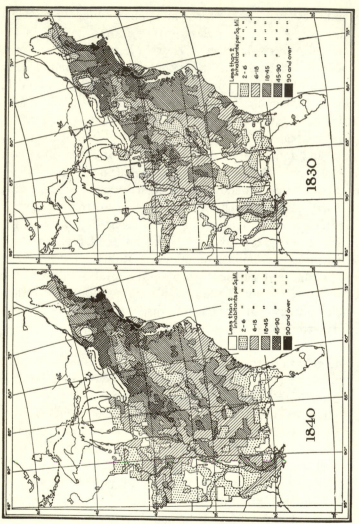

FILLING IN THE MIDDLE WEST (1830–1840)

Southern and Northern influence); in the Southwest
(demand for cotton lands, slavery interests revived, new
type of slavery); numbers; new states; political importance of West (votes in Congress, balance between
North and South, emergence of Western leaders).

2. The growth of commerce and economic independence.
Internal commerce: specialization of the sections in-
duces interchange; the East (manufactures and commerce); the Northwest (farm crops, food products,
wool); the South and Southwest (staple crops, cotton,
tobacco). The merchant marine: New England trade in
colonial days; intermittent prosperity (1775–1815); expansion after 1815 (packet ships on the Atlantic, clipper
ships on the Pacific); a close race with English merchant
marine till 1860.

3. Jacksonian democracy. Commerce and frontier influences
bred more liberal spirit; political democracy; helped by
panic of 1819; way led by the West; new constitutions
liberal; abolition of test oaths, religious and property
qualifications for voting and office-holding; representation based on population instead of on taxpayers; more
elective offices; education more widespread; reaction on
East (example of Connecticut, 1818; effect of church
conditions); Jackson's election (a victory for Western
democracy, "Let the people rule"); democracy extended to management of parties; "Death of King
Caucus"; organized politics; the spoils system. Western traits; opinions of foreign observers (Hall, Trollope,
De Tocqueville, Martineau, Kemble, Dickens); crudity;
self-reliance, adaptibility, inventiveness, love of "the
game"; uniformity ("eighteen million bores"); idealism; "manifest destiny."

REQUIRED READING

One of the following:

BASSETT, J. S. *A Short History of the United States*, chaps. 19, 20.

BEARD, C. A. and M. R. *History of the United States*, 1921 ed., chaps. 10, 11; 1929 ed., chaps. 11, 12.

FARRAND, MAX. *The Development of the United States*, chaps. 7, 8.

FORMAN, S. E. *Our Republic*, 261–270 or 295–315.

HARLOW, R. V. *The Growth of the United States*, 302–317 (the New West); 344–353 (Jackson).

MACDONALD, WILLIAM. *Three Centuries of American Democracy*, chap. 6.

MARTIN, A. E. *History of the United States*, I, chaps. 17–19; I, Enlarged Edition, chap. 23.

MORISON, S. E., and COMMAGER, H. S. *Growth of the American Republic*, 377–386 (America's awkward age: the New West); 386–389 (industrial development).

MUZZEY, D. S. *The United States of America*, I, 329–347.

SPARKS, E. E. *Expansion of the American People*, chap. 23.

TURNER, F. J. *Rise of the New West*, chap. 5.

REFERENCES

ABERNETHY, T. P. *From Frontier to Plantation in Tennessee: a Study in Frontier Democracy.*

ADAMS, J. T. *The Epic of America.*

ADAMS, J. T. *The March of Democracy.* 2 vols. 1932–1933.

BASSETT, J. S. (Editor). *Correspondence of Andrew Jackson.* 5 vols.

BASSETT, J. S. *The Life of Andrew Jackson.*

BOWERS, C. G. *The Party Battles of the Jackson Period.*

BRANCH, E. D. *Westward.*

BROOKS, GERALDINE. *Dames and Daughters of the Young Republic.*

CHANNING, EDWARD. *History of the United States.*

FISH, C. R. *The Rise of the Common Man.*

FOREMAN, GRANT. *Advancing the Frontier, 1830–1860.*

GOODWIN, C. L. *The Trans-Mississippi West.*

HART, A. B. *National Ideals Historically Traced.*

HOCKETT, H. C. *Political and Social History of the United States, 1492–1828.*

JAMES, MARQUIS. *Andrew Jackson, the Border Captain.*

MacDonald, William. *Jacksonian Democracy, 1829-1837.*
McMaster, J. B. *History of the People of the United States.*
Meigs, W. M. *The Life of Thomas Hart Benton.*
Morison, S. E. *The Oxford History of the United States.*
Nevins, Allan. *American Social History recorded by British Travellers.*
Ogg, F. A. *The Reign of Andrew Jackson.*
Parton, James. *Life of Andrew Jackson.*
Paxson, F. L. *History of the American Frontier.*
Pease, T. C. *The United States.*
Peck, C. H. *The Jacksonian Epoch.*
Riegel, R. E. *America Moves West.*
Schlesinger, A. M. *New Viewpoints in American History,* chap. 9.
Sumner, W. G. *Andrew Jackson as a Public Man.*
Turner, F. J. *Rise of the New West.*

Lecture XLIX. Manifest Destiny

The Extension of the United States to the Pacific

Introductory. The "Shadow of Europe in the West" gave way to a shadow of the United States in the West. The Anglo-Americans drove a wedge between Canada and Mexico, and by 1848 the domain of the young nation was extended from Louisiana to the Pacific. This was the other side of the Monroe Doctrine.

Many factors aroused interest in the Far West. The way was led by the vanguard of Boston coast traders, overland fur men, Northwestern missionaries, and official explorers. For twenty years all these Americans west of Louisiana were intruders into foreign or disputed territory. Interest was stimulated by sectional rivalry and by fear of foreign nations. Behind all these was the spirit of "manifest destiny" — confidence that the United States was destined to embrace and regenerate the continent. Pathfinders beckoned; government tried to follow. By purchase or diplomacy it essayed to acquire all the vast region between Louisiana and the Pacific. Mexico did not wish to sell, and England was stubborn; so officials resorted to watchful waiting. Wilkes, Ap Jones, Larkin, and Frémont all typify the government's hope that something would "turn up."

While government watched, settlers moved in. Invited, Americans colonized Texas, arose in revolt, and sought annexation. Covered wagons creaked their way to Oregon; then England yielded half of the disputed area. Uninvited,

other covered wagons invaded California; their occupants
set up the Bear Flag Republic. When something thus turned
up Frémont was on hand. Uninvited, Mormons poured into
the Great Basin, also Mexican territory. Soldiers and diplomats now supplemented the work of the settlers. Texas was

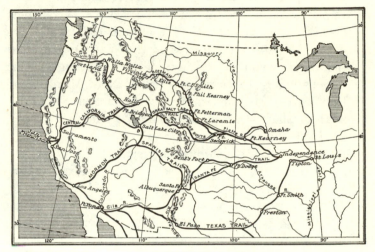

TRAILS TO THE FAR WEST

annexed; Mexico went to war, and was forced to yield half
of her domain. The purchase of the Gadsden strip and
Alaska completed the epic of growth on the mainland.

   This vast extension of territory was highly significant. It
made the United States the dominant power in North America
and gave her a frontage on the Pacific. It enabled her to
assimilate more millions of Europeans. Built on the national
domain, the West continued to be a nationalizing force. The
process of growth kept the nation young with continued frontier experience; it prolonged opportunity for social experimentation and perpetuated early American characteristics.

1. Expansion at the expense of neighbors. List of acquisitions (Texas, Oregon, Mexican cession of 1848, Gadsden Purchase, Alaska), chiefly at the expense of Mexico.
2. The growth of interest in the Far West. The vanguard of pioneers precede the flag; fur-traders and explorers in the Great Basin and on the Pacific; coastwise traders in California; missionaries in the Oregon country; efforts of the United States to possess the West; expansionist sentiment; manifest destiny; fear of foreign powers; various offers to purchase Texas, New Mexico, and California; watchful waiting; Frémont in California; settlers follow the explorers (Texas, California, Oregon, Utah).
3. The winning of Texas through settlement, revolution, and annexation. The American settlement of Texas (1821–1835): empresario grants; Moses and Stephen F. Austin; other empresarios. The Texan revolution (1835–1836): causes; Santa Anna's efforts to crush; declaration of independence (March 2, 1836); the fall of the Alamo; Houston's victory at San Jacinto. The Republic of Texas (1836–1845): Mexico's efforts to reconquer; Texan expansion efforts. Annexation: United States' fear of England and France; Texas in politics; failure of treaty of annexation; annexation by joint resolution (1845).
4. Half of Oregon secured. Joint occupation after 1818; British influence dominant; diplomacy fails to settle boundary; growth of American influence (settlers); the Oregon Trail; immigration to California; Oregon and Texas in the campaign of 1844 ("Fifty-four forty or fight"); Polk's aggressive policy; treaty of 1846 (Oregon divided).

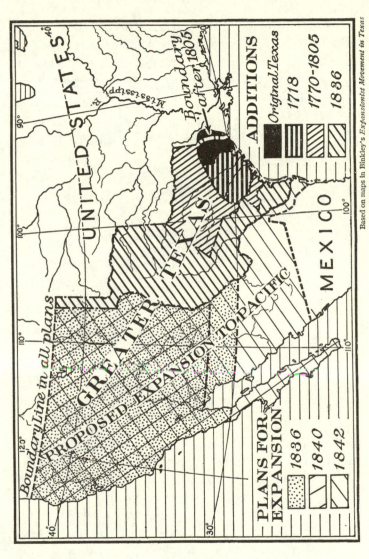

ADDITIONS

Original Texas
1718
1770-1805
1836

PLANS FOR EXPANSION
1836
1840
1842

TEXAN DREAMS OF EMPIRE (1836–1842)

Based on maps in Binkley's *Expansionist Movement in Texas*

5. The Mormons in the Great Basin. Rise of the Mormons (Smith, Young); persecuted in the Middle West; the migration to Utah (then Mexican territory); the State of Deseret.

6. The war with Mexico and the Mexican cession (1846–1848). Causes of the war: annexation of Texas; claims; Slidell's mission; the rupture on the border (1846). The campaigns of the war: Taylor's advance across the Rio Grande; Scott's advance from Vera Cruz to Mexico City; Kearny's expedition (New Mexico, Chihuahua, California); Sloat, Stockton,

THE AREA DISPUTED BY MEXICO AND THE UNITED STATES (THE WHOLE OF TEXAS)

and Frémont in California. The Mormon battalion. The territorial cession (1848). Settlement in the cession; the Mormons in Utah; gold and the "Forty-niners."

7. The Gadsden Purchase. Boundary difficulties after 1848; desire for expansion; filibustering raids; need of a southern railroad route; Indian raids; the question of an Isthmian railroad route; Mexico's financial need; the Gadsden Treaty (1853–1854).

8. The Alaska Purchase. Offered by Russia (remoteness, fear of England), 1867; Seward's prompt bargain.

REQUIRED READING
One of the following:

BASSETT, J. S. *A Short History of the United States*, 438–450.
BEARD, C. A. and M. R. *History of the United States*, 1921 ed., chap. 12; 1929 ed., chap. 13.
FARRAND, MAX. *The Development of the United States*, chap. 9.
FORMAN, S. E. *Our Republic*, chap. 16.
GARRISON, G. P. *Westward Extension*, chaps. 6, 11.
HARLOW, R. V. *The Growth of the United States*, 396–416.
MARTIN, A. E. *History of the United States*, I, chaps. 21–22; I, Enlarged Edition, chaps. 27–28.
MORISON, S. E., and COMMAGER, H. S. *Growth of the American Republic*, 441–450 (Oregon), 451–470 (Texas and the Mexican War).
MUZZEY, D. S. *The United States of America*, I, chap. 8.
PRIESTLEY, H. I. *The Mexican Nation*, chaps. 16, 18.
SPARKS, E. E. *Expansion of the American People*, chaps. 25–28.

REFERENCES

BARKER, E. C. *The Austin Papers*. 3 vols.
BARKER, E. C. *The Life of Stephen F. Austin.*
BARKER, E. C. *Mexico and Texas, 1821–1835.*
BELL, J. C. *Opening a Highway to the Pacific.*
BIEBER, R. B. (Editor). *Adventures in the Santa Fé Trade, 1844–1847*, by J. J. Webb.
BIEBER, R. B. (Editor). *Frontier Life in the Army, 1854–1861*, by Eugene Bandel.
BIESELE, R. L. *The History of the German Settlements in Texas, 1831–1861.*
BINKLEY, W. C. *The Expansionist Movement in Texas.*
BROSNAN, C. J. *Jason Lee, Prophet of the New Oregon.*
CALLAHAN, J. M. *The Alaska Purchase and Americo-Canadian Relations.*
CANFIELD, C. L. *The Diary of a Forty-niner.*

CANNON, C. L. (Editor). *A Journal of the Santa Fé Expedition under Colonel Doniphan*, by Jacob S. Robinson.

CANNON, C. L. (Editor). *Route across the Rocky Mountains*, by Overton Johnson and W. H. Winter, of the Emigration of 1843.

CAUGHEY, J. W. (Editor). *The Emigrant's Guide to California*, by Joseph E. Ware.

CENDRARS, BLAISE. *Sutter's Gold*. (Fiction.)

CHASE, M. K. *Négociations de la République du Texas en Europe, 1837–1845*.

CHITTENDEN, H. M. *The American Fur Trade of the Far West*.

CREER, L. H. *Utah and the Nation*.

COY, O. C. *The Great Trek*.

DELLENBAUGH, F. S. *Frémont and '49*.

DRUMM, S. T. (Editor). *Down the Santa Fé Trail and into Mexico. The Diary of Susan Shelby Magoffin*.

DUFFUS, R. L. *The Santa Fé Trail*.

FALCONER, THOMAS (F. W. Hodge, Editor). *Letters and Notes on the Texan Santa Fé Expedition, 1841–1842*.

FOREMAN, GRANT. *Indian Removal: the Emigration of the Five Civilized Tribes of Indians*.

FOREMAN, GRANT. *Indians and Pioneers: the Story of the American Southwest before 1830*.

FULLER, G. W. *A History of the Pacific Northwest*.

GARRISON, G. P. *Westward Extension*.

GHENT, W. J. *The Early Far West: a Narrative Outline, 1540–1850*.

GHENT, W. J. *The Road to Oregon*.

GILBERT, E. W. *The Exploration of Western America, 1800–1850: an Historical Geography*.

GOODWIN, CARDINAL. *John Charles Frémont: an Explanation of his Career*.

GOODWIN, CARDINAL. *The Trans-Mississippi West*.

HAFEN, L. R., and GHENT, W. J. *Broken Hand: the Life Story of Thomas Fitzpatrick, Chief of the Mountain Men*.

HANNUM, A. P. *A Quaker Forty-Niner: the Adventures of Charles Edward Pancoast on the American Frontier*.

HART, S. H., and HULBERT, A. B. (Editors). *Zebulon Pike's Arkansaw Journal*.

HOWLAND, C. P. (Editor). *American Relations in the Caribbean*.

HULBERT, A. B. *Forty-Niners: the Chronicle of the California Trail*.

HULBERT, A. B. (Editor). *The Call of the Columbia.*

HULBERT, A. B. (Editor). *Southwest on the Turquoise Trail: the First Diaries on the Road to Santa Fé.*

HULBERT, A. B. (Editor). *Where Rolls the Oregon.*

JAMES, MARQUIS. *The Raven: A Biography of Sam Houston.*

JOHNSON, W. F. *A Century of Expansion.*

LOWRIE, S. H. *Culture Conflicts in Texas, 1821–1836.*

McCORMAC, E. I. *James K. Polk, a Political Biography.*

McPHERSON, H. M. "The Interest of William McKendrie Gwin in the Purchase of Alaska, 1854–1861," in *Pacific Historical Review*, III (1934), 28–38.

MANNING, W. R. *Early Diplomatic Relations between the United States and Mexico.*

MORISON, S. E. *The Oxford History of the United States.*

NEIHARDT, J. G. *The Splendid Wayfaring.*

NEVINS, ALLAN. *Frémont; the West's Greatest Adventurer.*

PAXSON, F. L. *History of the American Frontier.*

PAXSON, F. L. *Last American Frontier.*

POWELL, F. W. (Editor). *Hall J. Kelley on Oregon.*

QUAIFE, M. M. *The Kingdom of Saint James: a Narrative of the Mormons.*

REEVES, J. S. *American Diplomacy under Tyler and Polk.*

RIPPY, J. F. *The United States and Mexico.*

RIVES, G. L. *The United States and Mexico, 1821–1848.*

SCHAFER, JOSEPH. *History of the Pacific Northwest.*

SEARS, L. M. *John Slidell.*

SMITH, J. H. *The Annexation of Texas.*

SMITH, J. H. *The War with Mexico.*

STEPHENSON, N. W. *Texas and the Mexican War.*

TURNER, F. J. *The Frontier in American History.*

TURNER, F. J. *Rise of the New West.*

VESTAL, STANLEY. *Kit Carson: the Happy Warrior of the Old West.*

WHITE, S. E. *The Forty-niners.*

WYLLYS, R. K. *The French in Sonora, 1850–1854.*

Lecture L. Sectional Strife

Introdu tory. Territorial expansion was attended by severe growing pains. Many of them arose out of sectional interests. When the nation was formed the union was far from complete, and the nature of the Federal bond was disputed by strict and loose constructionists. For many years the logic of events was strongly toward nationalism and the increase of Federal authority, a tendency that was clearly revealed in the "American System," the Monroe Doctrine, and the buoyant spirit of manifest destiny.

Running counter to this current of nationalism was the rising tide of sectionalism. Geographic differences between North and South produced economic and social contrasts, with resulting disagreements on public questions. For thirty years the sections maintained peace by compromise. States were admitted in pairs, one from the North and one from the South. Disputes which threatened to rend the Union were settled by mutual yielding. The most notable of these sectional struggles were over questions of tariff, territorial growth, and the extension of slavery into the territories. At bottom was the ambition of both sections for political power.

Missouri demanded admission as a state with a constitution permitting slavery. Long and heated debates ensued; then Congress settled the matter by compromise. Missouri was admitted with slavery, but elsewhere the institution was excluded from all the Louisiana Purchase north of latitude 36°30'. A decade later the ship of state struck another rock. The tariff of 1828, harmful to the South, was branded the "Tariff of

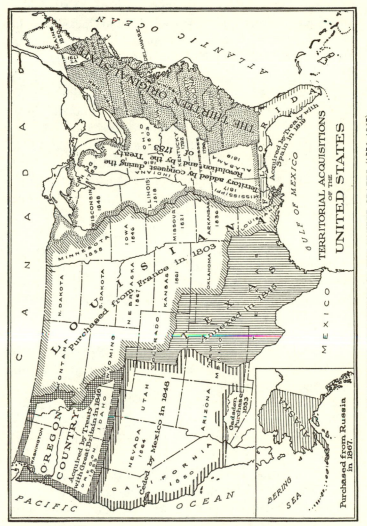

TERRITORIAL EXPANSION OF THE UNITED STATES (1776–1867)

Abominations." It called forth opposing views of the Federal
bond. South Carolina became defiant, and Jackson replied
with a threat to use force. Then Congress, led by Clay, provided for a compromise tariff, and the danger subsided.

Sectional strife attended the various acquisitions of new
territory. Expansion was a national impulse, but each section
was ambitious to go faster than the other. The addition of
Texas, Oregon, and the conquests from Mexico each aroused
sectional animosities. Polk, taking a national view, combined
them all in one compromise program — and succeeded. The
status of slavery in these acquisitions was a special cause for
strife, but when the Union seemed about to be rent asunder,
peace was restored by the Compromise of 1850.

But compromise no longer served. The Kansas-Nebraska
Act and the Dred Scott decision were Southern victories.
The North was outgrowing the South, and it in turn became
aggressive. Lincoln's election tipped the scale toward Northern supremacy, and the South became desperate.

1. The incompleteness of the early union. Uncertainty of
   meaning of the Constitution at first. Two views of interpretation : strict construction (doctrines of express
   powers, state rights, nullification, secession, early examples) ; liberal construction (doctrines of implied,
   necessary, and proper powers ; influence of Hamilton and
   Marshall and of events such as the Louisiana Purchase
   and westward expansion).

2. Growth of nationalism after War of 1812. Stimulated by
   the war spirit ; by internal commerce and growth of
   economic independence ; shown in nationalistic legislation (the "American System," internal improvements,
   protective tariffs) ; by the Monroe Doctrine.

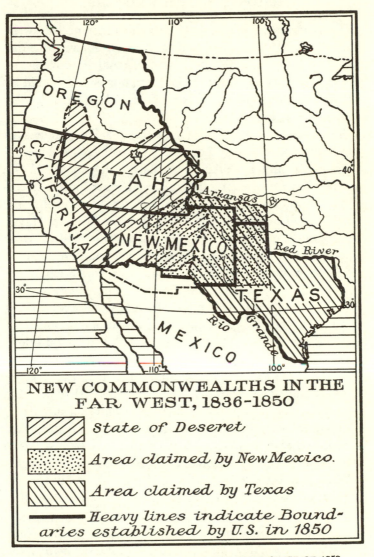

NEW COMMONWEALTHS IN THE
FAR WEST, 1836-1850

State of Deseret

Area claimed by New Mexico.

Area claimed by Texas

Heavy lines indicate Boundaries established by U.S. in 1850

BOUNDARY DISPUTES SETTLED BY THE COMPROMISE OF 1850

3. Divergence of the sections. Geographic differences between North and South; economic and social differences; disagreement on public questions (internal improvements, tariff, slavery extension); Southern opposition caused by injurious legislation and fear of loss of political leadership; East versus West.

4. Conflict and compromise (1820-1850). The balance of power maintained by admitting states in pairs, by compromises, and by alliance of the South and the West; the Missouri Compromise (1820), a question of expansion, not of slavery in the old states. The tariff; the "Tariff of Abominations" (1828); the Webster-Hayne debate; the doctrine of nullification; the tariff of 1832; nullification tested; Jackson's attitude; the "Force Bill"; Clay's compromise tariff of 1833. Territorial expansion, not primarily a sectional question but involved with politics and sectional interests (manifest destiny); Texas and Oregon in politics; the abolitionists and the "gag rule"; the Mexican War; the Cuban question; slavery in the Mexican cession; the Wilmot Proviso (1846); California's "gross impertinence"; the struggle over admitting California; Webster's "Seventh of March" speech; the Compromise of 1850 (California admitted, squatter sovereignty in Utah and New Mexico, new Fugitive Slave Law, western boundaries adjusted, etc.).

5. The balance of power broken (1850-1860). The Kansas-Nebraska Act (Douglas's railroad program); bill for two new territories; "squatter sovereignty"; repeal of Missouri Compromise; "Bleeding Kansas"; the Dred Scott decision; the rise of the Republican party; the North inflamed by Abolitionists; *Uncle Tom's Cabin*; the "underground railroad"; new party devoted to restric-

tion of slavery; defeat of Frémont (1856); Northeast
and Northwest welded by railroads; balance reversed;
the Lincoln-Douglas debates; the issue defined; Lincoln
elected.

REQUIRED READING

One of the following:

BASSETT, J. S. *A Short History of the United States*, chap. 21.
BEARD, C. A. and M. R. *History of the United States*, 1921 ed.,
307–342; 1929 ed., 335–367.
FARRAND, MAX. *The Development of the United States*, 212–222.
FORMAN, S. E. *Our Republic*, chap. 18, 19, or 20.
HARLOW, R. V. *The Growth of the United States*, 318–325 (cotton and
slavery); 353–358 (Webster-Hayne, nullification); 383–385 (the
plantation system); 387–395 (the abolitionist crusade); 417–427
(Compromise of 1850); 435–467 (civil war precipitated).
MACDONALD, WILLIAM. *Three Centuries of American Democracy*,
chap. 7.
MARTIN, A. E. *History of the United States*, I, chaps. 25–28; I, En-
larged Edition, chaps. 31–34.
MORISON, S. E., and COMMAGER, H. S. *Growth of the American Re-
public*, 495–507 (the irrepressible conflict, 1854–1859); 508–525
(Lincoln, secession, civil war).
MUZZEY, D. S. *The United States of America*, I, chap. 9.

REFERENCES

AUCHAMPAUGH, GERALD. *James Buchanan and his Cabinet on the Eve
of Secession*.
BANCROFT, FREDERIC. *Calhoun and the South Carolina Nullification
Movement*.
BANCROFT, FREDERIC. *Slave-trading in the Old South*.
BARNES, G. H. *The Anti-Slavery Impulse, 1830–1844*.
BEVERIDGE, A. J. *Abraham Lincoln, 1809–1858*. 2 vols.
BROWN, W. G. *The Lower South in American History*.
BUTLER, PIERCE. *Judah P. Benjamin*.
CARPENTER, J. T. *The South as a Conscious Minority, 1789–1861*.
CHANNING, EDWARD. *History of the United States*.

CLAY, T. H. *Henry Clay.*

COLE, A. C. *The Irrepressible Conflict.*

CRAVEN, AVERY. *Edmund Ruffin, Southerner: a Study in Secession.*

DODD, W. E. *The Cotton Kingdom.*

FLEMING, W. L. *Civil War and Reconstruction in Alabama.*

FUESS, C. M. *Daniel Webster.* 2 vols.

HART, A. B. *Slavery and Abolition, 1831–1841.*

HOUSTON, D. F. *A Critical History of Nullification in South Carolina.*

HUNT, GAILLARD. *John C. Calhoun.*

JOHNSON, ALLEN. *Stephen A. Douglas.*

MCMASTER, J. B. *History of the People of the United States.*

MACY, JESSE. *The Anti-Slavery Crusade.*

MORISON, S. E. *The Oxford History of the United States.*

NICHOLS, R. F. *Franklin Pierce, Young Hickory of the Granite Hills.*

PEASE, T. C. *The United States.*

PHILLIPS, U. B. *American Negro Slavery.*

PHILLIPS, U. B. *Life and Labor in the Old South.*

PHILLIPS, U. B., and GHENT, J. D. *Florida Plantation Records from the Papers of George Noble Jones.*

RAMSDELL, C. W. *Reconstruction in Texas.*

RAY, P. O. *The Repeal of the Missouri Compromise.*

RHODES, J. F. *History of the United States from the Compromise of 1850.*

SCHLESINGER, A. M. *New Viewpoints in American History.*

SHEPARD, E. M. *Martin Van Buren.*

SMITH, T. C. *Parties and Slavery, 1850–1859.*

TURNER, F. J. *Rise of the New West.*

TURNER, F. J. *The Significance of Sections in American History.*

TYLER, L. G. *The Letters and Times of the Tylers.*

VAN DEUSEN, J. G. *Economic Bases of Disunion in South Carolina.*

WESLEY, C. H. *Negro Labor in the United States, 1850–1925.*

WHITE, L. A. *Robert Bunwell Rhett, Father of Secession.*

LECTURE LI. DIVISION AND REUNION

Introductory. Slavery was endangered, and the South applied the extreme remedy of secession. Compromise was tried once more, but Lincoln said "No." First the lower South and then the middle South withdrew; the border states remained in the Union. The seceding states formed a Confederacy with its capital first at Montgomery, and then at Richmond. The pessimistic prophecies of Europeans seemed about to come true. Buchanan was supine, but Lincoln answered secession with a call for volunteers to preserve the Union.

The combatants were unequal, and Northern victory was inevitable. The North had the advantage of population and resources, though weakened by divided sentiment and political quarrels. In military leadership the advantage at first was with the South. Both sides appealed to Europe. England attempted to maintain neutrality, but did so with difficulty; Russia favored the North and France the South. Both sides were unprepared. Volunteers were relied on at first, with bad results; then came the draft. Three million men took part in the combat, and three fourths of a million paid the extreme price. The war was financed by taxes, loans, and paper-money issues. At the end the Union debt was three billion dollars. Yet the war stimulated industry and commerce; great fortunes were made in the North, and a new aristocracy founded.

The major strategy of the war was simple. The South was blockaded, but the brilliant blockade-runners won the applause of the world. In the East each side aimed at the other's capi-

tal: "On to Richmond" was echoed by "On to Washington."
In the West the Union aim was to cut the Confederacy in two.
Under the superb leadership of Lee and "Stonewall" Jackson,
for two years the South was generally victorious. In despera-
tion, and purely as a war measure, Lincoln issued the Emancipation Proclamation. Grant and Sherman now arose to Union
command. The tide turned at Vicksburg and Gettysburg,
Sherman cut a devastating swath through the exhausted
South, and the war ended at Appomattox.

Reconstruction was almost as disastrous for the South as
war. Lincoln favored clemency; Congress demanded retri-
bution. Lincoln was assassinated, and Congress had its way.
Amendments to the Constitution freed the slaves and gave
them civil rights. Negro legislatures and carpetbaggers embittered the whites; the Ku-Klux Klan terrorized the blacks.
By 1870 all the seceding states had been readmitted to the
Union, and by 1877 the whites were again in control. But
the Old South was gone.

1. Secession and the formation of the Southern Confederacy.
   The effect of Lincoln's election; the lower South secedes;
   failure of the Crittenden compromise; seizure of Federal
   property (Buchanan's inactivity, Lincoln's view of secession); fall of Fort Sumter; the middle South secedes;
   the border states remain in the Union (West Virginia
   secedes from Virginia); the Confederacy (government,
   capitals, officers, constitution).
2. The combatants. The North won because of preponderant
   resources; advantages (population, food supply, manufactures, railroads, navy); disadvantages (offensive warfare, divided sentiment, political quarrels); military
   leadership (advantage with the South at first).

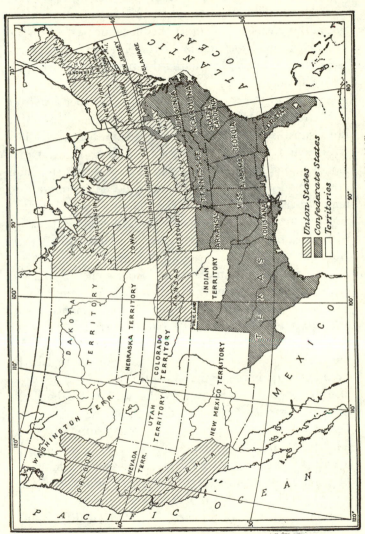

THE UNITED STATES DURING THE CIVIL WAR (1861–1865)

3. Europe and the war. The question of England: opinion in England divided (aristocracy and manufacturers versus working class); effect of the blockade; effect of the Emancipation Proclamation; the *Trent* affair; privateers (the *Alabama*); Charles Francis Adams. France and Russia.

4. The people and the war. The war not altogether a matter of battlefields; raising the armies (volunteers, the draft riots, substitutes, bounty-jumpers); numbers of soldiers (North and South); war finance (taxes, loans, paper money); industry and commerce in the North (high prices, food products, the Homestead Act, immigration, importance of farm machinery, manufactures); in the South (effect of blockade, blockade-running, export by way of Mexico, manufactures, overland trade with North).

5. Emancipation as a war measure. Lincoln's views; warning proclamation (September, 1862); the proclamation of January 1, 1863; where applied; gradual emancipation.

6. The strategy of the war. The blockade and naval war: purposes of the blockade; Farragut; the *Monitor* and the *Merrimac*; Southern privateers; damage to Northern merchant marine; the *Alabama* and the *Kearsarge*. Military strategy: the war in the West; the borders; the river forts and Union advance to the line of the Tennessee River; opening the Mississippi and the splitting of the Confederacy (Farragut); Vicksburg; in the East; the struggle for Richmond and Washington; long series of Confederate successes; the North invaded (Antietam, Gettysburg); the turn of the tide; Sherman's march to the sea; the fall of Richmond; Appomattox.

7. Reconstruction. The Thirteenth Amendment; the presidential policy; Congressional opposition; the "black codes"; the Freedman's Bureau; Civil Rights Bill and the Fourteenth Amendment; the Congressional plan of reconstruction; carpetbag government and negro rule; the Ku-Klux Klan; the Fifteenth Amendment; restoration of home rule in the South (1877).

REQUIRED READING

One of the following:

BASSETT, J. S. *A Short History of the United States*, chap. 28, 29, 30, or 31.

BEARD, C. A. and M. R. *History of the United States*, 1921 ed., chap. 15; 1929 ed., chap. 17.

FARRAND, MAX. *The Development of the United States*, 221–248.

FORMAN, S. E. *Our Republic*, chap. 22, 23, 24, or 25.

HARLOW, R. V. *The Growth of the United States*, 468–480 (secession and war); 481–504 (military aspects); 505–517 (nonmilitary aspects); 518–529 (foreign relations); 530–552 (reconstruction).

MACDONALD, WILLIAM. *Three Centuries of American Democracy*, chap. 8.

MARTIN, A. E. *History of the United States*, I, chaps. 29–33; I. Enlarged Edition, chaps 35–39.

MORISON, S. E., and COMMAGER, H. S. *Growth of the American Republic*, 532–536 (the two armies); 536–537 (strategy of the war); 541–546 (the blockade, European relations); 615–631 (aftermath of the war); 532–651 (reconstruction).

MUZZEY, D. S. *The United States of America*, I, chap. 10.

PEASE, T. C. *The United States*, chap. 24.

REFERENCES

BEALE, H. R. *The Critical Year: a Study of Andrew Johnson and Reconstruction.*

BOWERS, C. G. *The Tragic Era.*

CALLAHAN, J. M. *The Diplomatic History of the Southern Confederacy.*

CALLAHAN, J. M. *Russo-American Relations during the American Civil War.*

CHARNWOOD, G. R. B. *Abraham Lincoln.*
CUTTING, E. B. *Jefferson Davis, Political Soldier.*
DODD, W. E. *Jefferson Davis.*
DODD, W. E. *Statesmen of the Old South.*
DUMOND, D. L. *The Secession Movement, 1860–1861.*
DUNNING, W. A. *Reconstruction.*
ECKENRODE, H. J. *Rutherford B. Hayes, Statesman of Reunion.*
FLEMING, W. L. *The Sequel of Appomattox.*
HACKER, L. M., and KENDRICK, B. B. *The United States since 1865.*
HOSMER, J. K. *The Appeal to Arms.*
HOSMER, J. K. *Outcome of the Civil War.*
JORDAN, DONALDSON, and PRATT, E. J. *Europe and the American Civil War.*
KIRKLAND, E. C. *The Peace Makers of 1864.*
LONN, ELLA. *Desertion during the Civil War.*
MCMASTER, J. B. *A History of the People of the United States during Lincoln's Administration.*
MAURICE, MAJOR GENERAL SIR FREDERICK. *An Aide-de-camp of Lee, being Papers of Colonel Charles Marshall . . . , 1862–1865.*
MILTON, G. F. *The Age of Hate: Andrew Johnson and the Radicals.*
MORISON, S. E. *The Oxford History of the United States.*
NEVINS, ALLAN. *The Emergence of Modern America, 1865–1878.*
OWSLEY, F. L. *King Cotton Diplomacy: Foreign Relations of the Confederate States of America.*
PAXSON, F. L. *The Civil War.*
PERKINS, DEXTER. *The Monroe Doctrine, 1826–1867.*
POLLARD, E. A. *The Lost Cause.*
RANDALL, J. G. *Constitutional Problems under Lincoln.*
RHODES, J. F. *History of the Civil War.*
ROBINSON, W. M., JR. *The Confederate Privateers.*
SMITH, E. C. *The Borderland in the Civil War.*
STEPHENSON, N. W. *Abraham Lincoln and the Union.*
STEPHENSON, N. W. *The Day of the Confederacy.*
STRYKER, L. P. *Andrew Johnson: a Study in Courage.*
TAYLOR, A. A. *The Negro in the Reconstruction of Virginia.*
WILSON, WOODROW. *Division and Reunion.*
WOOD, WILLIAM. *Captains of the Civil War.*

Lecture LII. Peopling the Far West and Welding the Nation

Introductory. The Union had been preserved. It was now enhanced by the peopling of the Far West. Far-flung and sprawling, it was welded together by the building of transcontinental railroads, the economic reconstruction of the South, and the reorganization of industry and commerce on a national scale.

In 1858 the Far West was sparsely settled except in a few spots. By 1830 an Indian country had been set aside west of the 95th meridian, and in the next quarter-century there was little settlement between that line and the Pacific Coast. The New Mexico, Oregon, California, and Utah migrations merely passed through the Indian reserve. In 1854 Kansas and Nebraska were carved out of the Indian lands and settlement there begun. Otherwise the vast area between the Missouri Bend and the Pacific Slope was unoccupied by white men. But this space was now invaded on both sides.

In and after 1858 astonishing gold and silver deposits were found all through the Rockies. So rapid was mining development that five new territories were erected within six years. Much of this mining activity was a backwash from California. To form new commonwealths old territories were cut down. Each mining region witnessed a typical succession of events. Strikes were followed by rushes and mushroom towns; each camp had its bad men; demand for decency found expression in law and order associations and vigilance committees; territorial governments soon followed.

Greater still was the rush to the prairie farms. New markets, farm machinery, and the Homestead Act caused the demand for agricultural lands to soar. In two decades (1860–1880) five million Europeans came to the United States, and most of them went to the West. Prairie farms, once neglected, now became the rage. Here, too, each district had its typical

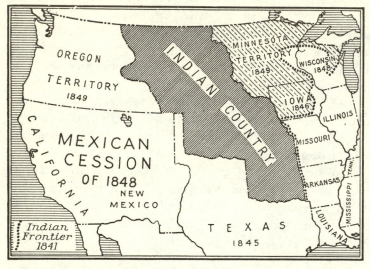

POLITICAL ORGANIZATION OF THE WEST IN 1849 (SHOWING ENCROACH-
MENT ON THE INDIAN COUNTRY SINCE 1841)

scenes. Lines of prairie schooners streaked the horizon, sod houses went up overnight, and bonanza wheat fields were planted. Grasshoppers, cyclones, Indians, claim-jumpers, and bad men were the prairie pests; vigilantes, claims associations, territorial and county governments followed as a sign of order. Beyond the prairies lay the Great Plains, rich in grazing lands. Thither flocked cowmen to open vast ranches or make the Long Drive. Rustlers and sheep wars broke the monotony.

Each advance of the white man impinged on the Indian. New land cessions were demanded. The red man resisted in a long series of wars led by chiefs with picturesque names. Always the Indian had to yield and move to narrower reservations. It was the old story, repeated all the way from the Atlantic to the Pacific — one of America's dark tragedies.

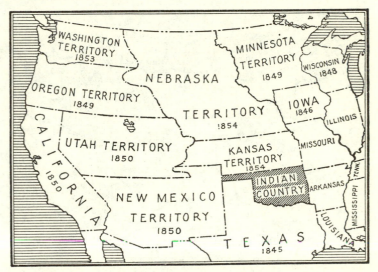

POLITICAL ORGANIZATION OF THE WEST IN 1854 (SHOWING REDUCTION OF THE INDIAN COUNTRY IN 1854)

Settlement in the West created a demand for better means of communication. The Pacific Slope showed signs of secession, and quicker travel was looked to for a remedy. Stagecoach and pony express gave way to the railroad. By 1884 five bands of steel bound the Far West to the East. In greater volume now the people rushed in, and by 1891 the whole Northwest had achieved statehood. Indian Territory was opened, and another commonwealth founded over night.

Meanwhile the Old South was transformed by industry into the New South, and all sections were pervaded by a spirit of national solidarity.

1. The frontier in 1858. The Indian line of 1830; the 95th meridian; settlement beyond the line in 1858 (portions of

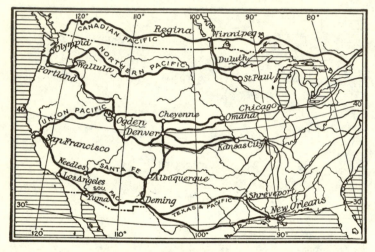

RAILROADS TO THE PACIFIC (1869–1886)

Kansas, Nebraska, Texas, New Mexico, Utah, California, and the Oregon country); political divisions (1860).

2. The mines and the new territories. Gold discoveries in the Rockies (1858–1864) caused the political subdivision of the region; typical scenes; Colorado ("Pikes Peak or bust," 1859; Denver territory, 1859–1861); Nevada (the Comstock Lode; territory erected, 1861; state, 1863); Arizona (placers on Bill Williams Fork, 1862; territory, 1863); Idaho (strikes in Snake River valley, Lewiston, Boise, Owyhee; territory, 1863); Montana

(Missoula, 1861; Bannack City, 1862; Virginia City, 1863; Helena, 1864; territory, 1864); vigilance committees; a demand for order and decency.

3. Prairie farming and the cow country. The prairie farm lands invaded: demand for agricultural lands (new markets, farm machinery, the Homestead Act, immigration); the rage for prairie farming; prairie schooners, grasshoppers, Indians, bad men (Jesse James), vigilance committees, new territories, new states. The cow country opened: grazing lands, great ranches, the Long Drive ("North of '36"), bad men, rustlers, sheep wars, fence wars.

4. Indian resistance. The Indian frontier; country beyond 95th meridian; closed to settlement, 1830–1850; intrusions (trails to Far West, pressure for lands); new cessions; resistance during Civil War (Minnesota, Little Crow), 1862; the Cheyenne War (Black Kettle), 1864; the Southern Sioux War (Red Cloud), 1866; Black Kettle's last raid, 1868; Northern Sioux (Sitting Bull, the Custer massacre), 1876; the Modoc War, 1872–1873; the Nez Percé War, 1877; the Apache War (Cochise and Geronimo), 1860–1886.

5. The transcontinental railroads. Overland mail and pony express; early demand for railroads; official explorations (1853–1855); danger of secession; railroads chartered (land grants, subsidies), 1862–1873; the Union Pacific completed (Stanford, Crocker, Huntington, Hopkins), 1869; others completed by 1884 (Northern Pacific, Santa Fe, Southern Pacific); Canadian Pacific, 1886.

6. The inrush of people and the new states. Numbers; new states (the Dakotas, Montana, Idaho, Wyoming, Washington), 1889–1890; the opening of Indian Territory

(the Dawes Act, 1887; "sooners" and "boomers"); the last of the states (Utah, Oklahoma, Arizona, New Mexico), 1896–1912; the rush to Southern California; over the borders into Canada and Mexico; the arid lands and irrigation projects.

7. The West as a nationalizing force. Settlement on the national domain; national aid (lands, protection, railroads); commerce a nationalizing force; the West and Populism.

8. The New South. Break-up of plantations; industrial development; lumber and turpentine; iron and coal; water power; Northern capital; education; the national spirit.

REQUIRED READING

One of the following:

BEARD, C. A. and M. R. *History of the United States*, 1921 ed., chap. 18; 1929 ed., chap. 20.

FARRAND, MAX. *The Development of the United States*, chap. 12.

FORMAN, S. E. *Our Republic*, 536–542, 621–626.

HARLOW, R. V. *The Growth of the United States*, 572–589.

MARTIN, A. E. *History of the United States*, II, chap. 6.

MORISON, S. E., and COMMAGER, H. S. *Growth of the American Republic*, 652–670 (the passing of the frontier); 671–685 (transportation and its control); 626–631 (the New South).

PAXSON, F. L. *Last American Frontier*.

SPARKS, E. E. *Expansion of the American People*, chap. 30.

REFERENCES

AUSTIN, MARY. *Land of Little Rain*.

BECKER, C. L. *Kansas*. (Turner Essays.)

BRADLEY, G. D. *The Story of the Pony Express*.

BURNS, W. N. *The Saga of Billy the Kid*.

BURNS, W. N. *Tombstone: an Iliad of the Southwest*.

CANNON, C. L. (Editor). *Scout and Ranger, being the Personal Adventures of James Pike of the Texas Rangers in 1859–1860*.

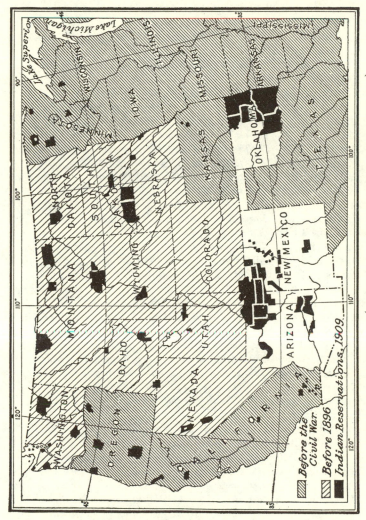

FILLING IN THE FAR WEST (SHOWING NEW STATES BETWEEN 1861 AND 1897)

Before the Civil War
Before 1896
Indian Reservations, 1909.

CAREY, C. H. (Editor). *The Emigrants' Guide to Oregon and California*, by Lansford W. Hastings.

CASSON, H. N. *The Romance of the Reaper.*

CAUGHEY, J. W. (Editor). *The Emigrants' Guide to California*, by Joseph E. Ware.

CLELAND, R. G. *A History of California: the American Period.*

COY, O. C. *Gold Days.*

COY, O. C. *The Humboldt Bay Region, 1850–1875.*

DAGGETT, STUART. *Chapters on the History of the Southern Pacific.*

DAVIS, BRITTON. *The Truth about Gerónimo.*

DAVIS, J. P. *The Union Pacific Railway.*

DONDORE, D. A. *The Prairie and the Making of Middle America.*

ELLISON, JOSEPH. *California and the Nation, 1850–1869.*

FARQUHAR, F. P. (Editor). *Up and Down California in 1860–1864: the Journal of William H. Brewer.*

FOLWELL, W. W. *A History of Minnesota.*

GITTINGER, ROY. *Formation of the State of Oklahoma.*

GOODWIN, C. L. *The Establishment of State Government in California.*

GRINNELL, G. B. *The Story of the Indian.*

HACKER, L. M., and KENDRICK, B. B. *The United States since 1865.*

HAFEN, L. R. R. *Colorado, the Story of a Western Commonwealth.*

HAFEN, L. R. R. (Editor). *The Past and Present of the Pike's Peak Gold Regions*, by Henry Villard.

HANEY, L. H. *A Congressional History of Railways in the United States, 1850–1877.*

HAWORTH, P. L. *The United States in our Own Times.*

HEBARD, G. R. *Washakie: an Account of Indian Resistance to the Covered Wagon and Union Pacific Railroad Invasions of the Territory.*

HOUGH, EMERSON. *The Passing of the Frontier.*

HOUGH, EMERSON. *Story of the Outlaw.*

HUTCHINSON, W. T. *Cyrus Hall McCormick.*

LESLEY, L. B. (Editor). *Uncle Sam's Camels.*

LEWIS, E. R. *America, Nation or Confusion* (immigration).

LOCKWOOD, F. C. *Pioneer Days in Arizona.*

LOMAX, J. A. *Cowboy Songs.*

MEANY, E. S. *History of the State of Washington.*

MITCHELL, BROADUS. *The Industrial Revolution in the South.*

MOODY, JOHN. *The Railroad Builders.*

MOODY, JOHN. *Romance of the Railways.*
OSGOOD, E. S. *The Day of the Cattleman.*
PAXSON, F. L. *History of the American Frontier.*
PAXSON, F. L. *When the West is Gone.*
PHILLIPS, P. C. (Editor). *Scenery of the Plains, Mountains and Mines,* by Franklin Langworthy.
PYLE, J. G. *The Life of James J. Hill.*
RICHARDSON, R. N. *The Comanche Barrier to South Plains Settlement.*
RISTER, C. C. *The Southwestern Frontier, 1865–1881.*
ROBINSON, DOANE. *A Brief History of South Dakota.*
ROLLINS, P. A. *The Cowboy.*
ROOT, F. A., and CONNELLEY, W. E. *The Overland Stage to California.*
RYE, EDGAR. *The Quirt and the Spur.*
SABIN, E. L. *Building the Pacific Railway.*
SCHAFER, JOSEPH. *The Pacific Northwest.*
SHINN, C. H. *Mining Camps.*
SHINN, C. H. *The Story of the Mine.*
SHIPPEE, L. B. *Recent American History.*
SIRINGO, CHARLES A. *Riata and Spur.*
SMALLEY, E. V. *The Northern Pacific Railroad.*
SMITH, C. H. *The Coming of the Russian Mennonites.*
STEPHENSON, G. M. *The Political History of the Public Lands.*
TRIMBLE, W. J. *Mining Advance into the Inland Empire.*
TWAIN, MARK. *Roughing It.*
VAN HISE, C. R. *The Conservation of Natural Resources in the United States.*
VESTAL, STANLEY. *Sitting Bull, Champion of the Sioux: a Biography.*
WARMAN, CY. *The Story of the Railroad.*
WEBB, W. P. *The Great Plains.*
WHITE, S. E. *The Forty-niners.*
WILLARD, J. F., and GOODYKOONTZ, C. B. *Experiments in Colorado Colonization, 1869–1872.*
WILLARD, J. F., and GOODYKOONTZ, C. B. (Editors). *The Trans-Mississippi West.*
WILLIAMS, M. F. *History of the San Francisco Committee of Vigilance of 1851.*

LECTURE LIII. BIG BUSINESS AND NATIONAL CONTROL

Introductory. Political nationality was achieved concurrently with economic nationality. Industries formerly local became continent-wide in scope, so changed was life by the Industrial Revolution — the discovery and invention of new processes and devices and their application to industry. Railways made it possible to settle the Great West, agricultural machinery to exploit the Western lands, the Bessemer process to utilize coal and iron deposits, refrigerator cars to market the fruit products of the Far West and the New South.

Business organization was now reshaped. A multitude of local concerns gave way to units embracing the whole country. The new era bred also a new type of captains of industry — bold, imaginative, self-made men, often ruthless in proportion to their wealth. "Law! What do I care for law? Ain't I got the power?" said Cornelius Vanderbilt. Gould, Hill, Rockefeller, Carnegie, Frick, Stanford, Huntington, Hopkins, and Crocker typify this age.

Among the progeny of big business was monopoly, that entity caricatured as the Octopus. Simple partnerships gave way to vast corporations and trusts. Basic industries became absorbed by a few great concerns, of which the prototype was the Standard Oil Company. By acquiring control of refineries, terminals, pipe lines, and other essential factors, Rockefeller was able to crush out competition and control the entire oil business of the nation.

While monopolies prospered the people grew discontented. They saw the rich growing richer, and the poor poorer. They

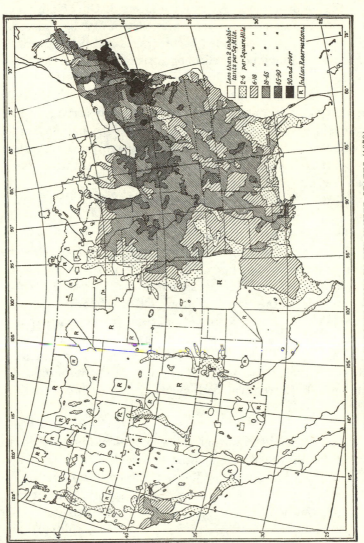

DISTRIBUTION OF POPULATION IN THE UNITED STATES (1870)

saw the nation's resources wasted or misused. Out of individual discontent came class consciousness, shown first by industrial laborers. Unions demanded better wages and better working conditions. Employees relied on strikes and other forms of violence; employers retaliated with lockouts. In the American Federation of Labor separate trades merged their interests in a nation-wide contest. Farmers more slowly arrived at class consciousness, but eventually the sons of the middle border found voice. Then, as Patrons of Husbandry (Grangers) or Populists, they demanded reform in transportation rates, banking, currency, and the abuse of the lobby.

Discontent and class organization had their effect. The old doctrine of laissez faire was replaced by a demand for public control. The Octopus must be curbed, and one by one his members were chained. The first great fight came with the railroads and trusts. For a long time it was a losing battle. But laws "with teeth" were enacted, Roosevelt took up "trust-busting," and the day was won. Other victories followed. Pure-food legislation, conservation, reclamation, restriction of immigration, the establishment of the Bureau of Labor and the Department of Agriculture all are examples of the demand for public control of big business and natural resources. By the end of the century both political and economic nationality had been achieved.

1. The Industrial Revolution. New inventions and their applications: the Bessemer process; development of steam, electrical, and gasoline power; the perfection of the internal-combustion engine; the telephone; the radio; refrigeration; application of these inventions and processes to manufactures, transportation (the railroad), and agricultural machinery on a large scale. These inven-

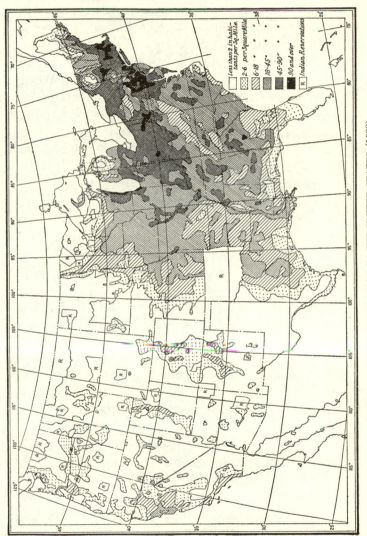

DISTRIBUTION OF POPULATION IN THE UNITED STATES (1880)

Less than 2 inhabitants per Sq. Mile.
2-6 " "
6-18 " "
18-45 " "
45-90 " "
90 and over
R Indian Reservations

tions and their applications made it possible to develop the vast natural resources of the country.

2. Large-scale production. Business formerly small, individualistic, local; reorganized on a national scale (transcontinental railroads, American Express Company, Western Union, Bell Telephone Company, United States Steel Corporation, Standard Oil Company); captains of industry; new type of leader self-made, aggressive, far-seeing (Vanderbilt, Rockefeller, Carnegie, Huntington, Stanford, Crocker, Hill, Harriman); new type of millionaire (railroad, oil, steel "magnates").

3. Monopolies and trusts. New type of business organization (corporations, trusts); corporation yields to monopoly (the Standard Oil Company, Carnegie and steel, the great railroads, agricultural machinery, the Bell Telephone Company, the sugar trust, etc.); abuses of the railroads and monopolies.

4. Discontent and class consciousness. Discontent (hard times, low wages, bad labor conditions, big business and railroads in politics, waste of the public domain); labor organizations (labor class consciousness, unions, better wages and conditions, strikes and lockouts, collective bargaining, the Knights of Labor, the American Federation of Labor); farmers' organizations (agrarian class consciousness; the Patrons of Husbandry (Grangers); demand for reforms in transportation, marketing, banking, credit, currency; Populism); demand for national control of big business and natural resources.

5. Steps toward national control. The fight with the railroads: rebates, pools, passes, lobbying; the Interstate Commerce Act, 1887; the Interstate Commerce Commission; lack of power to fix rates; Roosevelt; the Hepburn

Act (1906); power to fix rates; the Adamson Act
(1916); power to determine wages; Federal operation
(McAdoo), 1917. Regulation of trusts: the Sherman
Anti-Trust Law (a law without teeth), 1890; Roosevelt
and the prosecution of the trusts. Pure-food legislation
(Bureau of Animal Husbandry): Oleomargarine Act
(1886); Meat Inspection Act (1890); inspection of
drugs etc. Conservation and reclamation: clamor
against railroad grants; revision of public-land policy;
act of 1891; reservation of reservoir sites; forests,
mineral lands. National recognition of the labor question: Bureau of Labor; Arbitration Act (1888);
Adamson Act (1916). National immigration policy:
demand for restriction; Chinese Exclusion Act (1882);
Immigration Act of 1883; Contract Labor Act (1885);
recent immigration policy; Alien Land Act. Federal aid
to agriculture: land-grant colleges (1862, 1890); experiment stations (1887); Department of Agriculture; tariff
revision.

REQUIRED READING

One of the following:

FARRAND, MAX. *The Development of the United States*, chap. 13
  or 15.
HARLOW, R. V. *The Growth of the United States*, 590–598 (Big Business); 599–604 (organized labor); 622 ff. (the Granger movement);
  640–647 (antitrust legislation; Populism); 671–677 (Big Business
  triumphant).
MARTIN, A. E. *History of the United States*, II, chap. 20.
MORISON, S. E. *The Oxford History of the United States*, chap. 57
  or 58.
MORISON, S. E., and COMMAGER, H. S. *Growth of the American Republic*,
  686–701 (the economic revolution); 702–723 (labor and immigration).

MUZZEY, D. S. *The United States of America*, II, chap. 2, 4, or 7.
PEASE, T. C. *The United States*, chap. 28, 29, 32, or 33.
SCHLESINGER, A. M. *Political and Social History of the United States*,
chap. 15 or 16.

REFERENCES

BEARD, C. A. *Contemporary American History.*
BEARD, C. A. and M. R. *The Rise of American Civilization.*
BEARD, M. R. *A Short History of the American Labor Movement.*
BISHOP, J. B. *Theodore Roosevelt and his Time.*
BOGART, E. L. *Economic History of the United States.*
BOWERS, C. G. *Beveridge and the Progressive Era.*
BUCK, S. J. *The Agrarian Crusade.*
BUCK, S. J. *The Granger Movement.*
CARLTON, F. T. *The History and Problems of Organized Labor.*
CASSON, H. N. *The Romance of Steel.*
CROLY, HERBERT. *Marcus Alonzo Hanna.*
DEWEY, D. R. *National Problems.*
DE WITT, B. P. *The Progressive Movement.*
DODD, W. E. *Woodrow Wilson and his Work.*
FAULKNER, H. U. *The Quest for Social Justice, 1898–1914.*
HACKER, L. M., and KENDRICK, B. B. *The United States since 1865.*
HART, A. B. *National Ideals Historically Traced.*
HAYNES, F. E. *Third Party Movements since the Civil War.*
HENDERSON, G. C. *The Federal Trade Commission.*
HENDRICK, B. J. *The Age of Big Business.*
HENDRICK, B. J. *The Life of Andrew Carnegie.* 2 vols.
HICKS, J. D. *The Populist Revolt.*
HOVEY, CARL. *The Life Story of J. Pierpont Morgan.*
HOWLAND, HAROLD. *Theodore Roosevelt and his Time.*
JONES, ELIOT. *Principles of Railway Transportation.*
JOSEPHSON, MATTHEW. *The Robber Barons; the Great American Capi-
talists, 1861–1901.*
LAUCK, W. J. *The Causes of the Panic of 1893.*
LAUGHLIN, J. L. *History of Bimetallism in the United States.*
LINGLEY, C. R. *Since the Civil War*, chaps. 3, 8, 9, 11, 14, 22.
MCMURRY, D. L. *Coxey's Army: a Study of the Industrial Army
Movement of 1894.*
MALIN, J. C. *An Interpretation of Recent American History.*

MERRIAM, C. E. *American Political Ideas.*

MOODY, JOHN. *The Masters of Capital.*

MOODY, JOHN. *The Railroad Builders.*

MOTE, C. H. *Industrial Arbitration.*

NEVINS, ALLAN. *Grover Cleveland: a Study in Courage.*

OBERHOLTZER, E. P. *A History of the United States since the Civil War.* 4 vols.

OBERHOLTZER, E. P. *Jay Cooke, the Financier of the Civil War.*

OGG, F. A. *National Progress.*

ORTH, S. P. *The Armies of Labor.*

PAXSON, F. L. *The New Nation,* chaps. 10, 18.

PAXSON, F. L. *Recent History of the United States.*

PAXSON, F. L. *When the West is Gone.*

PRINGLE, H. F. *Theodore Roosevelt: a Biography.*

RIEGEL, R. E. *The Story of the Western Railroads.*

SCHLESINGER, A. M. *The Rise of the City, 1878–1898.*

SHAW, ALBERT. *A Cartoon History of Roosevelt's Career.*

SHIPPEE, L. D. *Recent American History.*

SPARKS, E. E. *National Development.*

STANWOOD, EDWIN. *Tariff Controversies.*

STEPHENSON, N. W. *Nelson W. Aldrich, a Leader in American Politics.*

TARBELL, I. M. *The History of the Standard Oil Company.*

THOMPSON, HOLLAND. *The Age of Invention.*

TURNER, F. J. *Since the Foundation.*

VAN METRE, T. W. *Economic History of the United States,* chaps. 21, 24, 25.

WEYL, W. E. *The New Democracy.*

WRIGHT, C. D. *The Industrial Evolution of the United States.*

LECTURE LIV. ON THE THRESHOLD OF EMPIRE

Introductory. At the turn of the century the United States stepped upon the threshold of empire, extending her domain beyond the mainland area into the Pacific and the Caribbean. Unpremeditated, perhaps, the event was not sudden; it had been long preparing; it was just another case of the flag following traders and missionaries. The cry of "Eastward Ho!" was raised by merchants in Boston in the eighteenth century. Stout-hearted missionaries braved the soup kettles of the Pacific islands. Consular and treaty relations followed. A leading incident was the opening of trade with Japan. Nippon was then conservative, but where Biddle failed Perry succeeded. By "concert of power" the United States coöperated with European nations in establishing trade relations with Japan. In Samoa the prelude to concert was discord, and war with Germany was narrowly avoided there. By 1890 American traders operated in fifty or more islands of the Western Sea.

The Hawaiian Islands were a special focus of American interest, for they are an outpost of California. Other nations flocked thither, but Americans became dominant. Boston sails dotted the harbors; missionaries converted kings and entered politics. Official relations followed, and when French and English interfered, the Monroe Doctrine was read to them. The conquest of California accentuated American interest in Hawaiian sugar plantations. A movement for annexation failed, but reciprocity was carried over the stubborn opposition of Louisiana sugar men, and Pearl Harbor was acquired by treaty. Now the Lord greatly prospered Hawaii, the California

314

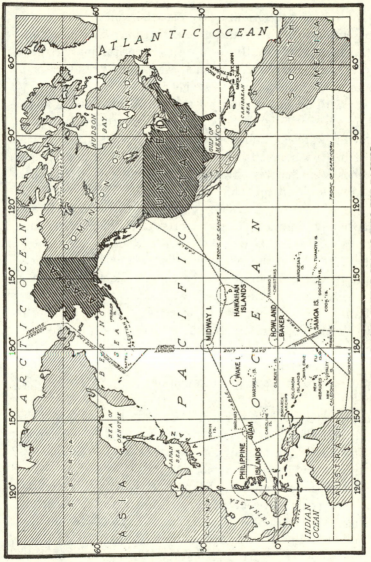

THE ENTRY OF THE UNITED STATES INTO THE PACIFIC

sugar kings, and the grandsons of early missionaries. Annexation sentiment revived, and a revolt against the queen furnished an opportunity. In the uprising American marines were in evidence; Dole, an American, was made president of a republic, and annexation was sought.

War with Spain now brought together United States interests in the Pacific and the Caribbean. Southern politicians had long watched Cuba. American filibusters had participated in Cuban revolts. In a new revolution there Spain's methods were harshly criticized. McKinley protested, the *Maine* was blown up, and war declared. "We'll set Cuba free," the slogan rang. Dewey captured Manila, Hawaii was immediately annexed, Cuban ports were blockaded, and Cervera's fleet destroyed. Roosevelt's Rough Riders coöperated with Shafter in Cuba, and Miles conquered Porto Rico. Unpreparedness and its consequences were shocking, but they were more than offset by Spain's weak resistance. The treaty of Paris left the United States an empire, with Cuba, Porto Rico, the Philippines, and Hawaii to dispose of or to govern. She now found herself a world power, with new responsibilities in the Far East and the Caribbean. She had launched her ship of state on the sea of world politics.

1. Early interests in the Pacific. Traders and missionaries; early official relations (consular agents, commercial treaties); the opening of Japan (Perry); the international conflict in the Samoan Islands.
2. Interest in the Hawaiian Islands. Relations before 1850: commercial, missionary, official; missionary influence in native government; the Monroe Doctrine applied (1842–1849). Provisional cession to United States (1851); uncompleted treaty of annexation (1854). Reciprocity:

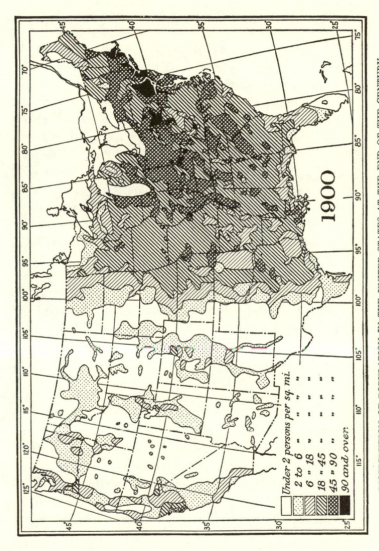

Under 2 persons per sq. mi.
2 to 6 " " "
6 " 18 " " "
18 " 45 " " "
45 " 90 " " "
90 and over: " "

1900

DISTRIBUTION OF POPULATION IN THE UNITED STATES AT THE END OF THE CENTURY

increased interest in the Islands; reciprocity proposals; reciprocity versus annexation; proposed treaties of 1855, 1863, 1867; the treaty of 1875–1876 (the "soul of the treaty"); prosperity in the Islands; efforts to abrogate the treaty; Southern sugar interests; treaty renewed (1887); cession of Pearl Harbor. The republic and annexation: Queen Liliuokalani (absolutist reaction); the uprising (1893); use of United States marines; provisional government; Dole president; treaty of annexation drawn; Cleveland's attempt to restore the queen; treaty withdrawn from Senate; Blount's inquiry; Dole refuses to yield; Congressional inquiry. Annexation completed (1897–1898): the cable controversy with England; new treaty opposed; joint resolution (1898); .effect of Dewey's victory (1898); annexation.

3. The War with Spain and the acquisition of island possessions. The outbreak of the war: early United States interest in Cuba; annexation prevented by sectional quarrels; revolutions in Cuba (1868–1878, 1895–1898); Weyler and reconcentrado camps; sympathy in the United States; protest to Spain (1897); destruction of the *Maine* (February 15, 1898), ultimatum (March 27, 1898); McKinley recommends forcible intervention (April 11); war declared (April 25). Dewey at Manila: the presence of foreign warships; the German squadron; Cámara's fleet turns back; Merritt's expedition from San Francisco (Guam); surrender of Manila. The Cuban campaign: the blockade; "bottling Cervera's fleet" (Hobson); the army in Cuba (Shafter, San Juan, Santiago); destruction of Spain's fleet (Schley); Porto Rico occupied (Miles, San Juan). The Treaty of Paris: Cuba, Porto Rico, Guam, the Philippines.

4. The United States becomes a world power. Cuban policy; policy in Porto Rico; in the Philippines (Aguinaldo, government of the Philippines, the Philippine Commission); annexation of Hawaii (policy in); the "open door" in Asia (European policy in China, spheres of influence and tariff, Kay's "open door" policy); the Boxer Rebellion (the United States and the "integrity of China"); influence of United States in Russo-Japanese War (Treaty of Portsmouth); the Japanese immigration question; business concessions in the Orient; increase of government interest in world politics.

REQUIRED READING

One of the following:

BEARD, C. A. and M. R. *History of the United States*, 1921 ed., chap. 20; 1929 ed., chap. 22.

FARRAND, MAX. *The Development of the United States*, chap. 16.

FORMAN, S. E. *Our Republic*, 653–658, 677–693.

HARLOW, R. V. *The Growth of the United States*, 656–657 (the Pacific islands); 678–690 (the Spanish war); 691–699 (beginnings of imperialism).

MARTIN, A. E. *History of the United States*, II, chaps. 16–17.

MORISON, S. E., and COMMAGER, H. S. *Growth of the American Republic*, 799–810 (the Spanish war and imperialism).

MUZZEY, D. S. *The United States of America*, II, chap. 5.

SPARKS, E. E. *Expansion of the American People*, chap. 36.

REFERENCES

BARROWS, D. P. *A History of the Philippines.*

CALDWELL, R. G. *James A. Garfield, Party Chieftain.*

CALLAHAN, J. M. *American Relations in the Pacific and the Far East, 1784–1900.*

CHADWICK, F. E. *The Spanish-American War.*

DARLING, A. B. (Editor). *The Public Papers of Francis G. Newlands.*

DAVIS, O. K. *Our Conquests in the Pacific.*

DENNETT, TYLER. *Americans in Eastern Asia.*

DENNETT, TYLER. *John Hay: from Poetry to Politics.*

DENNIS, A. L. P. *Adventures in American Diplomacy.*

ETHERTON, P. T., and TILTMAN, H. H. *The Pacific, a Forecast.*

FISH, C. R. *The Path of Empire.*

GREENBIE, SYDNEY and MARGERY. *Gold of Ophir.*

HACKER, L. M., and KENDRICK, B. B. *The United States since 1865.*

HORNBECK, O. K. *Contemporary Politics in the Far East.*

LATOURETTE, K. S. *The Development of China.*

MILLIS, WALTER. *The Martial Spirit: a Study of our War with Spain.*

MORISON, S. E. *Maritime History of Massachusetts.*

PAXSON, F. L. *Recent History of the United States.*

PAXSON, F. L. *When the West is Gone.*

PRINGLE, H. F. *Theodore Roosevelt: a Biography.*

ROBINSON, WILLIAM A. *Thomas B. Reed, Parliamentarian.*

ROOSEVELT, NICHOLAS. *The Restless Pacific.*

TREAT, P. J. *Diplomatic Relations between the United States and Japan, 1853–1895.* 2 vols.

TREAT, P. J. *The Far East.*

TYLER, A. F. *The Foreign Policy of James G. Blaine.*

VINACKE, H. M. *The Far East in Modern Times.*

WILLIAMS, E. T. *China Yesterday and Today.*

AMERICAN NEIGHBORS: DEVELOPMENT AND INTERRELATIONS

LECTURE LV. THE FEDERATION AND EXPANSION OF CANADA

Introductory. While the United States was achieving solidarity and power, the British provinces to the north were being welded into the Dominion of Canada. By 1850 these provinces had won responsible government. Now the tide of federation set strongly in. Union was prompted by community of interests, need of commercial coöperation, and fear of annexation to the United States. Obstacles were met in local hostilities and suspicion. Federation found able champions and determined opponents. In the Quebec Conference(1864)a plan of federation was drawn. Home government approved, and by the British North America Act the Dominion of Canada was founded (1867). The idea of federation came from the United States, but in details the constitutions are different. The Dominion is a centralized federation, with responsible government. One by one the older provinces joined. "A mari usque ad mare" became the slogan. Hudson's Bay Company relinquished its vast jurisdiction in the West, Manitoba and British Columbia entered, and the federation did indeed reach from sea to sea.

The loosely knit Dominion was now welded by transcontinental railroads and the development of the West. European immigrants thronged, Americans flocked across the border, and new prairie provinces were formed. Vancouver, the Canadian Pacific terminal, became a boom town; new railroads built up more northern cities in British Columbia, and mining rushes developed the Far Northwest. Growing rapidly, the Dominion now has a population of nearly ten millions. Culturally Canada combines the influences of an old French stock, close touch with England and the United States, and frontier experience. The World War stimulated Canadian loyalism on the one hand and British conciliation on the other. Canada now has equal membership with England in the British Commonwealth. A fine sentiment binds her to the Empire, but she is essentially an independent nation.

The interrelations of Canada and the United States have always been close, and their development has been in many ways parallel. By 1846 the old boundary questions had been adjusted. The mid-century was often disturbed by annexation talk that was seldom dangerous. For more than a decade reciprocity facilitated mutual commerce; then it was abrogated by the United States. The Civil War and Fenian raids caused friction. Fisheries and the Bering Sea were bones of contention; Blaine enjoyed twisting the British lion's tail; but eventually these disputes were amicably settled by arbitration. Partly in retaliation, but chiefly as a nationalist policy, Canada established a protective tariff. When Laurier and Taft tried to end it Laurier fell. All in all, with their common boundaries unfortified for a century, Canada and the United States have given the world a splendid example of helpful neighborliness.

1. Analogies and interrelations between Canada and the United States. Influence of American settlement; stages of frontier development; early particularism; the struggle for unification; the Dominion welded by railroads and western settlement; protective tariff and nationalism.

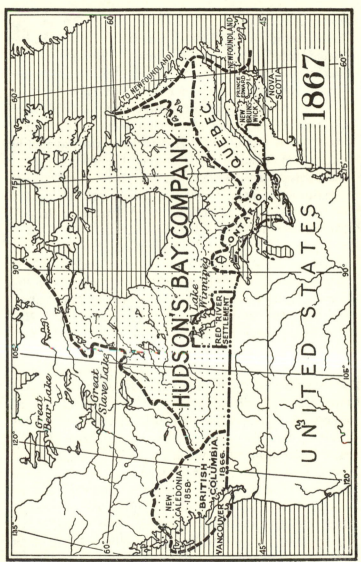

CANADA ON THE EVE OF CONFEDERATION (1867)

2. The movement for federation (1860–1873). Causes: political disturbances; fear of annexation to the United States; need of commercial union; expiration of reciprocity treaty with United States (1866). Obstacles: local jealousies; quarrels of French and English; Radicals and Liberals; lack of communication. Federation effected: leadership of Macdonald and Cartier, Tupper and Tilley; opposition by Howe; federation favored by imperial government; the Quebec Conference (1864); the British North America Act of 1867; the Canadian constitution (a centralized federation, responsible government); resistance of the Maritime Provinces (Howe); Newfoundland still outside the Dominion.

3. The Northwest brought into the union. Two centers of population; Red River (early history, Selkirk's colony, Winnipeg); Pacific Coast (Hudson's Bay Company; Victoria; the mining boom of 1858 in the Fraser Valley; the Cariboo Trail; provinces of Vancouver and New Caledonia; united into British Columbia, 1867); Hudson's Bay Company rights purchased (1869); Manitoba and British Columbia enter the union (1870–1871).

4. The Dominion welded by the railroads (1882–1914). The Canadian Pacific in politics (1867–1880); Macdonald and Smith; J. J. Hill; government land grants; European capital; Winnipeg reached (1882); Vancouver (1886); later transcontinental railroads.

5. Development of the Northwest (1882–1914). The prairie region: the early boom; growth of Winnipeg; depression and slow growth; competition of western United States lands; the great boom of 1893 (immigration policy, land policy); American and British immigrants; numbers (400,000 in 1900; 1,300,000 in 1910); Saskatche-

wan and Alberta provinces added. British Columbia
(1886–1914): growth of Vancouver; British Columbia
an isolated province; British character; Asiatic connec-
tions; new cities developed by new railroads; the Grand
Trunk Pacific; the Canadian Northern. The northern
jurisdictions: Yukon (Dawson); Northwest Territories.
6. Relations with the United States. Boundary settlements;
movement for annexation (short-lived), 1849; reciprocity in trade (relation to the slavery question),
1854–1866; relations during the Civil War; Canada
friendly to North at first; changed attitude; friction
after the war (reciprocity ended; Fenian raids, 1865–
1870; fisheries and Bering Sea questions; "twisting the
British lion's tail"); arbitration; Canada's protective-
tariff policy; a national movement; depression after
1873; anti-United States feeling; the tariff of 1879;
carried by Conservatives (Macdonald); maintained by
Liberals (1896–1911); reciprocity measures of Laurier
and Taft (1911); defeated; a declaration of anti-
American and national sentiment; failure of new annexation movement (hard times, Goldwin Smith), cir.
1890.
7. The Dominion of Canada in the British Commonwealth:
autonomous; an international entity.

REQUIRED READING

One of the following:

BRADLEY, A. G. *Canada*, chap. 3, 8, or 9.
COLQUHOUN, A. H. U. *The Fathers of Confederation*, chap. 6 or 13.
SKELTON, O. D. *The Canadian Dominion*, chap. 3.
SKELTON, O. D. *The Day of Sir Wilfrid Laurier*, chaps. 6, 10, 12.
WITTKE, CARL. *A History of Canada*, chap. 17, 18, or 27.

REFERENCES

BORDEN, SIR ROBERT. *Canada in the Commonwealth: from Conflict to Co-operation.*

BOURINOT, J. G. *Canada under British Rule, 1760–1905.*

BRADLEY, A. G. *Canada.*

BRADY, ALEXANDER. *Canada,* in The Modern World Series.

BRYCE, GEORGE. *A Short History of the Canadian People.*

BURPEE, L. J. *Sandford Fleming, Empire Builder.*

CHAMBERS, E. J. *The Unexploited West.*

COLQUHOUN, A. H. U. *The Fathers of Confederation.*

CORBETT, P. E., and SMITH, H. A. *Canada and World Politics: a Study of the Constitutional and International Relations of the British Empire.*

CURREY, C. H. *British Colonial Policy, 1783–1915.*

DAVID, L. O. *Histoire du Canada depuis la confédération, 1867–1887.*

DAWSON, R. M. *Constitutional Issues in Canada, 1900–1931.*

DECELLES, A. D. *Laurier et son temps.*

DENISON, G. T. *The Struggle for Imperial Unity.*

DEWEY, A. G. *The Dominions and Diplomacy: the Canadian Contribution.*

DUNNING, W. A. *The British Empire and the United States.*

GRANT, W. L. *The Tribune of Nova Scotia.*

GRESWELL, W. P. *History of the Dominion of Canada.*

HALL, W. P. *Empire to Commonwealth.*

HAYDON, A. L. *The Riders of the Plains.*

HOPKINS, J. C. *Progress of Canada in the Century.*

HURST, SIR C. B., and others. *Great Britain and the Dominions.*

INNIS, H. A. *A History of the Canadian Pacific Railway.*

KEENLEYSIDE, H. L. *Canada and the United States.*

KEITH, A. B. *The Constitutional Law of the British Dominions.*

KEITH, A. B. *Responsible Government in the Dominions* (Revised Edition). 2 vols.

KENNEDY, W. P. M. *The Constitution of Canada.*

LARSON, L. M. *England and the British Commonwealth.*

LAUT, A. C. *The Cariboo Trail.*

LEWIS, JOHN. *George Brown.*

LONGSTRETH, T. M. *The Silent Force: Scenes from the Life of the Mounted Police of Canada.*

LOWELL, A. L., and HALL, H. D. *The British Commonwealth of Nations.*
MCARTHUR, DUNCAN. *History of Canada.*
MACBETH, R. G. *Sir Augustus Nanton: a Biography.*
MACBETH, R. G. *Policing the Plains.*
MCINNES, TOM. *Oriental Occupation of British Columbia.*
MARKHAM, C. R. *The Lands of Silence.*
MARTIN, CHESTER. *Empire and Commonwealth.*
MORISON, S. E. *The Oxford History of the United States.*
MORRIS, K. *The Story of the Canadian Pacific Railway.*
MUNRO, W. B. *American Influences on Canadian Government.*
MUNRO, W. B. *Canada and British North America.*
NATHAN, MANFRED. *Empire Government: an Outline of the System Prevailing in the British Commonwealth of Nations.*
NEWTON, A. P., and EWING, J. *The British Empire since 1783.*
POPE, JOSEPH. *The Day of Sir John Macdonald.*
ROBERTS, C. G. D. *A History of Canada.*
SKELTON. O. D. *The Canadian Dominion.*
SKELTON, O. D. *The Railway Builders.*
SMITH, GOLDWIN. *Canada and the Canadian Question.*
SMITH, WILLIAM. *Political Leaders of Upper Canada.*
TALBOT, F. A. *The Canadian Pacific Railway.*
THOMPSON, NORMAN, and EDGAR, J. H. *Canadian Railway Development from the Earliest Times.*
TROTTER, R. G. *The British Empire-Commonwealth.*
TROTTER, R. G. *Canadian Confederation.*
WALLACE, W. S. *Sir John Macdonald.*
WHATES, H. R. *Canada, the New Nation.*
WILLISON, J. S. *Sir Wilfrid Laurier and the Liberal Party.*
WOOD, WILLIAM. *All Afloat.*
Cambridge History of the British Empire, VI (Canada and Newfoundland).

LECTURE LVI. THE RISE OF THE ABC POWERS

Introductory. Not alone in the United States and Canada have consolidation and expansion been the keynote of recent development; parts of Hispanic America have been traveling rapidly along the same road. The last half-century has been remarkable for the rise of Argentina, Brazil, and Chile. Uruguay, though small, has shown the same tendencies. These countries have all made steady progress toward stable government. In them the age of turbulence and dictators seems to have passed; constitutional succession to the presidency and constitutional government have become matters of practice as well as of theory.

Brazil was the first to acquire stability. Slavery was finally abolished in 1888, and in the next year the Republic was established. Subsequent crises have been successfully passed. With a population of over thirty millions and vast extent and resources, Brazil is the second power in America. Argentina, after 1852, underwent a long struggle between Buenos Aires and the provinces, and a war with Paraguay. Patagonia was subdued, crises weathered, and political stability finally established. To Chile the War of the Pacific gave control of rich nitrate beds at the expense of Peru and Bolivia. Since 1891 Chile has had relatively stable government, notable for its parliamentary system. Boundary disputes with Argentina have been adjusted, and a trans-Andean railroad has connected Chile with Buenos Aires and the Atlantic. Uruguay since 1897 has moved steadily toward political stability.

328

Aided by foreign immigration and capital all these countries have experienced tremendous material progress in recent years. Italians, Spaniards, and Germans have come to them by millions to make their homes. Railroads, plantations, nitrate works, mines, and oil wells have been developed on a large scale by English and German capital. Since the World War North American capital has played an increasingly large rôle. Indexes of progress are the great modern cities of Buenos Aires, Rio de Janeiro, and Santiago. Cultural progress has followed material advancement. Public-school systems have been established. Universities are being modernized, with strong faculties especially in medicine, law, and engineering. In international law South Americans have won especial distinction. Some of the great newspapers are equal to the best in the world. In art, architecture, and music, Hispanic America now as always leads English America. Historians and literary men of high rank are not lacking. As members of the Pan-American Congresses, the Hague Tribunal, the Paris Peace Conference, and the League of Nations, the A B C powers have begun to play a part in world politics.

1. The advanced and the retarded countries. Rise of the
   A B C powers (Argentina, Brazil, Chile) during the past
   half-century; Uruguay; retardation of other states;
   fundamental differences (race elements, latitude, economic opportunities, European immigration).
2. General features of development. Advance to stable
   government (age of turbulence and dictatorships passed,
   constitutional succession to presidency, constitutional
   government); material progress (aided by foreign immigration and capital); growth of population, industries,
   cities; cultural advance; influence in world affairs.

3. Brazil. First to acquire stability; the empire; advantage of deferring republic; four great movements in recent development. The abolition of slavery (1871–1888): decree of Princess Isabella; havoc with coffee plantations in south; place of negroes taken by Italians. Change from empire to republic (1889): weakening of the empire (loss of support of landholders through abolition of slavery; hostility of clergy over Masonic question and patronage; republican propaganda; Jardim; the revolt of the army, 1889); Pedro II banished; the United States of Brazil (constitution similar to United States, ultra-democratic); Civil War (1924). Economic progress: population; immigration (Italian, German, Japanese); railroads; waterways; commerce; cities (Rio de Janeiro, Bahia, Pernambuco, São Paulo); products (coffee, sugar, cotton, cattle, rubber, timber, etc.). Cultural progress: Brazil's contribution to international law.

4. Argentina. Consolidation and stable government: overthrow of Rosas (1852); new federal constitution (1853); struggle of provinces with Buenos Aires (Federalists and Centralists, Urquiza, Mitre, Roca); educational and industrial progress under Sarmiento; Buenos Aires federalized (1880); constitutional succession. Territorial expansion (1870–1880): conquest of Patagonia; General Roca; boundary dispute with Chile; arbitration (the Christ of the Andes). Material progress: population; immigration (Italian, Spanish, English, German); foreign capital (English, United States, German); railroads, docks, plantations, ranches; cities (Buenos Aires nearly 2,000,000); crisis of 1890–1900 (speculation, national debt); restored prosperity, peace. Cultural progress: education, newspapers, art, general culture.

THE AMERICAS IN 1928

5. Chile. Stable government since civil war of 1890 (presidential autocracy versus parliamentary aristocracy, Balmaceda versus Congress). Territorial expansion: conquest of the Araucanians; the War of the Pacific; causes (nitrate beds; Tacna and Arica; concessions by all governments; Chilean concessionaries driven out by Bolivia and Peru, 1873); war of 1879–1883 (Peru and Bolivia defeated by Chile, disputed area falls to Chile); Balmaceda and civil war (1886–1891). Growth of army and navy (army Prussian, navy English). Material prosperity: population; immigration (Italian, German); cities (Santiago, Valparaiso, Concepción, Antofagasta); trans-Andean railroads. Cultural advancement: schools, newspapers, writers.

REQUIRED READING

One of the following:

JAMES, H. G., and MARTIN, P. A. *The Republics of Latin America,* 110–136 (Brazil), 158–169 (Argentina), or 195–207 (Chile).

RIPPY, J. F. *Historical Evolution of Hispanic America,* chap. 12 (selections).

ROBERTSON, W. S. *History of the Latin-American Nations* (selected portions).

SHEPHERD, W. R. *Hispanic Nations of the New World,* chaps. 7–9.

SHEPHERD, W. R. *Latin America,* passim (see index under Argentina, Brazil, Chile).

SWEET, W. W. *History of Latin America* (selections).

WARSHAW, JACOB. *The New Latin America,* chap. 8 or 11.

WEBSTER, HUTTON. *History of Latin America,* 138–149 or chap. 9.

WILGUS, A. C. *A History of Hispanic America,* chaps. 22–26 (selections).

REFERENCES

THE HISPANIC-AMERICAN NATIONS AND THEIR INTERRELATIONS

Mexico, Central America, and the Caribbean

ASPINALL, A. E. *The Pocket Guide to the West Indies.*

BAERLEIN, HENRY. *Mexico, the Land of Unrest.*

BANCROFT, H. H. *History of Central America.*

BANCROFT, H. H. *History of Mexico.*
BLAKESLEE, G. H. (Editor). *Mexico and the Caribbean.*
BONSAL, STEPHEN. *The American Mediterranean.*
BUNAU-VARILLA, PHILIPPE. *Panama.*
DOMVILLE-FIFE, C. W. *Guatemala and the States of Central America.*
ENOCK, C. R. *The Republics of Central and South America.*
FISKE, A. K. *The West Indies.*
FORTIER, ALCÉE, and FICKLEN, J. R. *Central America and Mexico.*
FRANCK, H. A. *Tramping through Mexico, Guatemala, and Honduras.*
HASBROUCK, L. S. *Mexico, from Cortés to Carranza.*
JONES, C. L. *Caribbean Interests of the United States.*
KEANE, A. H. *Central and South America.*
LATANÉ, J. H. *The United States and Latin America.*
MUNRO, D. G. *The Five Republics of Central America.*
NOLL, A. H. *From Empire to Republic.*
NOLL, A. H. *Short History of Mexico.*
OBER, F. A. *Our West Indian Neighbors.*
O'SHAUGHNESSY, E. L. *Diplomatic Days.*
SCHOENRICH, OTTO. *Santo Domingo.*
SELVA, SILVIO. *The United States and Central America.*
VERRILL, A. H. *The Book of the West Indies.*

South America in general

AKERS, C. E. *History of South America.*
BROWN, H. W. *Latin America.*
COESTER, A. L. *Literary History of South America.*
COOPER, C. S. *Latin America.*
DENNIS, W. J. *Documentary History of the Tacna-Arica Dispute.*
GARCÍA CALDERÓN, FRANCISCO. *Latin America, its Rise and Progress.*
KOEBEL, W. H. *South America.*
REYES, RAFAEL. *The Two Americas.*
ROSS, E. A. *South of Panama.*
WARSHAW, JACOB. *The New Latin America.*
Cambridge Modern History, XII, chap. 21.

SEPARATE SOUTH-AMERICAN COUNTRIES

BÁEZ, CECILIO. *Resumen de la Historia del Paraguay.*
BLANCO ACEVEDO, PABLO. *Historia de la República Oriental del Uruguay.*

BOURGADE LA DARDYE, EMMANUEL DE. *Paraguay: the Land and its People.*

BOX, P. H. *The Origins of the Paraguayan War.*

CHAPMAN, C. E. *A History of the Cuban Republic.*

CLEMENCEAU, G. E. B. *South America Today.*

COOPER, C. S. *The Brazilians and their Country.*

CURTIS, W. E. *Venezuela.*

DENIS, PIERRE. *Brazil.*

ELLIOT, G. F. S. *Chile.*

ELLIOTT, L. E. *Brazil To-day and To-morrow.*

HAMMERTON, J. A. *The Real Argentine.*

HANCOCK, A. U. *A History of Chile.*

HERMANO, DAMASCENAS. *Ensayo de Historia Patria.*

HERVEY, M. H. *Dark Days in Chile.*

HUDSON, W. H. *The Purple Land.*

KIRKPATRICK, F. A. *A History of the Argentine Republic.*

KOEBEL, W. H. *Paraguay.*

LA GUARDIA, G. G. B. and C. G. B. *Argentina: Legend and History.*

LEVENE, RICARDO. *Lecciones de Historia Argentina.*

MARKHAM, CLEMENTS. *History of Peru.*

MARTÍNEZ, A. B., and LEWANDOWSKI, MAURICE. *The Argentine in the Twentieth Century.*

ORDÓÑEZ LÓPEZ, MANUEL, and CRESPO, L. S. *Bosquejo de Historia de Bolivia.*

PENNINGTON, A. S. *The Argentine Republic.*

REID, W. A. *Bolivia, the Heart of a Continent.*

RIBEIRO, JOÃO. *Historia de Brazil.*

SQUIER, E. G. *Peru.*

TEJERA, FELIPE. *Manual de Historia de Venezuela.*

VERDÍA, L. P. *Compendio de la Historia de México.*

VILLACORTA, C. J. A. *Historia de la América Central.*

WASHBURN, C. A. *History of Paraguay.*

WRIGHT, M. R. *Bolivia.*

WRIGHT, M. R. *The New Brazil.*

WRIGHT, M. R. *The Republic of Chile.*

ZAHM, J. A. *Following the Conquistadores.*

Lecture LVII. Tropical and Caribbean Spanish America

Introductory. "The first shall be last." In the tropics and around the shores of the Caribbean, Spanish America has made less progress than in the temperate regions. The areas which were most developed in early colonial days are now the most retarded. The reasons are plain. The Spaniards were first attracted to areas inhabited by advanced native peoples — the Mayas, the Aztecs, the Chibchas, and the Incas — or to the Spanish Main, which was easily accessible from the West Indies center.

The factor which then made most for progress has now become a hindrance. The advanced peoples were so numerous, their civilization so high, and their labor so profitable that they were not exterminated. Instead the Spaniards fused with them. As a result, population in those regions is still largely mestizo or Indian. If one counts mixed and full bloods, in Ecuador the population is 66 per cent Indian, in Peru 60 per cent, and in Bolivia 50 per cent. In Venezuela and Colombia, where the population is 15 or 20 per cent Indian, there is also a large Negro element. In contrast with these countries Brazil has only about 10 per cent of Indians, and Argentina and Uruguay practically none at all. In the tropical and Caribbean countries, therefore, the Indian constitutes "the white man's burden." There a small European element is serving as a leaven to raise a large native population to European standards of civilization. Geographic influence also has its part. Tropical climates are not conducive to a high display of energy. Much of the region is rough mountain country, and there are vast stretches of arid plain, tropical forest, and malarial swamp.

In political features the Caribbean and tropical countries are still particularistic and lack national cohesion. In most of them the period of dictatorship has continued longer than was the case farther south. They still often change rulers by means of revolutions instead of elections. Colombia, for example, has had twenty-seven civil wars. Sometimes, but by no means always, the revolutions are bloody. There are frequent changes of constitutions, Ecuador having had six in twenty-five years. In these countries the Church is frequently in politics, and in García Moreno Ecuador had a clerical dictator. Some of the dictators have been benevolent; others selfish. Some have resigned peaceably; others have waited to be overthrown. It is this political instability which has enabled the United States more and more to intervene in Central America and the island republics.

Economically also, these countries are retarded. Industries are still largely in the extractive stage. But all the countries offer great possibilities and promise. Indeed, the backwardness is only relative, and some of these regions are now attracting foreign capital at an unprecedented rate. In Central America United States capital has long been dominant, and everywhere since the World War it is playing a constantly larger part.

1. "The first shall be last." The first regions occupied: West Indies (trade, plantations); Central America, Mexico, Peru, Bolivia (advanced natives, gold, silver); Venezuela, Colombia (pearl fisheries, slaves); Paraguay (settled Indians, missions). Some of these regions now retarded.

2. Causes of retardation. Racial: highly civilized natives subjugated and retained, a mestizo race. Physiographic: climate relatively unattractive to Europeans; topography; communications poor. Results: internal disunion; intercity rivalry; little feeling of nationality.

3. Political features. Constant succession of dictators to present (twenty-seven civil wars in Colombia); revolutions instead of elections; Páez driven from Venezuela by Monagas, 1849; frequent constitutional changes (six constitutions in Ecuador in twenty-five years); revolutions sometimes sanguinary (Colombia, Ecuador), more often bloodless (Venezuela, Peru, Bolivia); clerical party important factor in revolutions (García Moreno in Ecuador, 1850–1875); dictators sometimes benevolent despots (Guzmán Blanco in Venezuela, 1850–1890); dictators sometimes withdraw peaceably (Santa Cruz in Bolivia, 1845; Reyes in Colombia, 1909); external domination of Central America and island colonies.

4. Economic features. Industries extractive: Colombia and Venezuela (gold, coffee, hides, cocoa); Ecuador (cocoa, tagua nuts); Peru (copper, silver, hides, cotton, sugar); Bolivia (minerals); Paraguay (quebracho wood, yerba maté). Lack of communication and capital chief hindrances. European influence. United States influence varies: Venezuela (Cleveland); Colombia (Panama); Ecuador (Guayaquil and Quito Railroad, Archer Harmon, sanitation of Guayaquil); Peru (Meiggs, Central Railroad, Cerro de Pasco Company, War of the Pacific); Bolivia (small); Paraguay (growth of American beef interests). Rapid increase of American investments since the World War. Future prospects: Venezuela (cattle industry on the llanos); Colombia (petroleum); Ecuador,

Peru, and Bolivia (montaña to the east of the Andes);
Paraguay (cattle, industry); Central America (fruit,
coffee); island colonies (sugar, tobacco).

REQUIRED READING

One of the following:

GARCÍA CALDERÓN, F. *Latin America*, 222–231 (the anarchy of the
tropics).

JAMES, H. G., and MARTIN, P. A. *The Republics of Latin America*,
233–240 (Peru) or 268–270, 283–285, 322 ,26 (Venezuela, Colombia,
Paraguay).

RIPPY, J. F. *Historical Evolution of Hispanic America*, chap. 10
(selections).

ROBERTSON, W. S. *History of the Latin-American Nations*, 1922 ed.,
chap. 13; 1932 ed., chaps. 18, 19, 20 or 21.

SHEPHERD, W. R. *Hispanic Nations of the New World.*

SWEET, W. W. *History of Latin America*, 1919 ed., chap. 15; 1929 ed.,
196–217.

WARSHAW, JACOB. *The New Latin America*, chap. 13.

WEBSTER, HUTTON. *History of Latin America*, 133–138.

REFERENCES

BOOKS OF TRAVEL AND DESCRIPTION RELATING TO
HISPANIC AMERICA [1]

General

BRYCE, JAMES. *South America: Observations and Impressions* (1912).
COOPER, C. S. *Understanding South America* (1918).
CURTIS, W. E. *Between the Andes and the Ocean* (1900).
MACKELLAR, C. D. *A Pleasure Pilgrim in South America* (1908).
MOZANS, H. J. *Along the Andes and down the Amazon* (1912).
MOZANS, H. J. *Up the Orinoco and down the Magdalena* (1910).
PECK, A. S. *The South American Tour* (1924).
ROSS, E. A. *South of Panama* (1914).
VAN DYKE, H. W. *Through South America* (1912).
WHITNEY, CASPAR. *The Flowing Road* (1912).

[1] Since dates of publication are especially important in a list of travel books,
they are given here.

Argentina
FRASER, J. F. *The Amazing Argentine* (1914).
HIRST, W. A. *Argentina* (1910).
KOEBEL, W. H. *Modern Argentina* (1907).
MILLS, G. J. *Argentina* (1914).

Bolivia
WALLE, PAUL. *Bolivia* (1914).
WRIGHT, M. R. *Bolivia* (1907).

Brazil
BENNETT, FRANK. *Forty Years in Brazil* (1914).
BRUCE, G. J. *Brazil and the Brazilians* (1915).
BULEY, E. C. *North Brazil* (1914).
BULEY, E. C. *South Brazil* (1914).
DOMVILLE-FIFE, C. W. *The United States of Brazil* (1910).
JAMES, H. G. *Brazil after a Century of Independence* (1925).
LANGE, ALGOT. *The Lower Amazon* (1914).
MULHALL, M. G. *Rio Grande do Sul and its German Colonies* (1873).
ROOSEVELT, THEODORE. *Through the Brazilian Wilderness* (1914).
WOODROFFE, J. F. *The Upper Reaches of the Amazon* (1914).

Central America
KOEBEL, W. H. *Central America* (1917).
MARTIN, P. F. *Salvador of the Twentieth Century* (1911).
PALMER, FREDERICK. *Central America and its Problems* (1910).
PUTNAM, G. P. *The Southland of North America* (1913).
WINTER, N. O. *Guatemala and her People of Today* (1909).

Chile
ELLIOTT, L. E. *Chile To-day and To-morrow* (1922).
KOEBEL, W. H. *Modern Chile* (1913).
MAITLAND, F. J. G. *Chile: its Land and People* (1914).
MILLS, G. J. *Chile* (1914).
WINTER, N. O. *Chile and her People of Today* (1912).

Colombia
BELL, P. L. *Colombia: a Commercial and Industrial Handbook* (1921).
EDER, P. J. *Colombia* (1913).
LÉVINE, V. *Colombia* (1914).
PETRE, F. L. *The Republic of Colombia* (1906).

Ecuador

ENOCK, C. R. *Ecuador* (1914).
MEJÍA, JOSÉ. *Ecuador* (1909).

Mexico

BLICHFELDT, E. H. *A Mexican Journey* (1912).
BULNES, FRANCISCO. *The Whole Truth about Mexico* (1916).
CARSON, W. E. *Mexico, the Wonderland of the South* (1909).
GILLPATRICK, O. W. *The Man who Likes Mexico* (1911).
MACHUGH, R. J. *Modern Mexico* (1914).
MARTIN, P. F. *Mexico of the Twentieth Century* (1907).
TWEEDIE, E. B. *Mexico as I saw It* (1901).

Panama

ARIAS, HARMODIO. *The Panama Canal* (1911).
EDWARDS, ALBERT. *Panama* (1911).
ROOSEVELT, THEODORE. *Fear God and take your Own Part* (1916).

Paraguay

KOEBEL, W. H. *In Jesuit Land* (1912).
KOEBEL, W. H. *Paraguay* (1917).
MASTERMAN, G. L. *Seven Eventful Years in Paraguay* (1870).
SCHURZ, W. L. *Paraguay: a Commercial Handbook* (1920).

Peru

ENOCK, C. R. *Peru* (1908).
MARTIN, P. F. *Peru of the Twentieth Century* (1911).
VIVIAN, E. C. *Peru* (1914).

Uruguay

KOEBEL, W. H. *Uruguay* (1911).

Venezuela

BELL, P. L. *Venezuela, a Commercial and Industrial Handbook* (1922).
DALTON, L. V. *Venezuela* (1912).
SCRUGGS, W. L. *The Colombian and Venezuelan Republics* (1905).

The island republics

CABRERA, RAIMUNDO. *Cuba and the Cubans* (1896).
GUITERAS, P. J. *Historia de la Isla de Cuba* (2 vols.) (1928).
ST. JOHN, SPENCER. *Hayti, or the Black Republic* (1884).
SCHOENRICH, OTTO. *Santo Domingo* (1918).

LECTURE LVIII. Díaz and the Aftermath
in Mexico

Introductory. Juárez carried through liberal reforms and
overthrew Maximilian. Now followed the remarkable rule of
a most remarkable man. Porfirio Díaz, half-breed Zapotec,
soldier hero, and follower of Juárez, became president on the
platform of no reëlection, and then held the office for eight
terms, seven of them in succession. Díaz became a dictator.
He aimed at good order, strong rule, and material progress.
The army was enlarged, a remarkable rural police force trained
(the Rurales), and disorder stamped out. The administration
was centralized, federalism undermined, and local government
dominated from the capital. A conservative, Díaz turned
for support to the old régime — the Church and the land-
owners. To develop industries he relied on foreign capital and
enterprise.

Mexico now experienced phenomenal material development.
National finance was put on its feet, railroads were built, mines
and oil wells opened. Immigrants established flourishing agricultural colonies. As a forward step, Díaz revived the old
National University. He became a world figure extravagantly
eulogized by foreign writers. The outside world saw Mexico in
a golden age. But prosperity was one-sided. Vast estates were
still intact, while millions of people needed land. Foreigners
and the aristocracy were getting rich, while peons were still
bound to the soil. Underneath the surface there were seeds
of revolution. The middle class evolved group consciousness,
which showed itself in hostility to foreigners, attempts at labor

341

organization, demand for land reform, and for free election of a successor to Díaz. But this program met little response.

Then followed ten years of revolution and strife. Madero led a revolt; the octogenarian president resigned and fled the country never to return. Huerta led a counter revolution. Madero was murdered, and in the Tragic Ten Days the streets of the old Aztec capital ran with blood. Three years were spent in eliminating Huerta and elevating Carranza. Wilson earnestly took a hand, and the A B C powers gave aid. Carranza parleyed for recognition and struggled with guerrillas led by Villa and Zapata.

Meanwhile the Constitution of 1917 was installed. Obregón and Calles have continued with eight years of socialistic reform. The declared aims are Mexico for the Mexicans, rights for the common man, education for the common people. Large estates have been cut up, natural resources nationalized, and foreign influence curbed. Critics maintain that some of these reforms are more apparent than real and that the leaders have not been wholly unselfish. In so radical a change vested interests have inevitably suffered. In the struggle the Church has been inextricably involved.

1. The work of Juárez a temporary triumph for liberalism and constitutional government. The victory over the Centralists; election of Lerdo de Tejada (1872); constitutional government sustained.
2. Peace and prosperity under Díaz. Porfirio Díaz: his Indian blood; early career; his adherence to Juárez; his election (Lerdistas, Iglesistas, Porfiristas), 1876. His aims and ideas: good order through strong rule; benevolent despotism (paternalistic measures to improve the people); material development through foreign aid

(capital, immigration); friendship with the United
States; support of Church, landholders, and foreign
capitalists. His methods of government: revolution
stamped out (army, Rurales, ley fuga); national finance
(loans, banks, Limantour); railroads (foreign capital);
nationalization begun at end of rule; mines; agriculture
(foreign colonies); oil; education (schools; National
University, 1910). Díaz a world figure.

3. A one-sided prosperity. Large estates still intact; rural
laborers (peons) still dependent; industrial labor organizations discouraged; constitutional government ignored;
"Díazpotism."

4. Ten years of revolution (1911–1920). The Madero revolt (1911–1912): growing discontent (political self-
consciousness, hostility to foreigners, demand for free
election of successor to Díaz, fear of Corral, demand
for land reforms); the Madero revolt; resignation and
expatriation of Díaz. Huerta: the Científico reaction;
the Tragic Ten Days (1912); the elimination of Huerta
(Wilson, the A B C powers, Carranza, the Tampico
incident, United States intervention in Vera Cruz, the
Niagara Conference, the fall of Huerta). Carranza
(1915–1920): victory over Villa and Zapata; struggle for
recognition (the conference of the American powers,
watchful waiting, recognition awarded); friction with
the United States (the Villa raid on Columbus, 1916; the
Pershing expedition); the Constitution of 1917 (radical,
antiforeign); the question of subsoil property; oil.

5. Obregón, Calles, and nationalism. Demand for free elec-
tion; revolution (1920); assassination of Carranza;
Obregón elected; the question of recognition by the
United States. Calles: election in 1924; vigorous na-

tionalistic program (nationalization of natural resources, agrarian reform, education for the masses, elimination of foreign influence, socialistic legislation); the Church question; the oil question and relations with the United States; Obregón assassinated (1928).

REQUIRED READING

One of the following:

JAMES, H. G., and MARTIN, P. A. *The Republics of Latin America*, 343–347.

PRIESTLEY, H. I. *The Mexican Nation*, chap. 23 (Díaz), chap. 24 (Madero), chaps. 25–27 (Huerta, Carranza, relations with the United States).

ROBERTSON, W. S. *History of the Latin-American Nations*, 1922 ed., 495–520; 1932 ed., 654–686.

SWEET, W. W. *History of Latin America*, 1919 ed., 208–210; 1929 ed., 265–272.

WILGUS, A. C. *A History of Hispanic America*, chap. 25.

REFERENCES

PORFIRIO DÍAZ

BAERLEIN, HENRY. *Mexico, the Land of Unrest.*
BEALS, CARLETON. *Porfirio Diaz.*
BELL, E. I. *The Political Shame of Mexico.*
BULNES, FRANCISCO. *The Whole Truth about Mexico.*
CORNYN, J. H. *Díaz y México.*
CREELMAN, JAMES. *Diaz, Master of Mexico.*
FLANDRAU, C. M. *Viva Mexico!*
FORNARO, CARLO DE. *Diaz, Czar of Mexico.*
HANNAY, DAVID. *Diaz.*
LUMMIS, C. F. *The Awakening of a Nation.*
MADERO, F. I. *La Sucesión Presidencial en 1910.*
SMITH R. W. *Benighted Mexico.*
THOMPSON, WALLACE. *The People of Mexico.*
TURNER, J. K. *Barbarous Mexico.*
TWEEDIE, E. B. *Porfirio Diaz.*

MADERO

BELL, E. I. *The Political Shame of Mexico.*
CASE, A. B. *Thirty Years with the Mexicans.*
RUSSELL, T. H. *Mexico in Peace and War.*
SMITH, R. W. *Benighted Mexico.*
TROWBRIDGE, E. D. *Mexico To-day and To-morrow.*
TWEEDIE, E. B. *Mexico from Diaz to the Kaiser.*
WINTON, G. B. *Mexico Today.*
ZAYAS, ENRÍQUEZ RAFAEL. *The Case of Mexico.*

HUERTA

BULNES, FRANCISCO. *The Whole Truth about Mexico.*
CALERO, MANUEL. *The Mexican Policy of President Woodrow Wilson.*
O'SHAUGHNESSY, E. L. *Diplomatic Days.*
O'SHAUGHNESSY, E. L. *A Diplomat's Wife in Mexico.*
O'SHAUGHNESSY, E. L. *Intimate Pages of Mexican History.*
ZAYAS, ENRÍQUEZ RAFAEL. *The Case of Mexico.*

CARRANZA

ACKERMAN, C. W. *Mexico's Dilemma.*
BLAKESLEE, G. H. (Editor). *Mexico and the Caribbean.*
BLASCO IBÁÑEZ, VICENTE. *Mexico in Revolution*
BURGES, W. H. *A Hot-house Constitution.*
CALLCOTT, W. H. *Liberalism in Mexico, 1857-1929.*
CHAMBERLAIN, G. A. *Is Mexico worth Saving?*
CREEL, GEORGE. *The People Next Door.*
DE BEKKER, L. J. *The Plot against Mexico.*
DILLON, E. J. *Mexico on the Verge.*
FORNARO, CARLO DE. *Carranza and Mexico.*
GIBBON, T. E. *Mexico under Carranza.*
JONES, C. L. *Mexico and its Reconstruction.*
LAWRENCE, DAVID. *The Truth about Mexico.*
RIPPY, J. F., VASCONCELOS, JOSÉ, and STEVENS, GUY. *American Policies Abroad, Mexico.*
TANNENBAUM, FRANK. *The Mexican Agrarian Revolution.*
TANNENBAUM, FRANK. *Peace by Revolution, an Interpretation of Mexico.*
VERA ESTAÑOL, JORGE. *Carranza and his Bolshevik Régime.*

LECTURE LIX. THE INTERNATIONAL RELATIONS OF HISPANIC AMERICA

Introductory. The most intimate international relations of the Hispanic American countries have been their dealings with each other. There have been boundary disputes on many borders, but most of them have been adjusted by arbitration, in which Hispanic America has set a model before the world. A few rivalries have resulted in strife — notably the war on Paraguay and the War of the Pacific. In general Hispanic America has shown solidarity against outsiders. Relations with Europe have been friendly in the main. There have been a few cases of friction with and danger from Europe, but more conspicuous has been the peaceful intercourse of commerce, investment, and immigration.

Early relations with the United States were amicable. The northern republic was the first to recognize the Hispanic states, and she championed them against reconquest. But this friendship was soon cooled. The United States extended her boundaries at the expense of Mexico and obtained concessions on the Isthmus. Mexico became embittered and the rest of Hispanic America suspicious.

After the Civil War relations with Mexico greatly improved. Lincoln gave Juárez support in the overthrow of Maximilian, and in the long reign of Díaz dealings were most cordial. This was the heyday of American investors south of the Rio Grande. But since the expulsion of Díaz the story has been one of almost continuous intervention in Mexico. Huerta was eliminated and Carranza elevated largely through Wilson's aid. Carranza

70° 50°

DEMARCATION LINE

Caracas
f.
e. VENEZUELA
Bogotá
COLOMBIA
GUIANA
c

ATLANTIC

d. 3
4
5
b Quito
ECUADOR
b Guayaquil

Pará

P E R U

6
Limá
Cuzco
Pernambuco

PACIFIC
Tacna
Arica
ARICA
La Paz
BOLIVIA
Sucre
Potosí

6

2.

1.

Bahia

20° 20°

TARAPACA
B

TROPIC OF CAPRICORN
Antofagasta
ANTOFAGASTA
A

a PARAGUAY
7
8

Rio de Janeiro

OCEAN
Asunción
9

OCEAN

ARGENTINA
Córdoba

Valparaiso
Santiago
Rosario
Buenos Aires
URU-
GUAY
Montevideo

EXPANSION OF
BRAZIL

1. The original Brazil
2. Added before 1850
3. From Venezuela, 1859,1905
4. From Colombia, 1907
5. From Ecuador, 1904
6. From Bolivia, 1867, 1903
7. From Paraguay, 1872
8. From Argentina, 1895
9. From Uruguay, 1851

THE QUESTION
OF THE PACIFIC

A. Yielded by Bolivia
    to Chile
B. Yielded by Peru
    to Chile
C. Disputed by Peru
    and Chile

SCALE OF MILES
0 50 100 200 300 400 500 600

OTHER DISPUTED
AREAS

a. The Gran Chaco
b. Ecuador, Colombia and
   Peru
c. Venezuela and England
   Disputed till 1899
d.)
e.) Boundary disputes
f.) between Colombia
     and Venezuela

AREAS OF FRICTION IN SOUTH AMERICA (NINETEENTH AND
TWENTIETH CENTURIES)

showed little gratitude, and bickering continued. For three years recognition was withheld from Obregón. The Constitution of 1917 threatened American investments in oil lands, and a decade of irritation followed, but the matter has now been partially adjusted.

Next to Mexico the United States has had closest relations with the Isthmus and the Caribbean area. Concessions were early acquired in Panama and Nicaragua, and the Panama Railroad was built. Negotiations with Colombia for a canal concession failed. Roosevelt thereupon supported a revolt in Panama, obtained a concession, and built the Panama Canal. Since 1898 the United States has constantly strengthened her influence in the Caribbean area and Central America. Porto Rico was acquired by war with Spain; the Virgin Islands by purchase from Denmark. Cuba and Panama are protectorates, and in Santo Domingo, Nicaragua, Guatemala, Salvador, and Honduras the United States exercises some form of financial control.

With South America relations have been less close than with Mexico and the Caribbean. In the main dealings have been friendly. South America felt apprehension at Olney's view of the Monroe Doctrine in the Venezuela disputes, and there has been much talk of the "Yankee peril." To offset it Pan-Hispanism and Pan-Iberism have been promoted. This in turn has been countered in the United States by the promotion of Pan-Americanism.

1. Relations of the Hispanic countries with each other. Boundary disputes: some adjusted (Argentina and Chile, arbitration, Christ of the Andes); some pending. International rivalries: the war against Paraguay (1865–1870); the War of the Pacific (1879–1884); jealousies among the

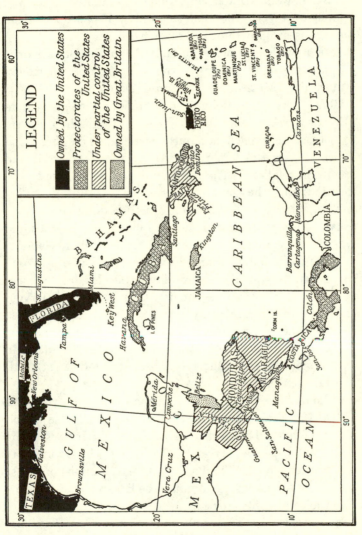

THE CARIBBEAN AREA IN THE TWENTIETH CENTURY

ABC powers. Underlying solidarity: united in face of foreign danger; the Bolívar ideal; Hispanic American congresses; growth of international law.

2. Relations with Europe. The Holy Alliance. Danger from Spain: recognition long withheld; attempts to restore authority (Mexico, 1829; Santo Domingo, 1861–1865; Chile, Peru, and Bolivia, 1867–1869). The French in Mexico: the "Pie War" (1838); Maximilian (1861–1866). The French in South America. The English in Central America; in South America. Commercial and cultural relations. The Calvo and Drago doctrines.

3. Relations with the United States.

   a. Early relations. The Monroe Doctrine declared.

   b. The United States and Mexico. From 1836 to 1853: United States aggressive; Texas; the Mexican War, Gadsden Purchase, filibustering. From the Civil War to 1911: generally friendly; Maximilian episode; border troubles; American investments; Díaz friendly. Intervention since 1911: army on the border; the Tampico incident; Huerta eliminated; the Pershing expedition; the Constitution of 1917 and the oil interests; delay in recognizing Obregón; recognition granted (1923); adjustment of oil question (1928).

   c. Isthmian questions. The Panama Railroad; conquest of California; treaty with New Granada (1848); railroad built. The Nicaragua route: British interests; the Clayton-Bulwer Treaty (1850); the Hay-Pauncefote Treaty (1901). The Panama Canal: various projects; negotiations with Colombia; the Panama revolt (1903); the canal built (1915).

   d. Intervention in the Caribbean area since 1898. The "Big Stick" policy; purposes and methods; United States

acquires possessions and protectorates. Cuba: the
Spanish-American War (1898); Cuba freed (1902); a
qualified freedom; the Platt Amendment; new intervention (1906). Panama: revolution of 1903; concessions to United States. Santo Domingo: danger of
foreign intervention; United States control of customs
(1907). Haiti: United States financial and police control (1915). Nicaragua: control of finances (1909);
troops landed (1912); Treaty of 1914 (exclusive canal
concessions, naval stations); recent intervention.
  e. The United States and South America. Relations reflect
     relations with Caribbean; early minor difficulties (Ar-
     gentina, 1831; Paraguay, 1850); difficulties with Chile,
     1881, 1891 (the *Itata* incident); friendly mediation;
     Colombia and Venezuela (see elsewhere); commercial,
     industrial, educational, and scientific contact.
  f. Recent aspects of the Monroe Doctrine. Original mean-
     ing; new applications and interpretations; the two
     Venezuela episodes; Olney's declaration; England and
     Germany forced to arbitrate (1896); relation to "Big
     Stick" policy; apprehension in Hispanic America; the
     "Yankee peril."
4. Pan-Americanism. Meaning; Blaine's leadership; the Pan-
   American congresses; the Pan-American Union; Pan-
   Hispanism.

REQUIRED READING
One of the following:
FORMAN, S. E. *Our Republic*, 683, 686–687, 708–714.
HARLOW, R. V. *The Growth of the United States*, 712–719 (Panama,
   the big stick, Santo Domingo); 749–754 (Mexico, Colombia);
   791–799 (the United States and the Caribbean).
JAMES, H. G., and MARTIN, P. A. *The Republics of Latin America*,
   chap. 13.

MORISON, S. E., and COMMAGER, H. S. *Growth of the American Republic*, 827–843 (the big stick).

PRIESTLEY, H. I. *The Mexican Nation*, chaps. 15, 18.

ROBERTSON, W. S. *History of the Latin-American Nations*, chap. 20.

SHEPHERD, W. R. *Hispanic Nations of the New World*, chap. 13.

SWEET, W. W. *History of Latin America*, 1919 ed., chap. 21; 1929 ed., chap. 26.

WEBSTER, HUTTON. *History of Latin America*, chap. 10.

WILGUS, A. C. *A History of Hispanic America*, chaps. 39–46 (selections).

REFERENCES

RELATIONS OF THE HISPANIC-AMERICAN COUNTRIES WITH EACH OTHER AND WITH EUROPE

ADAMS, E. D. *British Interests and Activities in Texas, 1838–1846.*

AKERS, C. E. *History of South America, 1854–1904.*

ALTAMIRA Y CREVEA, RAFAEL. *España en América.*

BOX, P. H. *The Origins of the Paraguayan War.*

CADY, J. F. *Foreign Intervention in the Rio de la Plata, 1838–1850.*

CHANDLER, C. L. *Inter-American Acquaintances.*

CONTRERAS, FRANCISCO. *Le Chile et la France.*

DENNIS, W. J. *Tacna and Arica.*

FLORES, PASTORIZA. *History of the Boundary Dispute between Ecuador and Peru.*

GALDAMES, LUÍS. *Estudio de la Historia de Chile.*

GOEBEL, JULIUS. *The Struggle for the Falkland Islands.*

HARING, C. H. *The Germans in South America.*

HARRISON, AUSTIN. *The Pan-Germanic Doctrine.*

INMAN, S. G. *Problems in Pan Americanism.*

KOEBEL, W. H. *British Exploits in South America.*

LOCKEY, J. B. *Pan-Americanism — its Beginnings.*

QUESADA, V. G. *Recuerdos de mi Vida Diplomática.*

RIPPY, J. F. *Latin America in World Politics.*

ROBERTSON, W. S. *History of the Latin-American Nations.*

WERTHEIMER, M. S. *The Pan-German League, 1890–1914.*

ZUBIETA, P. A. *Congresos de Panamá y Tacubaya.*

THE UNITED STATES AND HISPANIC AMERICA

BACON, ROBERT. *For Better Relations with our Latin American Neighbors.*

BARRETT, JOHN. *Pan-American Union: Peace, Friendship, Commerce.*

BLAKESLEE, G. H. (Editor). *Latin America.*

BROWN, P. M. *American Intervention in Central America* (Clark University Studies).

CHANDLER, C. L. *Inter-American Acquaintances.*

CHAPMAN, C. E. *A History of the Cuban Republic.*

CLEVEN, N. A. N. *Readings in Hispanic American History.*

COOLIDGE, A. C. *The United States as a World Power.*

COX, I. J. *Nicaragua and the United States, 1909–1927.*

EDGINGTON, T. B. *The Monroe Doctrine.*

ETTINGER, A. A. *The Mission to Spain of Pierre Soulé, 1853–1855: a Study in the Cuban Diplomacy of the United States.*

EVANS, H. C., JR. *Chile and its Relations with the United States.*

GARNER, J. W. *American Foreign Policies.*

HALL, A. B. *The Monroe Doctrine.*

HALL, A. B. *The Monroe Doctrine and the Great War.*

HILL, H. C. *Roosevelt and the Caribbean.*

HILL, L. F. *Diplomatic Relations between the United States and Brazil.*

INMAN, S. G. *Problems in Pan Americanism.*

JENKS, L. H. *Our Cuban Colony.*

JONES, C. L., NORTON, H. K., and MOON, P. T. *The United States and the Caribbean.*

KNIGHT, M. M. *The Americans in Santo Domingo.*

LATANÉ, J. H. *History of American Foreign Policy.*

LATANÉ, J. H. *The United States and Latin America.*

LOCKEY, J. B. *Pan-Americanism — its Beginnings.*

MANNING, W. R. (Editor). *Diplomatic Correspondence of the United States: Inter-American Affairs, 1831–1860.*

MOORE, J. B. *American Diplomacy, its Spirit and Achievements.*

PERKINS, DEXTER. *The Monroe Doctrine, 1826–1867.*

REDDAWAY, W. F. *The Monroe Doctrine.*

RIPPY, J. F. *The Capitalists and Colombia.*

RIPPY, J. F. *Latin America in World Politics.*

RIPPY, J. F. *Rivalry of the United States and Great Britain over Latin America.*

RIPPY, J. F. *The United States and Mexico.*

ROBERTSON, W. S. *Hispanic-American Relations with the United States.*

ROOT, ELIHU. *Latin America and the United States.* (Robert Bacon and J. B. Scott, Editors.)

RUBENS, H. S. *Liberty, the story of Cuba.*

SHEPHERD, W. R. "The Monroe Doctrine Reconsidered," *Political Science Quarterly,* March, 1924.

SHERMAN, W. R. *The Diplomatic and Commercial Relations of the United States and Chile, 1820–1914.*

SHERRILL, G. H. *Modernizing the Monroe Doctrine.*

STIMSON, H. L. *American Policy in Nicaragua.*

STUART, G. H. *Latin America and the United States.*

THOMAS, D. Y. *One Hundred Years of the Monroe Doctrine.*

UGARTE, MANUEL. *The Destiny of a Continent.* (J. F. Rippy, editor.)

USHER, R. G. *Pan-Americansim.*

WALLING, W. E. *The Mexican Question. Mexico and American-Mexican Relations under Calles and Obregón.*

WRIGHT, P. G. *The Cuban Situation and our Treaty Relations.*

ISTHMIAN DIPLOMACY [1]

ARIAS, HARMODIO. *The Panama Canal* (1911).

BENNETT, I. E. *History of the Panama Canal* (1915).

BIGELOW, JOHN. *Breaches of Anglo-American Treaties* (1917).

BISHOP, FARNHAM. *Panama, Past and Present* (1913).

BULLARD, ARTHUR. *Panama: the Canal, the Country, and the People* (1914).

BUNAU-VARILLA, PHILIPPE. *Panama: Creation, Destruction, and Resurrection* (1914).

CLEVEN, N. A. N. *Readings in Hispanic American History* (1927).

FORBES-LINDSAY, C. H. *Panama and the Canal Today* (1910).

GRAHAM, LEOPOLD. "Canal Diplomacy," *North American Review,* January, 1913.

JOHNSON, W. F. *Four Centuries of the Panama Canal* (1907).

KEASBEY, L. M. *The Nicaragua Canal and the Monroe Doctrine* (1896).

LATANÉ, J. H. *The United States and Latin America* (1920).

[1] In these special bibliographies it has seemed desirable to give publication dates of the authorities cited.

PRINGLE, H. F. *Theodore Roosevelt: a Biography* (1931).
RODRIGUES, J. C. *The Panama Canal* (1885).
THOMSON, NORMAN. *Colombia and the United States* (1914).
WILLIAMS, M. W. *Anglo-American Isthmian Diplomacy* (1916).
Diplomatic History of the Panama Canal, Senate Document No. 474,
 Sixty-third Congress, Second Session.

THE UNITED STATES AND MEXICO (1821–1913)

BANCROFT, H. H. *History of Mexico* (1914).
BURKE, U. R. *A Life of Benito Juárez* (1894).
CLEVEN, N. A. N. *Readings in Hispanic American History* (1927).
CORNYN, J. H. *Díaz y México* (2 vols.) (1910).
ENOCK, C. R. *Mexico* (1909).
GODOY, J. F. *Porfirio Diaz* (1910).
HACKETT, C. W. *The Recognition of the Díaz Government by the United
 States* (1924).
HANNAY, DAVID. *Díaz* (1917).
LATANÉ, J. H. *The United States and Latin America* (1920).
MACHUGH, R. J. *Modern Mexico* (1914).
MANNING, W. R. *Early Diplomatic Relations between the United States
 and Mexico* (1916).
NOLL, A. H. *From Empire to Republic* (1903).
RAMÍREZ, J. F. *México durante su Guerra con los Estados Unidos* (1905).
REBOLLEDO, MIGUEL. *México y Estados Unidos* (1917).
RIPPY, J. F. *The United States and Mexico* (1826), chaps. 1–19.
RIVES, G. L. *The United States and Mexico, 1821–1848* (2 vols.)
 (1913).
ROMERO, MATÍAS. *Mexico and the United States* (1898).
SMITH, J. H. *The War with Mexico* (1919).
TROWBRIDGE, E. D. *Mexico To-day and To-morrow* (1919).

THE UNITED STATES AND MEXICO (1914–1928)

BELL, E. I. *The Political Shame of Mexico* (1921).
BLAKESLEE, G. H. (Editor). *Mexico and the Caribbean* (1920).
BULNES, FRANCISCO. *The Whole Truth about Mexico* (1916).
CALERO, M. *Un Decenio de Política Mexicana* (1920).
CALLAHAN, J. M. *American Foreign Policy in Mexican Relations*
 (1932).

Chamberlain, J. P. "Property Rights under the New Mexican Constitution," *Political Science Quarterly* (September, 1917), XXXII.

Dillon, E. J. *Mexico on the Verge* (1921).

Hackett, C. W. *The Mexican Revolution and the United States, 1910–1926* (1926).

Hackett, C. W. *The New Régime in Mexico* (1921).

Inman, S. G. *Intervention in Mexico* (1919).

Inman, S. G. "Pan-American Conferences and their Results," *Southwestern Political and Social Science Quarterly* (December, 1923), IV.

Inman, S. G. *Problems in Pan Americanism* (1925).

Jones, C. L. *Mexico and its Reconstruction* (1921).

McCorkle, S. A. *American Policy of Recognition toward Mexico* (1933).

Priestley, H. I. "Relations between the United States and Mexico since 1910," *University of California Chronicle* (January, 1920), XXI.

Rippy, J. F. *The United States and Mexico* (Revised Edition) (1931).

Rowe, L. S. "The Mexican Revolution: its Causes and Consequences," *Political Science Quarterly* (June, 1912), XXVII.

Saenz, Moises, and Priestley, H. I. *Some Mexican Problems* (1926).

Trowbridge, E. D. *Mexico To-day and To-morrow* (1919).

Vasconcelos, José, and Gamio, Manuel. *Aspects of Mexican Civilization* (1926).

Zayas, E. R. de. *The Case of Mexico* (1914).

Investigation of Mexican Affairs, Senate Document No. 285, Sixty-sixth Congress, Second Session.

Series of articles on the Mexican situation, *Annals of the American Academy of Political and Social Science* (July, 1914), LIV.

"Settlement of the Mexican Oil Question," *Current History* (October, 1921), XXV.

Lecture LX. The Americas in the World War

Introductory. In 1914 the Americas faced the issue of the World War. Germany was pitted against nearly all the rest of Europe in a life-and-death struggle, and every American nation had to answer the question of participation or neutrality.

First of the American republics to enter the conflict was Canada. This was natural. The mother country needed help, and without hesitation aid was rendered. The day after war was declared recruiting began, and within six months thirty thousand Canadian troops were already in England. Before the war ended nearly half a million Canadians volunteered. In 1917 a draft law was adopted, and eighty thousand men were raised by conscription. French Canadians were slow to enlist, and in the province of Quebec the draft law was vigorously opposed. Canada's soldiers made a brilliant record on many fields. Her casualty list was 220,000, of whom 60,000 were left in graves "over there." Canada contributed liberally not only men but also money and supplies. In turn the war helped to put Canada and the other Dominions on a better political basis in the Empire. Before 1914 her position had been technically colonial. She emerged from the war with full national status.

The World War gave to the United States a more difficult problem than to Canada. The path of the Dominion was clearly marked; that of her neighbor was dimmed by uncertainty. At the outset Wilson declared for neutrality, a position more easily proclaimed than maintained. Both parties sought the support of the United States; both spread propaganda in the country. The dominant sentiment was for

357

the Allies, but eight million citizens were of German birth or parentage. Both contestants violated rights of neutrals on the sea. The situation was like that in the War of 1812, and for a time it looked like a choice between enemies. When a German submarine sank the *Lusitania*, with one hundred and fourteen American citizens on board, the country was ready for war, but President Wilson shrank from taking the step. For two years he used every resource of diplomacy to restrain Germany, with some success. His policy was approved by the nation, and he was reëlected on the slogan "He kept us out of war." But Germany resumed her unrestricted submarine program, and Congress declared war (April 6, 1917).

"Politics adjourned," and the country was now turned into a war machine. Wilson guided. A draft act was passed, officers' training camps were established, and in less than a year 2,000,000 men were trained and equipped. The Council of National Defense supervised the use of resources. National boards assumed control of food supplies, fuel, railroads, shipping, and war industries. In May (1917) American soldiers began to cross the Atlantic; by the end of the year 187,000 had reached France. In a single month (July, 1918) 297,000 men were transported. But they could not go fast enough, for the Allies were nearly exhausted. In numerous campaigns the American Expeditionary Force performed distinguished service, fighting beside the British and French armies. The United States navy, too, gave valuable aid. Superb work was done by the American Red Cross and the Belgian Relief Commission. The Americans did not "win the war." But the timely arrival of 2,000,000 fresh men enabled the tired Allies to finish the defeat of the Germans.

Hispanic America, too, was put in a serious position by the titanic European struggle. Until the United States joined the

THE AMERICAS IN THE WORLD WAR

Allies, all the southern republics remained neutral. Wilson invited them to coöperate, but in most cases the decision was not easy. The sympathy of the mass of the people was with France, whose culture had long been a potent influence among them. The example of the United States aroused enthusiasm. Germany's harsh methods injured South America and stirred resentment there. Some feared that a German victory would be followed by German conquest in South America. These sentiments were offset by German propaganda. In some places the clergy leaned strongly toward Germany. Then there was the fear of the "Colossus of the North." Under these circumstances, to many neutrality seemed wisest, safest, or most just. Nevertheless, of the twenty states to the south, eight joined the Allies. Five broke relations with Germany and seven remained neutral. Of the eight belligerents only Brazil and Cuba took an active part in the war. Three of the most important republics — Argentina, Chile, and Mexico — maintained neutrality.

Wilson's diplomacy struck at militarism a harder blow than was delivered by the American army. He appealed to the German nation against autocracy. In January, 1918, he drafted his famous Fourteen Points as a basis for peace. Foreseeing defeat, Germany's allies now deserted, her people turned against the militarists, an armistice was signed (November 11, 1918), the kaiser abdicated, and a republic was established.

The greatest achievement of the awful war, perhaps, was the hatred for war which it bred. To capitalize this sentiment Wilson led a movement for a League of Nations. At the Peace Conference most of his Fourteen Points went into the discard, but by bold fighting he made the Covenant of the League a part of the treaty — and then the treaty was rejected by the Senate of the United States. But Wilson's ideal is not dead;

it is still the inspiration of efforts to maintain international harmony.

The World War had profound effects upon the Western Hemisphere. In each country it strengthened the national bonds, and it shocked each republic into a clearer sense of national responsibility. It promoted Western Hemisphere solidarity. "The American nations became acutely conscious of a common heritage of ideals of democracy and liberty which the war had imperiled." Finally, the war gave the Western Hemisphere a new place in world politics. Canada emerged a full-fledged nation. Nine Hispanic American nations were represented at the Peace Conference at Paris. Several of them have participated in the League of Nations. The United States, led by Wilson, occupied a central position in the war settlements, and established her place as a World Power of first rank.

1. Canada in the World War. The outbreak of the war: the invasion of Belgium; England's breach with Germany; Canada proffers aid; special session of Canadian parliament. Organizing for war: recruiting begun; volunteers; French Canadians enlist slowly; the Military Service acts. The nation on a war basis: expansion of agriculture and industry; shipments of food and munitions; loans from the United States; domestic loans; Victory Loan; new taxation. Distinguished military service in many fields. Canada's new political status: the Imperial Conference at London, 1917; demand of dominions for autonomous nationality within the Empire; Borden, Botha, Smuts; dominions represented at War Cabinet meetings; at the Peace Conference; in the peace treaty with Germany; in the League of Nations; Canada has her own ambassador to the United States.

2. The United States in the World War.
    a. The period of neutrality. The outbreak of the war:
    neutrality declared; American opinion of the war;
    the clash over American trade; Germany's submarine
    campaign; the violation of American rights; the sink-
    ing of the *Lusitania*; the *Lusitania* notes; the election
    of 1916.
    b. United States participation in the war. Germany's re-
    newal of unrestricted submarine warfare; declaration
    of war with Germany (April 6, 1917); with Austria-
    Hungary (December 7); war aims; the selective draft;
    Liberty Loans and taxes; mobilizing the resources;
    the Espionage and Sedition acts; labor and the war;
    the American Expeditionary Force in France; the
    United States navy in the war; the American Red
    Cross; the Belgian Relief Commission (Hoover).
3. Hispanic America and the World War. General considera-
    tions: eight nations joined the Allies; five broke rela-
    tions with Germany; seven remained neutral; motives
    involved. Two active participants, Brazil and Cuba.
    Brazil in the war: Brazilian indignation; Ruy Barbosa's
    indictment; government supported by public opinion;
    precautions against Germans; war measures; aid to
    Allies in food supply. Cuba in the war: political
    rivalries suspended; propaganda neutralized. Policy of
    the other nations: Argentina; Chile; Uruguay; other
    South American republics; the Caribbean republics;
    Mexico. Effect of the war on Hispanic America.
4. The settlement at Versailles. The Peace Conference; the
    Supreme Council; the terms of settlement; the League
    of Nations; reception of the treaty in the United States;
    the League of Nations in the campaign of 1920; peace

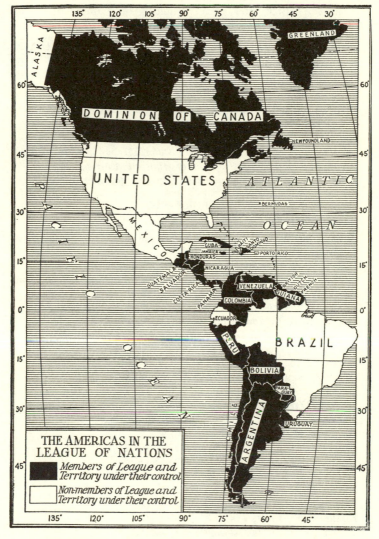

THE AMERICAS IN THE LEAGUE OF NATIONS (MAY 1, 1928)

and its problems; the Washington Conference; subsequent efforts toward preserving world peace.

5. America in the world today. Economic strength; political and social responsibilities and opportunities in world affairs.

REQUIRED READING

BEARD, C. A. and M. R. *History of the United States*, 1921 ed., chap. 25; 1929 ed., chap. 27.

HARLOW, R. V. *The Growth of the United States*, 755–790.

MARTIN, A. E. *History of the United States*, II, chaps. 25–29.

RIPPY, J. F. *Historical Evolution of Hispanic America*, chap. 24.

WITTKE, C. *A History of Canada*, chaps. 27, 30 (selections).

REFERENCES

ADAMS, R. G. *History of the Foreign Policy of the United States.*

ARMSTRONG, W. E. *Canada and the League of Nations: the Problem of Peace.*

BAKER, R. S. *Woodrow Wilson and World Settlement.*

BAKER, R. S. (Editor). *Woodrow Wilson: Life and Letters.* 4 vols.

BASSETT, J. S. *Expansion and Reform, 1889–1926.*

BRADY, ALEXANDER. *Canada.*

CLARKSON, G. B. *Industrial America in the World War.*

DAVISON, H. P. *The American Red Cross in the Great War.*

DODD, W. E. *Woodrow Wilson and his Work.*

FORMAN, S. E. *Our Republic.*

GOMPERS, SAMUEL. *American Labor and the War.*

HACKER, L. M., and KENDRICK, B. B. *The United States since 1865.*

HALÉVY, DANIEL. *Le Président Wilson.*

HAYES, C. J. H. *A Brief History of the Great War.*

HOUSTON, D. F. *Why we Went to War.*

HOWLAND, H. J. *Theodore Roosevelt and his Times.*

JAMES, H. G., and MARTIN, P. A. *The Republics of Latin America*, 472–488.

KELLY, F. F. *What America Did.*

KIRKPATRICK, F. A. *South America and the War.*

KOLBE, P. R. *Colleges in War Time.*

LATANÉ, J. H. *From Isolation to Leadership.*

LAVALLE, J. B. *El Perú y la Gran Guerra.*

LINGLEY, C. R. *Since the Civil War*, chap. 25.

LOW, A. M. *Woodrow Wilson, an Interpretation.*

LUGONES, LEOPOLDO. *Mi Beligerancia.*

McMASTER, J. B. *The United States in the World War.*

MANNING, C. A. W. *The Policies of the British Dominions in the League of Nations.*

MARTIN, CHESTER. *Empire and Commonwealth.*

MARTIN, P. A. "Latin America and the War," *League of Nations*, II, No. 4, August, 1919.

MATHEWS, J. M. *Conduct of American Foreign Relations.*

MUZZEY, D. S. *The United States of America.*

PAXSON, F. L. *Recent History of the United States*, chaps. 44–57.

ROBERTSON, W. S. *Hispanic-American Relations with the United States*, 223–227, 412–416.

ROBERTSON, W. S. *History of the Latin-American Nations* (see index under World War).

ROBINSON, E. E., and WEST, V. J. *The Foreign Policy of Woodrow Wilson.*

ROGERS, LINDSAY. *America's Case against Germany.*

ROOSEVELT, THEODORE. *America and the World War.*

SCOTT, J. B. *Survey of International Relations between the United States and Germany.*

SEYMOUR, CHARLES. *Woodrow Wilson and the World War.*

SHIPPEE, L. B. *Recent American History.*

SILVA VILDÓSOLA, CARLOS. *Le Chile et la Guerre.*

SILVA VILDÓSOLA, CARLOS, and LÓPEZ, N. F. *South American Opinions on the War.*

SLOSSON, P. W. *The Great Crusade and After, 1914–1928.*

SOWARD, F. H. *Canada and the League of Nations.*

TROTTER, R. G. *The British Empire-Commonwealth: a Study in Political Evolution.*

YOUNG, E. W. *Wilson's Administration and the Great War.*

PRINTED IN THE UNITED STATES OF AMERICA